Bill Haley and His Comets and LaVern Baker concert, Sports Arena, Hershey, Pennsylvania, April 23, 1956, by Ed Feingersh.

Elvis Presley concert, University of Dayton Fieldhouse, Dayton, Ohio, May 27, 1956, by Phillip Harrington.

WHY ROCK'N'ROLL? [12]
A CONVERSATION BETWEEN ALAIN DOMINIQUE PERRIN AND GREGG GELLER

THE ROOTS OF ROCK'N'ROLL [38]
FROM BOOGIE-WOOGIE TO RHYTHM AND BLUES

BOOGIE-WOOGIE [46] / SWING BANDS [54] / GOSPEL [64]
BLUES [72] / COUNTRY [80] / RHYTHM AND BLUES [88]
TEXTS BY ROBERT PALMER, PETER GURALNICK, AND FLORENT MAZZOLENI

THE ROCK'N'ROLL EXPLOSION [126]
ELVIS, TEENAGERS AND ROCK'N'ROLL ATTITUDE

TEENAGERS [134] / ELVIS PRESLEY [172]
TEXTS BY DAVID HALBERSTAM, PETER GURALNICK, AND LINE RENAUD
ELVIS PRESLEY PORTFOLIO BY ALFRED WERTHEIMER

THE GOLDEN AGE OF ROCK'N'ROLL [278]
FROM BILL HALEY TO BUDDY HOLLY

BILL HALEY [284] / BO DIDDLEY [294] /
CHUCK BERRY [300] / FATS DOMINO [310]
LITTLE RICHARD [324] / JERRY LEE LEWIS [334]
BUDDY HOLLY [344] / CARL PERKINS [368]
GENE VINCENT [370] / EDDIE COCHRAN [372]...
TEXTS BY CHARLIE GILLETT AND PETER GURALNICK
BUDDY HOLLY PORTFOLIO BY WILLIAM EGGLESTON

SEVEN RECORDS BY GREIL MARCUS [392]
BIOGRAPHIES BY GREGG GELLER [409]
39–59 CHRONOLOGY BY GREGG GELLER [411]

WHY ROCK 'N' ROLL?

A CONVERSATION BETWEEN ALAIN DOMINIQUE PERRIN AND GREGG GELLER

Gregg Geller: I think that you and I are probably about the same age?

Alain Dominique Perrin: I don't know. I was born in October 1942.

We both came of age in the years after World War II.

Yes, yes.

And I'm wondering what your earliest memories of music are. For me they are from when I was driving in the car with my father with the radio on, playing the music of the early 1950s: Tony Bennett, Johnnie Ray, Teresa Brewer, that kind of thing.

Now, funnily enough, my father was not fond of music, so I was not raised with it. In fact, the earliest memories I have of music that really touched me are of Charles Aznavour when I was ten. And I must say, not long after that came Bill Haley and Elvis Presley. I was twelve or thirteen when I heard Bill Haley for the first time. He was all the rage for one year or so. Then Elvis came and it was very funny, like in a football match. You know, you had the Bill Haley fans and the Elvis Presley fans, and they were not usually the same people. What I remember most is that the music, all of a sudden, around 1954 and 1955, played a stronger role in my daily life.

So you became a fan?

Not really a fan, but in looking back I realize that although I didn't seek it out, the music came to me, through friends and in the cafes. A friend would tell you at school that he'd just bought a new record and we would listen to it on a small record player—it only played 45 rpm records and it was like a little suitcase that you brought wherever you went. We listened to American music more and more. It was a fresh sound and totally different from what had been popular before. Jukeboxes played this new music all the time, everywhere we went. This change began in 1955 and got bigger and bigger.

The first record I ever bought was "Sixteen Tons" by Tennessee Ernie Ford...

Yes! "Sixteen Tons." I remember that was the record that people learned to dance to. It was very easy to do.

Very simple beat. Finger snaps. Very, very simple. Was there any opportunity in France to actually see any of these musicians in person?

No, these people did not come to France back then. But we saw them in the movies, rock 'n' roll movies like *High School Confidential* with Jerry Lee Lewis and *The Girl Can't Help It* with Jayne Mansfield—there was a lot of music in that one.

Let's jump forward to this exhibition. It seems to me to be an unusual show for the Fondation Cartier.

It is. I don't think that there has ever been an exhibition like this anywhere in the world; one that explores the origin of rock 'n' roll but is not simply about the music. I've always been interested in contemporary art, not only because of the art itself, but also because of the freedom of expression that it embraces, which every society needs. Rock 'n' roll helped provoke a very important transformation in society, a very dramatic change in spirit. And this has altered America and the world. In the years following World War II, I remember how much we loved the Americans. I still have in my mind the memory of the American soldiers. I remember the American cars, the first time I tasted chewing gum, the beginning of blue jeans, and all that stuff. However, when I became a bit older, I realized that American society was in deep trouble due to the racial problems in the South, which shocked me. We sometimes forget that the law in the South did not allow mixed schools, buses, cinema houses, or restaurants. Today, European restaurants have non-smoking and smoking areas. At that time, you had black and white areas. When you think of it today, it's just a horror. To me, America was both good and bad: it was powerful and came to save Europe from the Nazis, but it was also divided, segregated. This America was so rich, Puritan, racist, and reactionary. A man on television comes to mind, a father, who broke a record in public saying that rock 'n' roll had to go, the footage of which is shown in the exhibition. Rock 'n' roll was the devil, it was hell. It was decadence, it allowed the mixture of black and white!

Do you think that rock 'n' roll from that era has an ongoing influence on contemporary culture?

Definitely, it caused a big change in many parts of the arts, and the influence it had on teenagers has stayed with us and continues to affect the way we move, walk, dance, dress. The rock 'n' roll attitude in turn is strongly linked to the rebelliousness of new stars like Marlon Brando and James Dean who talked, thought, and dressed in a new way. There are photos of Elvis and Brando on motorcycles, wearing caps, and you can't tell one from the other. When Elvis was young, he started wearing pink jackets with black shirts—that was a new way of dressing and it influenced fashion tremendously. When you look at what fashion became just after the beginning of the rock 'n' roll revolution and still today, it is inspired by music.

The exhibition itself looks back on these developments, which took place fifty years ago. Perhaps I'm mistaken, but my impression has been that generally your exhibitions focus on living, breathing, truly contemporary art.

Not all of them, but most of them. But, you know, in the past the Fondation Cartier has presented exhibitions on the 1960s and 1980s, as well as on the Yanomami Indians from the Brazilian Amazon. So we do not only show the work of living young artists; we examine society as well.

You have mentioned in the past that this is an exhibition that you've wanted to do for a very long time.

Oh, absolutely, for over twenty years. From the day I started the Fondation Cartier, when I hired the first curator, Marie-Claude Beaud, I told her I wanted to do something on rock 'n' roll.

So in a way it's a dream come true.

Exactly, and I'm happy that we did it a bit later, finally, because twenty years ago I would not have stopped at 1959, I'm sure. I would have let it go through the 1960s and 1970s because it's true that in the story of rock 'n' roll, there are very important groups like the Rolling Stones and so many others. But I feel that 1959 was the end of rock 'n' roll—a kind of end. By the end of 1958, Elvis left the stage for the Army. I always remember the famous phrase: "Elvis has left the building."

By 1959, Little Richard had turned to the ministry. Chuck Berry would soon be in trouble with the law. Jerry Lee Lewis had married his cousin . . .

Buddy Holly was dead, Ritchie Valens was dead . . . and soon Eddie Cochran would be dead, too.

They all, all the great ones, faded from the scene.

It was exactly the time when rock 'n' roll came to Europe with European singers—Cliff Richard in England, Johnny Hallyday, Eddy Mitchell, and Danyel Gérard in France, for instance. European rockers were the ones who were selling records, more than the Americans. Then, in the 1960s, rock 'n' roll became European, even in America, where the Beatles and the Rolling Stones became the biggest stars. When Europe takes over, it's not rock 'n' roll anymore. So it's a rupture. It's the end of the story, really, the end of an era.

How was 1939 the beginning?

It was the beginning of the war in Europe, a dramatic, historical date, a turning point, even though America was not yet involved in the war. It was also the year of the emergence of Albert Ammons from the *Spirituals To Swing* concerts at Carnegie Hall and the boogie-woogie craze which ultimately led to rock 'n' roll. The date of 1939 allows us to show how rock 'n' roll was born as a music.

Have you included any contemporary art in the exhibition that comments on rock 'n' roll?

No, however, we do make reference to an extremely important artist from that time: Jackson Pollock. We are showing a short film about him.

The one where he's dripping the paint?

Exactly. Jackson Pollock dripping is Elvis singing or moving on stage. The same impulse, the same freedom. And they were the same age, more or less. Jackson Pollock was a bit older. The style of Pollock's painting is very, very close to the spirit of rock 'n' roll music to me, it was a kind of rebellion in the way you sing and the way you move and in the way you see, from Pollock to James Dean to Elvis. I think that everything you look at, paintings, photography, sculpture, everything was changing. We also highlight the art of the age, the record covers, and all the poster design. It's very typical of the time. When you look at it, it's pop art! They used funny and clever color combinations, and their manner of treating typography is also interesting: each letter, for example, started to move. They brought rhythm to the look of the graphics.

How do you think the younger generation today views Elvis Presley and the other founders of rock 'n' roll?

I would divide the younger generation into two categories—the musicians and more sophisticated followers of music, and everybody else. Elvis is huge in the memory and spirit of the music industry but, unfortunately, for everyone else, the most recent memory is the one that lasts, the memories of his concerts from the mid-1970s. His last great performance was the *Comeback* special on television in 1968, the one where he's in black leather. I was lucky enough to see him in Las Vegas in 1970. He was thin, looked good, sang perfectly well, but it wasn't the same. From there, he became a caricature, not only of himself, but of America at the time. He wasn't the rebel that we all loved in the 1950s, whose attitude, by the way, the photographer Alfred Wertheimer was able to capture, just before Elvis became a superstar. We are lucky enough to have a special exhibition on a selection of these photographs in our show, and we have added many of them to the Fondation Cartier's collection.

So you hope that one thing the exhibition will accomplish is to reinforce the earlier image of Elvis in the public's mind.

Not only Elvis. Elvis is only part of the exhibition. Elvis is big, but he's not the only one. If you look at every art movement, there's always one major figure, though he is not always the first, like Picasso for Cubism. So, when you look at rock 'n' roll, it's obvious that Elvis Presley became the leader, but there was also Bill Haley, Chuck Berry, Little Richard. . . . We are also trying to incorporate lesser known players, like the composer-producers Jerry Leiber and Mike Stoller. They were the most important guys behind the scenes, absolutely the biggest ones. We would like to pay tribute to artists like them who are key to the history of the period.

Do you think that in a sense rock 'n' roll, the story of rock 'n' roll—the story of Elvis as emblematic of rock 'n' roll—says anything about the American dream?

Yes, it's all about the American dream—the freedom, the possibilities. This exhibition shows the American dream—we will even have a Cadillac on display! It's a walk through the origins of rock 'n' roll and is 100% American. There is not one piece of French or European music or art in this exhibition. It reflects our view of the America of the 1940s and the 1950s, and of the music that generated a new society in America and all over the world. The young generation of today does not necessarily know that. It does not realize that young guys like Elvis, who was a truck driver, contributed to a huge change in our civilization, a great change in music. And it was all done, as always, by young chaps.

Alain Dominique Perrin is the President of the Fondation Cartier pour l'art contemporain and Chief Curator of the exhibition *Rock 'n' Roll 39-59*, presented at the Fondation Cartier in Paris from June 22 to October 28, 2007.
Gregg Geller is an A&R man, the producer of compilations and reissues, and is the Creative Consultant of the exhibition.

Chopping cotton on rented land, near White Plains, Greene County, Georgia, June 1941, by Jack Delano

Worker's child playing a phonograph in a cabin home, Transylvania Project, Louisiana, January 1939, by Russell Lee.

Pawnshop and secondhand clothing store on Beale Street, Memphis, Tennessee, November 1939, by Marion Post Wolcott.

Newspaper extra announcing the Japanese attacks on Pearl Harbor, Redding California December 7, 1941, by Russell Lee.
A workman reads about the United States' decision to go to war, Shasta County, California, December 1941, by Russell Lee (opposite).

December 7, 1941, allied with Germany since 1936 and fighting against China since 1937, Japan launches an air attack that effectively destroys an American naval base on Pearl Harbor, provoking the United States to enter World War II. *Life* magazine cover, December 22, 1941.

Atomic bomb tests over Bikini Lagoon, July 25, 1946. The Eniwetok and Bikini atolls in the Marshall Islands territory were used as nuclear test sites from 1946 to 1958. *Life*, magazine cover, February 27, 1950.

After returning from the Korean war, a U.S. Marine is welcomed by his family, Brooklyn, New York, September 10, 1953.

Consumer products, c.1950, by Philippe Halsman.

Hot Shot Eastbound. A drive-in movie theater, Iaeger, West Virginia, August 2, 1956, by O. Winston Link.

Cars sitting outside of a drive-in restaurant, West Los Angeles, December 31, 1944, by Nina Leen.

Suburban housing, California, July 11, 1949, by Loomis Dean

"WE CAN SOLVE A HOUSING PROBLEM OR WE CAN TRY TO SOLVE A RACIAL PROBLEM. BUT WE CANNOT COMBINE THE TWO."

WILLIAM J. LEVITT,
HOUSING DEVELOPER, 1954

A sign at a Greyhound bus terminal, Rome, Georgia, 1943, by Esther Bubley (above). Public restrooms, c.1960 (below).

Water fountains, North Carolina, 1950, by Elliott Erwitt (above). A movie theater entrance, Belzoni, Mississippi, 1939, by Marion Post Wolcott (below).

At its headquarters, 69 Fifth Avenue, the NAACP (National Association for the Advancement of Colored People) flew a flag to report lynchings, until, in 1938, the threat of losing its lease forced the association to discontinue the practice. New York City, 1938.

"SOUTHERN TREES BEAR A STRANGE FRUIT, BLOOD ON THE LEAVES AND BLOOD AT THE ROOT, BLACK BODY SWINGING IN THE SOUTHERN BREEZE, STRANGE FRUIT HANGING FROM THE POPLAR TREES."

BILLIE HOLIDAY, "STRANGE FRUIT" (WRITTEN BY LEWIS ALLAN IN 1937)

THE RO
ROCK'I

FROM BOOGIE-W
TO RHYTHM A

OOTS OF N'ROLL

OOGIE AND BLUES

ROCK BEGINS 40
BY ROBERT PALMER

SISTER ROSETTA THARPE 69
BY PETER GURALNICK

HOWLIN' WOLF 77
BY PETER GURALNICK

RHYTHM AND BLUES: ROCK BEFORE ROCK 88
BY FLORENT MAZZOLENI

ROCK BEGINS

BY ROBERT PALMER

Several dozen black dancers shuffled around the floor of the tiny rural church, stamping out a steady rocking beat on the floorboards and clapping their hands in complex cross-rhythms. A hoarse-voiced leader shouted out one-line phrases in a kind of singsong, the dancers answering with whiplash responses. When the song leader fell back on a bench, overcome by the shuddering rhythms, the heat, and the furious pace of the singing, a second leader took over, half-singing, half-gurgling in an unknown tongue.

O my Lord
O my Lordy
Well, well, well
I've gotta rock
You've gotta rock
Wah wah ho
Wah wah wah ho

In a corner of the church two white folklorists, John Lomax and his son Alan, sat transfixed as their bulky portable recording rig transcribed the music onto an aluminum disc. The year was 1934, and the Lomaxes had stumbled upon a survival of one of the oldest varieties of African-American religious songs, a genuine backcountry ring shout. But they had also stumbled upon the future. The rhythmic singing, the hard-driving beat, the bluesy melody, and the improvised, stream-of-consciousness words of this particular shout—eventually issued by the Library of Congress as "Run Old Jeremiah"—all anticipate key aspects of rock 'n' roll as it would emerge some twenty years later.

The Lomaxes were just beginning to record folk music on location in the rural South in 1934, but rock prototypes were already abundant. In Mississippi the sedate spiritual singing of earlier generations was being replaced by a new style, emphasizing the deliberate rhythms of the archaic ring shouts. The style was called "rocking and reeling," and it probably originated in the maverick Sanctified or Holiness churches, where guitars, drums, and horns were as acceptable as the piano or the organ, and more easily afforded. Moreover, it was a style that was already beginning to influence secular music. The Graves Brothers of Hattiesburg, Mississippi, who had recorded "rocking and reeling" spirituals for Paramount in 1929, made several blues records as the Mississippi Jook Band in 1936. Their songs "Barbecue Bust" and "Dangerous Woman" featured fully formed rock 'n' roll guitar riffs and a stomping rock 'n' roll beat.

40

It is possible, with the help of a little hindsight, to find rock roots at almost every stratum of American folk and popular music during the mid-1930s. In Chicago transplanted Southern bluesmen like Tampa Red and Big Bill Broonzy were taming irregular rural forms to the demands of the urban accompaniment, often including horns, piano, bass, and drums. In the Midwest jump bands were keeping their fans dancing with hard-riffing instrumental blues, featuring gruff-toned tenor saxophone solos and a four-to-the-bar walking rhythm that was an urban descendant of the down-home sanctified stomp. In Nashville two white hillbillies named Alton and Rabon Delmore were entertaining radio audiences with their hit "Brown's Ferry Blues," a black-influenced, two-guitar dance tune as redolent of things to come as the music of the Mississippi Jook Band. In Texas and Oklahoma large, white western swing bands such as Bob Wills and His Texas Playboys and Milton Brown's Musical Brownies were mixing big-band jazz, black blues, and white country music into a heady brew.

Rock 'n' roll was an inevitable outgrowth of the social and musical interactions between blacks and whites in the South and Southwest. Its roots are a complex tangle. Bedrock black church music influenced blues, rural blues influenced white folk song, and the black popular music of the northern ghettos —blues and black pop—influenced jazz and so on. But the single most important process was the influence of black music on white. Rock might not have developed out of a self-contained African-American tradition, but it certainly would not have developed had there been no African Americans.

In a very real sense rock was implicit in the music of the first Africans brought to North America. This transplanted African music wasn't exactly boogie-woogie or jazz, but it did have several characteristics that survive in American music today. It was participatory; often a song leader would be pitted against an answering chorus, or a solo instrument against an ensemble, in call-and-response fashion. It sometimes attained remarkable polyrhythmic complexity and always had a kind of percussive directionality or rhythmic drive. Vocal quality tended to be hoarse or grainy by European standards, though there was also considerable use of falsetto. Melodies fell within a relatively narrow range and often incorporated flexible pitch treatment around certain "blue notes." There was some improvisation, but always within the limits of more or less traditional structures.

All these characteristics are evident in quite a few rock 'n' roll records. For example, in "What'd I Say" Ray Charles calls out a lead melody while a chorus responds and riffing horns answer his piano figures. His band's rhythm section drives relentlessly and superimposes fancy accent patterns over the basic beat. His voice has a hoarse, straining quality, with occasional leaps into falsetto. His melody is narrow in range and blues-like, and the improvisations that occur never threaten the continuity of the song's gospel-derived metric and harmonic structure.

One shouldn't conclude from these similarities that pure African music was somehow transformed into rock 'n' roll. Music in Africa was always flexible, ready to accommodate new influences from the next village or from foreign cultures, and in America plantation owners and preachers tried to stamp it out entirely. Accordingly, it adapted. The traits that survived without much alteration tended to be of two kinds. Some were musical imponderables, like vocal quality or rhythmic drive, aspects of style so basic to the culture they were rarely considered consciously and were therefore immune to conscious change. Others—blues scales, call-and-response forms—were close enough to some varieties of European folk music to be assimilated and perpetuated by whites.

The acculturation of black Americans to mainstream musical values proceeded more and more rapidly as the twentieth century gathered momentum, but pockets of tradition remained. In 1940, when Charlie Christian and T-Bone Walker were already playing modern jazz and blues on electric guitars, a team of interviewers in the Georgia Sea Islands found elderly residents who still knew songs in African languages and knew how to make African drums. Elsewhere, the bedrock African culture persevered most tenaciously in the black church, just as in Africa itself religion, magic, and music had been closely linked in a kind of composite cultural focus. This is why the most African-sounding rock 'n' roll has always come from the church, from gospel-inspired blues shouters such as Ray Charles or from former gospel singers such as the Isley Brothers, whose "Shout" was an old-fashioned ring shout done up with band accompaniment.

But there is more to rock 'n' roll than this single primordial strain. The roots of "What'd I Say" and "Shout" are not necessarily identical to the roots of Chuck Berry's "Johnny B. Goode" or of Carl Perkins' "Blue Suede Shoes." It would take at least one book, if not a library, to trace these various kinds of rock 'n' roll back through their myriad sources. Here we can only indicate some of the most important contributors and trace a few of the most prominent developmental processes.

The music brought to America by European settlers determined most of the forms in which both old and new song materials would be set. Song stanzas of four and eight bars were a heritage of European epic poetry and narrative ballads; there are examples of such things in some traditional African music, but only as one formal scheme among many. The narrative ballad itself, with its objective performer who comments on but does not become involved in the action, was a European product very foreign to the mainstream of black tradition. A ballad vogue among blacks during the late nineteenth century did produce memorable songs such as "Stagger Lee" and "Frankie And Johnny," several of which were revived by early rockers.

In isolated rural areas, particularly Appalachia and the Ozarks, traditional English, Scotch, and Irish dance music survived, along with folk fiddling. But even there the African banjo became as popular as the fiddle. The guitar, which had been derived by the Spanish and Portuguese from the African Moors, came later. During the late nineteenth century and early twentieth centuries, white country musicians developed a tradition of virtuosity on all these instruments. Their repertoires retained many old-time folk ballads, dance tunes, and hymns, but black-influenced minstrel tunes, blues-like ballads, and camp meeting songs were also popular.

African Americans had developed their own distinctive and diverse body of folk music by 1900 alongside the relatively pure African strains that survived in some church music and in the work songs sung by gang laborers. The black creations that whites knew best were minstrel songs—lively, often humorous tunes that tended to resemble Anglo-American jigs and reels. Many minstrel songs were composed by whites such as Dan Emmett (composer of "Dixie") and Thomas D. Rice ("Jump Jim Crow"), but all of them were inspired ultimately by the black plantation orchestras that had regaled visitors in the antebellum South. Both the black groups and their white imitators consisted of banjos, fiddles (an instrument with numerous West African precedents), and various percussion instruments, notably tambourines, triangles, and bone clappers. The earliest plantation orchestras had probably played African dance music like that performed by the lute- and fiddle-playing *griots* of the African savanna today. But by the time we heard of them, they had learned enough European dance tunes to satisfy their white patrons, and the fiddlers were paying some attention to European musical standards. The white minstrels, who copied black playing styles and tunes as closely as they could, became the rage of America and Europe during the years just before the Civil War. For the first time, an essentially black music, albeit in diluted form, had found favor with a large white audience. Oddly enough, many popular minstrel songs were absorbed back into black tradition following the war. They turned up in the repertoires of black banjo- and guitar-playing minstrels, or songsters, well into the twentieth century.

During the first decades of the century a new kind of black secular song emerged. The songs were originally known as "one-verse songs" because they repeated a single line several times. Gradually an *aab* stanza form replaced the older *aaa*, and the songs began to be called the blues. They may have represented an attempt by rural blacks to accommodate the demands of guitar accompaniment within the free-following strains of their field cries and work songs. In any case, the blues spread rapidly, first through the tent-show performances of such vaudeville singers as Gertrude "Ma" Rainey, then through the polished blues-based compositions of W.C. Handy, and finally, after 1926, through recordings by authentic rural bluesmen such as Blind Lemon Jefferson. Along with blues recordings, which were popular among northern blacks as well as in the South, came records of singing black preachers and of holy dance music from the Sanctified churches.

The rise of the recording industry in the 1920s accelerated musical syntheses. For the first time, white guitar players from Kentucky were able to listen carefully to the music of black bluesmen from Texas, and rural medicine show entertainers could hear the latest cabaret hits from New York. Early recordings documented musical changes rather than determining them, but by the mid-1930s records were the primary source of inspiration for many musicians.

In white country music, the largely traditional repertoires of performers like Uncle Dave Macon became outmoded as younger musicians popularized their own hybrid material. Among the most influential of these were Jimmie Rodgers, the "singing brakeman" from Meridian, Mississippi, and the Alabama-born Delmore Brothers. Both acts recorded black-influenced blues and blues-like dance tunes. The Monroe Brothers, Bill and Charlie, popularized a more Anglo-American brand of country music. In a sense they helped preserve white folk traditions by dressing them up with a new vocal intensity and unprecedented instrumental flash. But even mandolinist Bill Monroe, who went on to become the "father of bluegrass," injected a great deal of blues feeling into his playing. Early in his career he had been impressed by a black guitarist and fiddler named Arnold Schultz, who reportedly exercised a decisive influence on Ike Everly and Merle Travis as well. In the West, western swing bands combined country music, black-oriented repertoires, horns, drums, and hot improvised solos from another black musical source, jazz.

Jazz itself was growing in several different directions, but in the Southwest it was heavily indebted to vocal blues. Bands like Count Basie's ("the band that plays the blues") concentrated on the twelve-bar blues form almost exclusively and often played "head" arrangements: blues riffs developed by the musicians on the spur of the moment. Rhythmically, Basie and the other southwestern bands played a danceable, even, four-to-the-bar pulse that gradually replaced the jerky 2/4 associated with Dixieland. The bluesiness, the riffing horns, the tough tenor saxophone solos, and the driving rhythm of these groups had a profound impact on western swing —which led in turn to country boogie and rockabilly—and on black popular music, which led to rhythm and blues and rock 'n' roll.

As rural bluesmen moved to urban centers, their music lost much of its delicacy and lilt. In keeping with the pace of city life, rhythms became heavier, more insistent and faster. An indication of this shift came from Memphis as early as the 1920s. There, several two-guitar teams worked out a characteristic differentiation of parts in which one played lead lines while the other provided bass notes and chords. (Earlier, country blues guitar duets had tended toward a more intricate, more democratic counterpoint.) Memphis blues rhythms were already harder and steadier than those of the surrounding countryside.

Big Bill Broonzy, a Mississippian who relocated to Chicago, took these ideas a step further by working with washtub-and-string bassists and with the percussive washboard of Washboard Sam. During the 1930s Broonzy and his Chicago friends, among them Sam and Tampa Red, became America's most popular blues performers. Harmonically, they were increasingly influenced by jazz, while rhythmically they favored the easy, relaxed swing of the southwestern bands. When horns, drums, and piano were added to their accompaniments, these ties to jazz became even more apparent.

Meanwhile, southwestern blues and jazz musicians were experimenting with a revolutionary new instrument, the electric guitar. Eddie Durham seems to have recorded the first solos on the amplified instrument in 1938 with the Kansas City Five and Six, groups recruited from the Count Basie band. In 1939 Charlie Christian, an Oklahoman, recorded on electric guitar with Benny Goodman. His virtuoso hornlike single-string lines and the deep, bluesy character of his playing set standards for jazz guitar playing that have yet to be superseded. But Christian was a former country bluesman. As a youngster he performed with an older guitarist, Aaron "T-Bone" Walker, who had recorded country blues (as Oak Cliff T-Bone) as early as 1929.

If Christian invented modern jazz guitar (and helped to invent modern jazz), it was T-Bone Walker who invented modern blues, setting the style that almost all subsequent blues and rock lead guitarists would follow, from B.B. King through Eric Clapton. The jazzy flash of Walker's work was not in itself revolutionary. While the Memphis bluesmen were developing early lead guitar styles within a relatively simple framework, Eddie Lang and Lonnie Johnson were working in New York City as jazz soloists, playing single-note lines on their acoustic guitars on recordings by Bix Beiderbecke, Duke Ellington, and other prominent figures.

Their techniques were exemplary, and necessarily so, for they had to fill with their virtuosity the spaces left by their instrument's rapidly decaying notes and relatively thin sound. Christian continued their style of rapid runs. But it took Walker to really exploit electricity. By using his amplifier's volume control to sustain pitches and combining this technique with the string-bending and finger vibrato practiced by traditional bluesmen, Walker in effect invented a new instrument. He was able to reproduce both the linear urgency of jazz saxophonists and the convoluted cry of blues and gospel singers. In addition, he developed a chordal style on fast numbers, a pumping guitar shuffle that led eventually to the archetypal rock 'n' roll style of Chuck Berry.

Jazz, which was a popular music with mass appeal through much of the 1930s, continued to produce black pop hits during the 1940s and early 1950s. But slick, sophisticated jazz bands did not appeal to a significant number of urban African Americans who were either born in the country or only a generation removed from it. To cater to their tastes, a raunchier, more down-home jazz style emerged. Lionel Hampton, a vibraharpist who had worked with Benny Goodman, produced the definitive record in the new genre in 1942. It was "Flying Home," a riff-based number with a heavy beat. Hampton, who was also a drummer, is credited with being the first popular jazz percussionist to make a habit of turning the sticks around and hitting the drums with the blunt ends. But "Flying Home" had more than a big beat; it had a grainy, shrieking saxophone solo by the Texas-bred Illinois Jacquet. Hampton now says he was influenced to move in this direction by guitarist Charlie Christian and other southwestern musicians, and Jacquet was one of a long line of Texas tenors who screamed and honked like sanctified preachers in spiritual paroxysms. There can be little doubt that the new idiom, often called "jump blues," was originally a Texas-Oklahoma phenomenon.

Louis Jordan, an Arkansas-born alto saxophonist and vocalist, played in a lighter, more urbanely humorous style, but his novelty hits of the 1940s— "Saturday Night Fish Fry," "Caldonia," "Blue Light Boogie"—moved out to a rocking southwestern boogie beat, and his alto solos were speech-inflected and gritty. Soon saxophone-dominated band blues, usually with a boogie rhythm and T-Bone-derived guitar leads, became a dominant strain in black popular music. The headquarters for this music was the West Coast, where war industry jobs attracted thousands of blacks from the southwest and where a number of early jump-blues artists made records that were practically rock 'n' roll—Amos Milburn's "Down The Road Apiece" (1946) and Little Willie Littlefield's "K.C. Loving" (1952, the same Leiber-Stoller tune later made famous as "Kansas City") are good examples. But the style's outreach was national. Roy Brown, from New Orleans, made the most seminal of all jump-blues hits, "Good Rockin' Tonight," in 1947, and the Nashville pianist Cecil Gant prefigured the Jerry Lee Lewis piano style in 1950 with "We're Gonna Rock."

Even black vocal harmony groups were affected by the emergence of band blues. Many of these groups had roots in the quartet singing that had been an important part of black religious music since the 1920s, but rather than base their styles on those of the more abandoned sanctified singers, they usually emulated the smooth pop harmonies of the Ink Spots. During the mid-1940s, however, the Spots' popularity waned, and some of the vocal groups adopted a harder approach that was much closer to Southern blues and gospel.

In some cases this was the result of suggestions by white record producers. Independently operated record companies such as Savoy, Aladdin, Atlantic, Modern, Imperial, and King recorded a majority of the black music popular after World War II. (For the most part, the "majors," including Columbia and Victor, either concentrated on middle-of-the-road pop or continued to issue "race" discs by prewar favorites.) The independents were successful in part because they were run by men who knew black music. Many of the producers were collectors of blues, jazz and gospel records, and even when they were working with northern musicians and singers they attempted to give their records a Southern flavor.

The increasing prominence of rocking boogie rhythms in black popular music during the 1940s and early 1950s was an important but not particularly surprising phenomenon. Old-time southwestern musicians remember people playing rocking boogies as far back as 1910—Texas pianist Sammy Price recalls Blind Lemon Jefferson referring to the style as "booger rooger"—and the supercharged "Pinetop's Boogie Woogie" by Alabama-born pianist Clarence "Pinetop" Smith was a "race record" hit in 1928. More interesting, for the purposes of the present study, is the fact that the boogie fever that swept America beginning in the late 1930s and continuing through the early 1950s, right up to the beginnings of rock 'n' roll, was a biracial phenomenon. It began, for all practical purposes, in 1938, when the white jazz collector and entrepreneur John Hammond brought black music to Carnegie Hall for his first *From Spirituals To Swing* concert. Featured on the bill were the rotund Kansas City blues shouter Joe Turner and his pianist Pete Johnson (who together made music that rocked as hard as the hits Turner would cut for Atlantic during the 1950s), along with two first-generation Chicago boogie-woogie pianists, Meade Lux Lewis and Albert Ammons. Turner and the three pianists settled in for a five-year run at New York's Cafe Society following the concert, and they made a number of recordings. Before long the infectious boogie-woogie beat was finding its way into the mainstream of white popular music. Tommy Dorsey scored a hit with "Boogie Woogie," a record so kinetic it is still cited as a favorite by one of rock's founding fathers, Sun Records producer Sam Phillips. The Andrews Sisters did "Boogie Woogie Bugle Boy." Country artists started making boogie records, too. The Delmore Brothers, who were no strangers to black rhythms, set the pace in 1945 with their "Hillbilly Boogie," which lent an entire movement its name. By 1950, when Louis Jordan's "Blue Light Boogie" was a #1 rhythm and blues hit, Tennessee Ernie Ford was hitting the top of the country charts with "Shotgun Boogie." Black country bluesmen made raw, heavily amplified boogie records of their own, especially in Memphis, where guitarists like Joe Hill Louis, Willie Johnson (with the early Howlin' Wolf Band) and Pat Hare (with Little Junior Parker) played driving rhythms and scorching, distorted solos that might be counted the distant ancestors of heavy metal.

Memphis in the early 1950s was a hotbed of musical activity, and many of the artists who were making a new kind of Southern city blues there—B.B. King, Bobby "Blue" Bland, Roscoe Gordon—would go on to shape the rhythm and blues and soul music of the 1960s. Perhaps the most important and influential record to come out of this ferment was "Rocket '88', " cut at Sam Phillips' Memphis Recording Service, credited to Jackie Brenston on the Chess label, but actually by the Ike Turner Band, with saxophonist Brenston taking the lead vocal. Turner, a pianist and aspiring guitarist from the Mississippi Delta, was acting as talent scout for the Modern and RPM labels of Los Angeles and leading a band, the Delta Rhythm Kings, that took the West Coast jump-blues groups as its models. "Rocket '88' " could almost have been a Wynonie Harris or Amos Milburn jump record, but the saxophone solo (by Raymond Hill) was wilder and rougher than the work of West Coast sax men like Maxwell Davis, and the boogie-woogie beat that kicked the performance along was carried by a fuzzed-out, overamplified electric guitar. (The story behind the guitar sound turns out to be prosaic enough: the amplifier fell off the top of Turner's automobile on the way to Memphis, and Sam Phillips stuffed some paper in the burst speaker cone in order to get on with the session.) These striking characteristics and the song's lyrics, which celebrate the automobile, have led some listeners to credit "Rocket '88', " a #1 rhythm and blues hit in 1951, as "the first rock 'n' roll record."

"Rocket '88' " was an unusually accurate indicator of what some early rock 'n' roll would sound like. It was also recorded by western swing musician Bill Haley and his group the Saddlemen as their first rhythm-and-blues-styled performance, for the small Essex label of Philadelphia. By 1952 Haley and his rechristened Comets were recording full-fledged rockers such as "Rock The Joint" in a similar style. Despite their lingering western swing touches, these early Haley recordings, which predate both his first national hits and Presley's first Sun records by several years, are authentic rock 'n' roll. So are numerous black records from the same period, 1951 to 1953, and by this time white disc jockeys, including Alan Freed in Cleveland and Dewey Phillips in Memphis, were beginning to program such records for a racially mixed but predominantly teenaged audience. The music was ready and waiting for America to discover it.

But America's musical tastes were changing across the board. Guitarist Les Paul, who had been among the first to use the electric instrument, was beginning to revolutionize pop music with his multitracked guitar overdubs. His wife, Mary Ford, sang sweetly enough, but Paul had been a friend of Charlie Christian's, and his playing was blues and jazz oriented. Johnnie Ray's "Cry," a record so emotionally bluesy it virtually parodied itself, was a pop and rhythm and blues hit in 1951. By this time urban rhythm and blues had begun to make way for the Southern sound. The 1952 rhythm and blues hits included Eddie Boyd's "Five Long Years" and Little Walter's "Juke," both Mississippi Delta blues played by musicians who had only recently moved to Chicago. The Caribbean-tinged rhythms of New Orleans were featured on two more rhythm and blues hits, Fats Domino's "Goin' Home" and Lloyd Price's "Lawdy Miss Clawdy" (with Domino on piano). B.B. King, the Beale Street Blues Boy, combined Southern intensity with T-Bone Walker's guitar style on his "3 O'Clock Blues" and "You Know I Love You." Many of the hits produced in the North, among them records by Ruth Brown and Willie Mabon, emulated Southern music or had themes and imagery rooted in the South. Billy Ward and the Dominoes' hits, featuring young Clyde McPhatter, were thinly secularized gospel, often with the stomping beat and rasping saxophone style of jump blues.

By 1954 the music on the rhythm and blues charts was even rawer. Guitar Slim's "The Things That I Used To Do" combined superamplified lead guitar with a vocal so country many urban listeners probably had trouble understanding the diction. The Midnighters' "Work With Me Annie" was a thinly disguised sexual metaphor; Etta James's similar "Roll With Me Henry" roared along in a raucous sanctified vein. Both records had follow-ups. James' "Hey Henry" resembled its predecessor, while the Midnighters' "Annie Had A Baby" left no doubt as to what the "working" in their earlier hit had been about. These records were widely attacked by white ministers and disc jockeys. Abandoned singing and suggestive lyrics were nothing new to black listeners, but black music was beginning to reach a sizable audience of white adolescents.

In 1954 the Crew-Cuts' version of the Chords' rhythm and blues hit "Sh-Boom" was the most successful of many white "covers" of black material. A year later Bill Haley and His Comets made #1 on the pop charts with "Rock Around The Clock," which was introduced to many Americans through the film *The Blackboard Jungle*. This was the original white rock 'n' roll hit, although the music and group's overall style were a somewhat crude copy of the Southern-influenced New York rhythm and blues sound exemplified by Joe Turner's "Shake, Rattle And Roll" (which Haley covered). That same year Elvis Presley scored his first C&W #1 with "I Forgot To Remember To Forget," backed with the black-influenced "Mystery Train" on Sun, while Chuck Berry (with his classic automotive epic "Maybellene") and Fats Domino had #1 rhythm and blues hits. By 1956 Presley, Berry, and Domino, along with newcomer Little Richard, had crossed over to the pop charts. The rock 'n' roll era had begun.

Each of these early rock 'n' rollers was firmly rooted in the music of earlier years. Presley and the other white singers groomed by Sun's Sam Phillips were raised on white country music, hillbilly boogie, and black blues. Presley, for one, knew the recordings of Roy Brown and Mississippi bluesman Arthur "Big Boy" Crudup well before he began recording; Sam Phillips encouraged him to go ahead and make that kind of music himself. Carl Perkins' classic "Blue Suede Shoes" and most of his other work was closer to hillbilly boogie, although his "Matchbox" was a twelve-bar blues that had been popularized by Blind Lemon Jefferson. Jerry Lee Lewis' piano style was shaped by the blues and boogie players he heard in Haney's Big House, a black nightclub in his native Ferriday, Louisiana, and perhaps by the recordings of white country boogie pianists like Moon Mullican and Merrill Moore.

Chuck Berry's guitar work was redolent of the fast shuffle playing of T-Bone Walker; it was his unique talent as a lyricist that made him one of the most original of the early rock 'n' rollers. Fats Domino had been making rhythm and blues records since 1949 and he did little to change his style. It was his astute producer and bandleader, Dave Bartholomew, who added guitar solos and other effects and also wrote many of the songs that Domino made into rock 'n' roll hits. Little Richard, who was backed by Bartholomew's band on many of his early recordings, simply sang novelty blues with the no-holds-barred enthusiasm of a particularly unabashed sanctified vocalist. Bo Diddley, the most primitive of the early black rock 'n' rollers, built his hits on blues and folk materials from backcountry Mississippi and on the Latin-like "hambone" beat.

Without Presley, Berry, and the rest, rock 'n' roll might have turned out differently. But the music was able to flourish and, eventually, to become the dominant popular music of the Western world precisely because it was firmly rooted in, and sustained by, the fertile soil of the South and Southwest.

FIRST PUBLISHED IN *THE ROLLING STONE ILLUSTRATED HISTORY OF ROCK AND ROLL*, EDITED BY JIM MILLER. NEW YORK: ROLLING STONE, 1980.

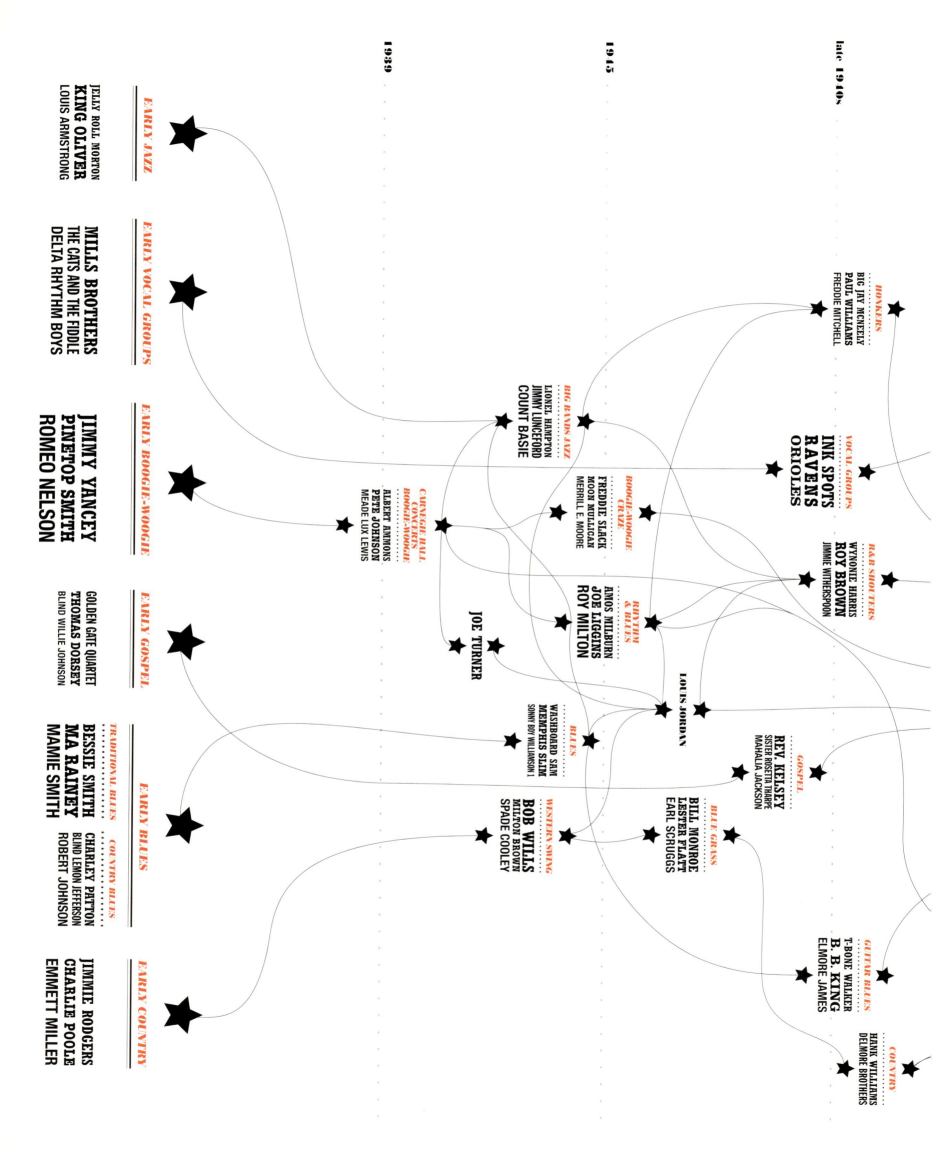

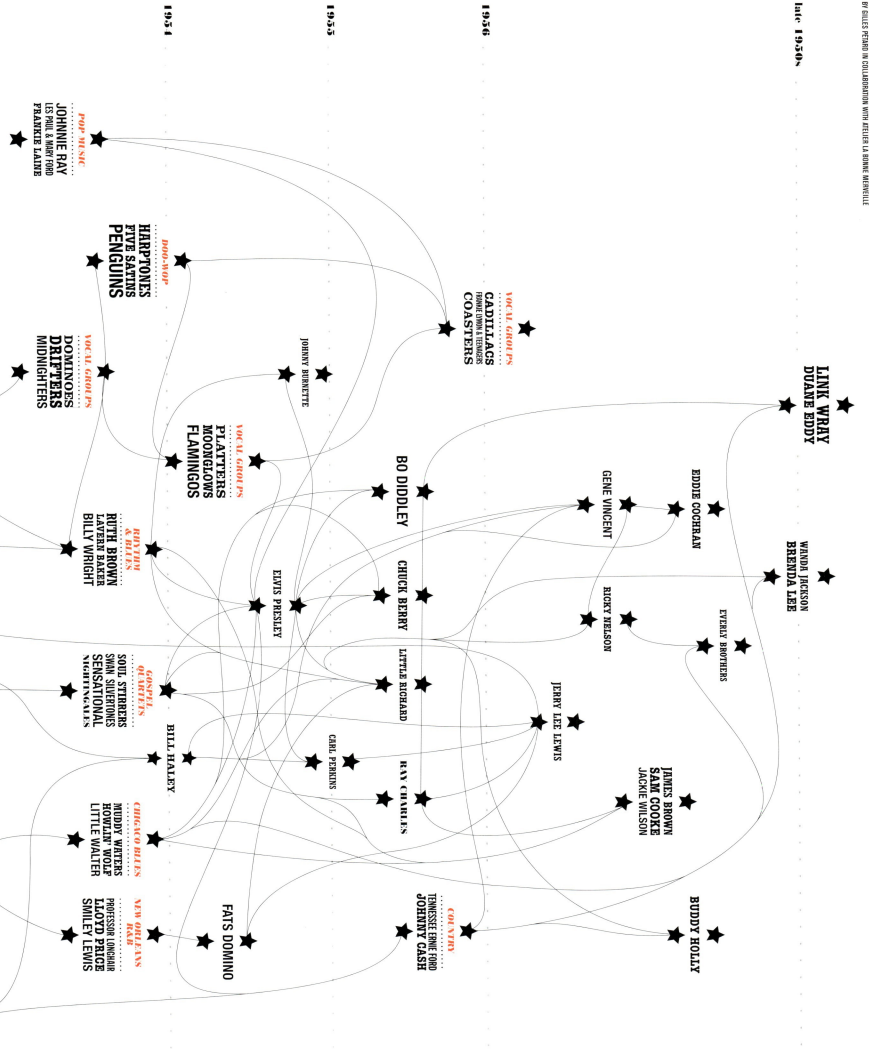

"NOW OUT IN OUR ALLEY EVERY NIGHT, THEY'RE DOIN' THIS THING AND IT'S JUST TOO TIGHT. WELL THEY CALL IT BOOGIE WOOGIE EVERYBODY'S DOIN' THAT BOOGIE WOOGIE NOW."

TAMPA RED, "THEY CALL IT BOOGIE WOOGIE," 1930-1931

Cars lined up outside shelters at Osceola migratory labor camp, Belle Glade, Florida, June 1940, by Marion Post Wolcott.

Albert Ammons and Pete Johnson, c.1942.

Meade "Lux" Lewis, c.1945.

Boogie Woogie Music, Decca, 78 rpm album, early 1940s.

Freddie Slack, *Boogie Woogie*, Capitol, 78 rpm album, early 1940s.

Boogie Woogie And The Blues, Commodore, 10" LP, early 1950s (recordings from the 1940s).

Albert Ammons, *Boogie Woogie Classics*, Blue Note, 10" LP, early 1950s (recordings from 1939).

"MEN CLIMBED OVER EACH OTHER, GIRLS PERCHED ON THEIR PARTNERS' SHOULDERS, BABIES WERE HELD ALOFT, THE YOUNGER GENERATION SCRAMBLED UP ON THE STANDS, CAR TOPS AND CONSTRUCTION WORK AT THE NORTH END OF THE FIELD AND <u>SWING</u> REALLY BROKE LOOSE." —LEE CARSON, *CHICAGO DAILY TIMES*, AUGUST 24, 1938

Savoy Ballroom, Harlem, New York, 1939, by Cornell Capa.

Jitterbug dancers, c. 1945.

Jitterbug dancers, Cholly Atkins on the right, c.1945.

Lionel Hampton and His Orchestra concert bill, c.1943 (above). Jimmie Lunceford and His Orchestra, c.1940 (below).

Glenn Miller and His Orchestra, c.1940 (above). Duke Ellington and His Orchestra, c.1940 (below).

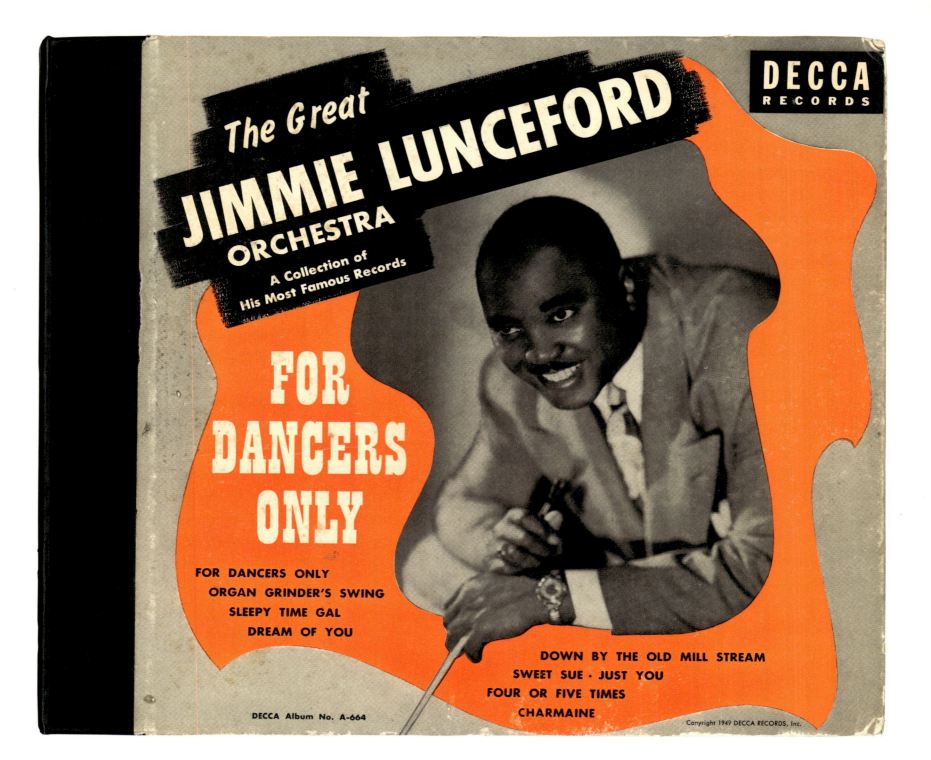

Jimmie Lunceford, *For Dancers Only*, Decca, 78 rpm album, mid-1940s (recordings from the late 1930s).

Lionel Hampton, *Hot Jazz*, RCA Victor, 78 rpm album, mid-1940s (recordings from 1937 to 1938).

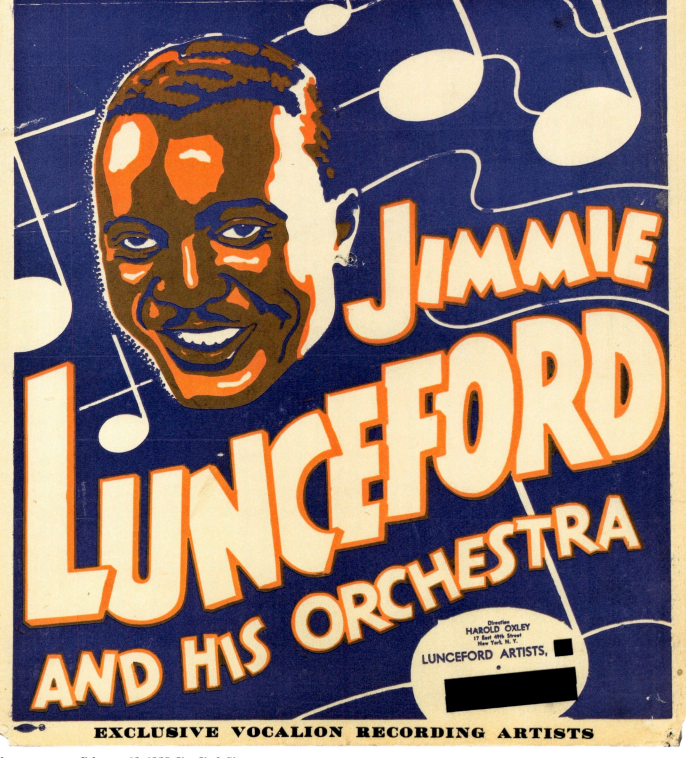

Jimmie Lunceford concert poster, February 12, 1939, New York City.

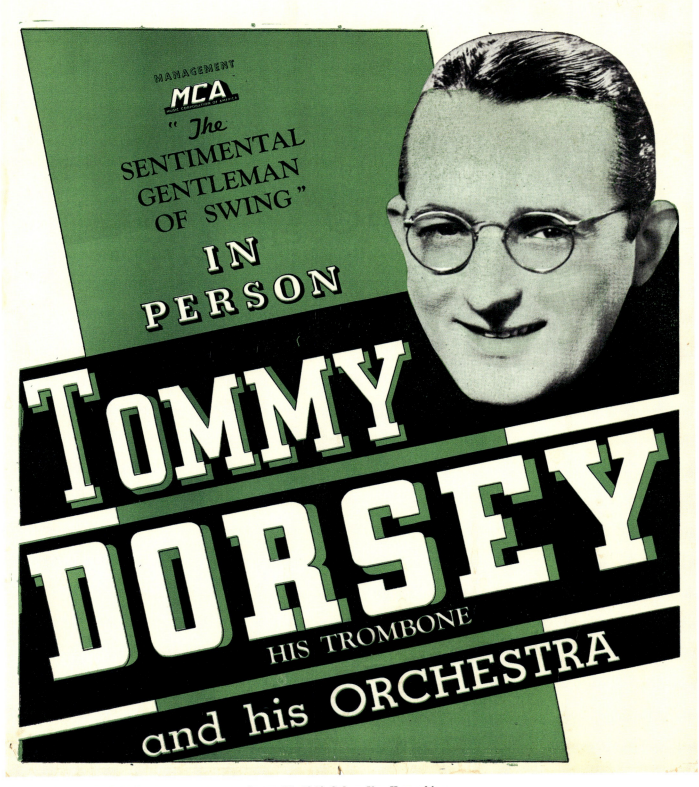

Tommy Dorsey, His Trombone and His Orchestra concert poster, August 30, 1940, Salem, New Hampshire.

"GOSPEL MUSIC IS STEEPED IN EMOTION, NOT LOGIC. WHILE GOSPEL MUSIC MAY MAKE PEOPLE THINK, ITS REAL GOAL IS TO MAKE THEM FEEL."

ACE COLLINS, MUSIC HISTORIAN, 1999

Gospel service, Chicago, Illinois, 1947, by Wayne Miller.

Religious signs along the highway, Georgia, May 1939, by Marion Post Wolcott.

SISTER ROSETTA THARPE

BY PETER GURALNICK

On December 4, 1956 Elvis Presley, Carl Perkins, Jerry Lee Lewis, and Johnny Cash all got together in Sun Studio at 706 Union Avenue in Memphis. It was an impromptu occasion, triggered by Elvis' visit to the little studio where he had gotten his start just eighteen months earlier. There was a Carl Perkins session in progress, with newcomer Jerry Lee Lewis on piano, and Sam Phillips called Johnny Cash to come in for a photo opportunity. Cash didn't stick around long enough to take part in the "jam session" that developed, but the other three sang and played for close to two hours, and when their picture was published in the Memphis paper the next day, they were dubbed the Million Dollar Quartet.

There was one person missing from that picture: gospel singer and guitarist extraordinaire Sister Rosetta Tharpe. She was not there in the flesh, of course, but she was indisputably present in spirit, for while the Million Dollar Quartet may have had much in common—including a love of bluegrass, an admiration for Chuck Berry, an omniverous knowledge and passion for music of every kind, and a certainty that they were on the cusp of a revolution—it was Sister Rosetta Tharpe who provided not just the bedrock of their musical foundation but the jump that lifted their music out of the room.

"Sister Rosetta Tharpe," Jerry Lee Lewis would later say, "I tell you, man, that woman could sing some rock 'n' roll! First time I ever heard her, in Natchez, Mississippi, I was eight or nine years old [this would have been, most likely, given the vagaries of memory, in the mid-to-late 1940s], and she was singing religious music, but she was hitting that guitar, man, she's shakin', and she is singing ROCK 'N' ROLL. I said, 'Whoo-oooo!'"

She was born Rosa (or Rosie Etta) Atkins in Cotton Plant, Arkansas, in 1915, started playing guitar by the age of six, and was on the road with her mother, Katie Bell Nubin, a traveling evangelist in the Church of God in Christ, before she turned twelve. From her earliest days she attracted attention not so much for the technical accomplishment of her playing and singing (though this was considerable) as for the *spirit* with which she imbued the music. "When you talked about Rosetta Tharpe, you talked about a ball of energy," gospel legend Ira Tucker of the Dixie Hummingbirds told her biographer, Gayle Wald. "You would wonder where she learned to play a guitar like that," said the musical director of Brooklyn's Washington Temple Church of God in Christ. "[It] made the people just go beserk."

Much like Jerry Lee Lewis (whose boogie-woogie piano playing owes a great deal to both the drive and whimsicality of her guitar runs), she was both a pure entertainer *and* a serious artist. In 1938 she sang at the celebrated Cotton Club, made her first recordings, and appeared in John Hammond's *From Spirituals To Swing* concert at Carnegie Hall. While she never abandoned her faith, she came in for a good deal of criticism from the gospel community for her various excursions into the world of secular music, not to mention a flamboyant 1951 showbiz wedding arranged primarily to sell tickets—over 20,000—at Washington D.C.'s Griffith Stadium. Nonetheless, she had some of the most popular gospel recordings of all time, with songs like "This Train," "Up Above My Head," "Ninety-Nine And A Half Won't Do" (with her mother), and, of course, "Strange Things Happening Every Day," which went to #2 on the "race" (rhythm and blues) charts in the spring of 1945.

For a whole generation of musicians, black and white, for every one of the Million Dollar Quartet, this was a seminal song—inspiring for its spiritedness as much as for its spirituality. As Carl Perkins said, "It was my Dad's favorite song. When I was a kid, that's one of the things I'd set there trying to learn. When people would come to our house, I'd always take my little old guitar, I'd always play 'Strange Things Happening Every Day.' It was rockabilly, that was it—it *was*."

"She is my all-time favorite gospel singer," said Johnny Cash, who, like Elvis and Jerry Lee, would later record the song, though his is the only version that survived. To another first-generation rockabilly from Arkansas, basso profundo Sleepy LaBeef, who like Elvis and Cash heard Sister Rosetta Tharpe on the radio as a kid, she was the key to his music, and for anyone who listens to her records today, the connection to all of this music remains undeniable. Her sound, in the language of that time, jumps right out of the jukebox—it lifts right off the digital groove. There is no denying the sly note of triumph in her singing and playing, there is no turning away from the joyful sense of celebration that was the heart of rock 'n' roll.

Sister Rosetta Tharpe, c.1948.

Mahalia Jackson, c.1947.

The Golden Gate Quartet, c.1945.

"**BLUES IS THE FOUNDATION OF ALL AMERICAN MUSIC. EVERYTHING COMES FROM BLUES—JAZZ, ROCK, FUNK—IT ALL COMES FROM THE BLUES.**"

ROBERT LOCKWOOD JR., MUSICIAN

John Lee Hooker at the Music Inn, Stockbridge, Massachusetts, c.1950, by Clemens Kalischer.

B.B. King with the Bill Harvey Band at the Hippodrome on Beale Street, Memphis, Tennessee, c.1950, by Ernest C. Withers.
Blues at the Maxwell Street flea market, Chicago, Illinois, 1947, by Wayne Miller (opposite).

HOWLIN' WOLF

BY PETER GURALNICK

When he first heard Howlin' Wolf in early 1951, Sam Phillips always liked to recall, "I said, 'This is for me. This is where the soul of man never dies.'"

Phillips never altered that view. If he could have recorded just one person to the end of his days, he said repeatedly and with conviction, it would have been the Howlin' Wolf, the greatest pure talent he ever encountered. "God, what I would give to see him [again] as he was in my studio, to see the fervor in his face, to hear the pure instinctive quality in that man's voice. He sang with his damn soul."

I don't think anyone who ever witnessed a live performance would disagree. The first time I saw him in person, he was playing in a little basement folk club, leaning on the metal posts that held up the ceiling as he sang and pounding on them occasionally for emphasis. It was a moment that could only put one in mind of the parable of Samson bringing down the temple around him. "If I had my way," sang street singer and traveling evangelist Blind Willie Johnson in his version of the story, "I'd tear this building down." And you believed that Wolf, fifty-five years old, six-foot-three and three-hundred pounds, not only could but very likely would—not due to his size but, as fellow blues singer Johnny Shines suggested, because of the sheer ferocity of his musical attack.

He was born Chester Arthur Burnett in West Point, Mississippi in 1910, grew up on the music of the great Delta bluesmen Charley Patton and Tommy Johnson, and embodied any number of contradictory qualities both in his music and in his person. He could be as thoughtful as he was ferocious. The instinctive qualities to which Sam Phillips alluded ("He gave the appearance of being almost totally unconcerned, but this was just a façade. He had the ability to read people without even letting you know he was doing it.") were matched by a dedication to education and self-improvement. He displayed a swaggering certitude, along with a sense of deep-seated hurt that could be traced to an unloving mother. And all of this came out in his music.

After a stint in the army, he moved to West Memphis in 1948 and got a fifteen-minute radio slot which was how Sam Phillips first heard him. He made some of his greatest recordings for Phillips, including two of his best-known songs (and biggest sellers), "Moanin' At Midnight" and "How Many More Years," which comprised his debut single release on the Chess label. When a battle broke out between Chess and Modern, the two companies to which Phillips had been licensing recordings (he would not start his own Sun label until the following year), Wolf signed with Chess and moved to Chicago in 1952. "I had a $4,000 car and $3,900 in my pocket," he told rock archivist Dave Booth. "I'm the onliest one that drove out of the South like a gentleman."

In Chicago he took up a rivalry with Muddy Waters—no rivalry at all, he would claim in expansive moments, when he was more than willing to declare himself "the king of the blues." In any case, while Muddy and virtually every other blues singer of their generation settled into a fairly fixed pattern of performance (Elmore James, had he lived, might have been the one bluesman to rival Wolf in intensity and spontaneity), the Mighty Wolf, as he not infrequently referred to himself, never subsided. Whether spurred on by inner demons, a sense of competition as much with himself as with any challenger, or simply the irrepressible need to express himself in exactly the way he felt at any given moment, Wolf refused to concede to either custom or age. You have only to watch him on the ABC network television show *Shindig!* from 1965, singing his magisterial "How Many More Years (Do I Have To Let You Dog Me Around)?" to grasp the power of the man and his music. There he is swaggering onto the national stage without a trace of self-consciousness or incongruity, ripping into his blues in a candy-cane setting with all the conviction that Sam Phillips had first glimpsed fifteen years earlier. He pops his eyes, waggles his hips, looks as if he is about to swallow the tiny harmonica in his mouth, then leaps up and down, with the Rolling Stones (the source of his *Shindig!* invitation) at his feet and the sense that not just the stage but the entire world has been shaken.

He was no less magisterial in old age. Gaunt, ill, the victim of a number of heart attacks, he carried on no less heroically, constricted only by the need to confine his engagements to cities in which he could receive dialysis treatment at a local Veterans Administration hospital. One of the last times I saw him, some nurses from the VA requested "I Can't Stop Loving You," and while he didn't know the song, Wolf graciously acceded to the request, sitting there with his legs splayed out, head tilted back, improvising lyrics to bandleader Eddie Shaw's accompaniment. "I can't stop loving you, baby," Wolf growled, "I can't get enough, I'll *never* get enough of your love." Later in the evening—or perhaps it was the next night—he was singing one of his signature numbers, flinging himself into it with characteristic abandon, when all of a sudden his body failed him, the color just seemed to drain from his face, and he sat there, eyes cast down, shaking his head as if at yet another in a series of inexplicable betrayals. "The great Howlin' Wolf!" called out Eddie Shaw, taking the microphone from him. "Let's hear it for the great Howlin' Wolf!" But Wolf would have none of it. He just sat there, continuing to shake his head until at last, as if by some superhuman effort, he roused himself and seized the microphone back, singing and blowing his harmonica with a force and determination that seemed unlikely ever to quit.

He made his last major appearance at an all-star blues concert in Chicago in late 1975, vying good-naturedly for the spotlight with contemporary stars Bobby "Blue" Bland, Little Milton, and B.B. King and remaining till the end of the show to watch B.B.'s headlining performance. A few days later he checked into the hospital, where he died on January 10, 1976, at the age of sixty-five.

There has probably never been a blues singer who more dramatically personified his music than Howlin' Wolf. He was the Mighty Wolf when he was feeling good, in other moods an object more to be pitied than feared ("Don't laugh at me, baby, please don't make fun of me," he sang, "I didn't make myself"). "I'm a taildragger," he would declare not infrequently, quoting the song, "I wipes out my tracks." He was a mountain wolf, a timber wolf, a lone wolf. But always the Wolf, "the wolf that howls, trying to be satisfied."

Howlin' Wolf, Memphis grocery store, Tennessee, early 1950s, by Ernest C. Withers.

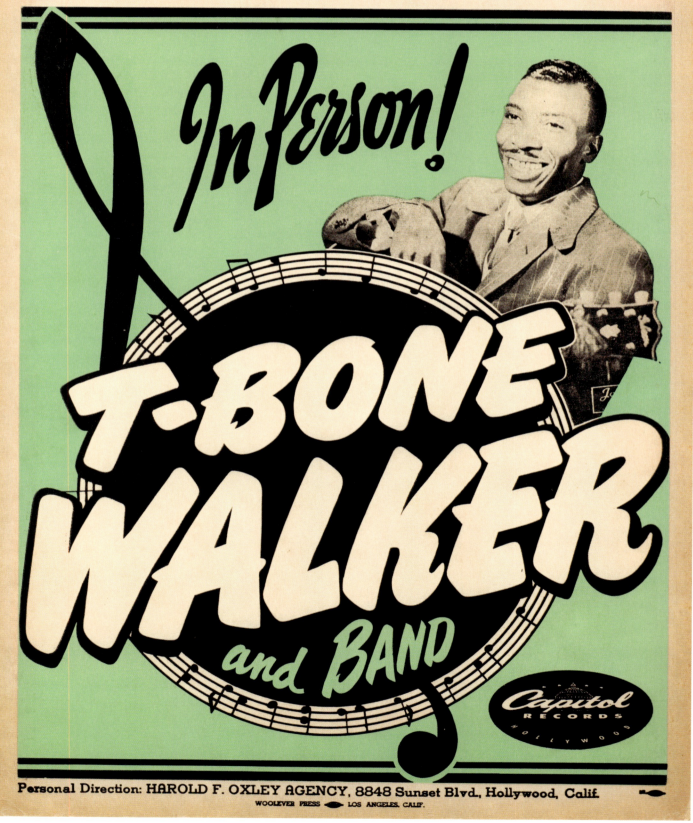

T-Bone Walker concert poster, May 14, 1950, Wichita, Kansas.

Muddy Waters concert poster, May 1, 1954, Clarksville, Tennessee.

"I'M A PLAIN OLD COUNTRY BOY A CORNBREAD LOVIN' COUNTRY BOY I RAISE CAIN ON SATURDAY BUT I GO TO CHURCH ON SUNDAY I'M A PLAIN OLD COUNTRY BOY A TATER EATIN' COUNTRY BOY I'LL BE LOOKIN' OVER THAT OLD GRAY MULE WHEN THE SUN COMES UP ON MONDAY." —"LITTLE" JIMMY DICKENS, "COUNTRY BOY" (WRITTEN BY FELICE AND BOUDLEAUX BRYANT IN 1949)

Fiddlers, Smoky Mountains, Tennessee, c.1948, by Clemens Kalischer.

A performance at the *Grand Ole Opry*, a country music radio program recorded in Nashville, Tennessee, November 1, 1956, by Yale Joel.
The Delmore Brothers, late 1940s (opposite).

Bill Monroe and His Blue Grass Boys concert poster, 1947, Nashville, Tennessee.

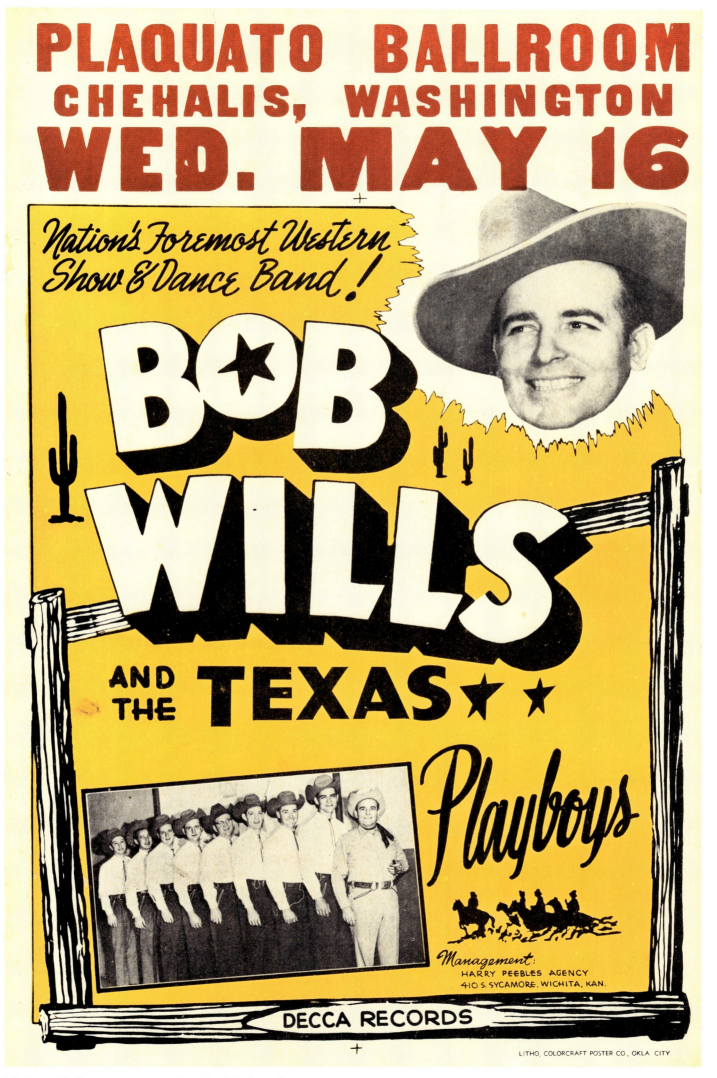

Bob Wills and the Texas Playboys concert poster, May 16, 1956, Chehalis, Washington.

A Hank Williams poster for a concert scheduled for January 1, 1953 in Canton, Ohio that the artist never gave.

20,000 Attend Hank Williams Funeral In Montgomery, Ala.

MONTGOMERY, ALA. — One of the greatest chapters in the life of Hank Williams was completed last Sunday, January 4, in Montgomery, Alabama. The more than 20,000 people who gathered at Montgomery's City Auditorium for the funeral services very vividly brought to mind the fact that among Hank's fans were people of every class and from every stand in life. The city's florists and communications offices were swamped with expressions of sympathy from all parts of the world. These were sent by everyone from fans who had never seen him to the heads of industries. There were expressions from almost everyone connected with the nation's music business. Several chartered airplanes brought capacity loads to Montgomery with all other transportation facilities filled.

After having passed away in his automobile enroute to a Canton, Ohio, personal appearance on January 1 at the age of 29, Hank's body had laid in state at the family home for twenty-four hours where an unending line of mourners passed the casket. The procession moved to City Auditorium at one p.m. Sunday where some 15,000 persons filed reverently by the casket.

The services were conducted by Dr. Henry L. Lyon, pastor of Montgomery's Highland Avenue Baptist Church, and Rev. Talmadge Smith, pastor of Ramer Baptist Church in Ramer, Alabama.

Dr. Lyon's message expressed the fact that, "No one could preach Hank's funeral—Hank had done that himself in the songs he wrote and sang in the language of all the people. His songs will continue the message of Hank Williams for centuries to come."

Nearly all of the artists and personnel from the radio stations on which Hank had worked were present, served as pallbearers, and sang songs in the service that Hank had been particularly fond of. Ernest Tubb sang "Beyond The Sunset"; Roy Acuff and a group of WSM artists sang Hank's own composition, "I Saw The Light"; Red Foley and the Statesman's Quartet sang "Peace In The Valley"; the Stateman's Quartet sang "Precious Memories" and a local colored quartet with which Hank had worked several years ago on Montgomery's WMGY sang "My Record Will Be There." Almost complete casts of the WSM "Grand Ole Opry" and KWKH "Louisiana Hayride" were present.

The funeral was broadcast over three local radio outlets who cancelled all programs to air the services as a public service to those who could not attend. Montgomery newspapers were at a premium with supplies of the Sunday edition exhausted early in the morning. The funeral procession was the longest ever seen by local Fire Chief R. L. Lampley.

The feeling was apparent that Hank's home had been changed but his parting word on each of his programs would still carry on—"If the good Lord's willing and the creeks don't rise between my house and yours, I'll be seeing you again." Yes, the life of Hank Williams was by no means completed! He would live on and on in the hearts of those who knew him and loved him and to whom he had given so much in the short span of his earthly life.

His recording affiliation and the publisher of all his songs expressed that their handling of Hank's material will go on uninterrupted as Hank himself had wanted it. The feeling is that Hank's greatest achievements are yet to come.

RHYTHM AND BLUES: ROCK BEFORE ROCK

BY FLORENT MAZZOLENI

Rhythm and blues, the immediate precursor of rock 'n' roll, embodied the superb exuberance of black music in the years from 1945 to 1950. Whether archaic or contemporary, profane or religious, rural or urban, this irresistible musical wave was swelled by all the currents of black music, and, boldly disregarding conventions with its direct, suggestive language, swept the country with its wild beat.

Rhythm and blues records received generous air time from DJs and were soon topping the charts. Throughout the course of the decade, Louis Jordan became known as the "king of the jukeboxes" in the rhythm and blues category and notched a record sequence of eighteen #1 hits. He was the leading figure among a whole host of remarkable artists and performers, such as T-Bone Walker, Illinois Jacquet, Amos Milburn, Roy Brown, and Wynonie Harris, who would transform American popular culture and pave the way for the success of the rock 'n' roll revolution.

In this period just after World War II, many of the big jazz bands and western swing groups had been decimated by the draft. They were now replaced by smaller, more economical groups known as "combos." In order to make themselves heard above the general hubbub of the bars, clubs, and rent parties where they played, the musicians began to amplify their instruments. Thanks to electric guitars and Hammond organs, the combos eventually managed to achieve the same kind of sound levels as the big bands. And while sophisticated music lovers tended to prefer the bebop jazz epitomized by Charlie Parker, this exciting electric music was hugely popular with black audiences, and soon spread beyond their neighborhoods to venues throughout America's big cities. It was a time of change; in these postwar years there was a new energy pulsing through all sectors of society. This was reflected in the effervescence of the music industry as a host of independent labels emerged in reaction to the bland products put out by the majors. The sharp-sighted new entrepreneurs behind King, Specialty, Imperial, Savoy, Chess, and Atlantic were much quicker on their feet than their more established counterparts due to their direct contact with the record stores and clubs in the cities. This exchange kept them abreast of the latest changes in the taste of black audiences, which is what determined musical fashions.

Since the end of the war, musicians from the rural South had begun migrating to the cities of the industrial North and West, bringing with them the musical culture of the Mississippi Delta. Dubbed "rhythm and blues" by journalist Jerry Wexler in 1949, the new style spawned by their new urban environment combined the stark intensity of the blues with the compelling rhythm of boogie-woogie. Its full, warm sound explored themes of black urban life and drew its inspiration from the street and the club scene. Sex and heavy drinking were featured prominently. The rise of rhythm and blues was abetted by the multitude of radio stations sprouting up across the country, which did a very effective job promoting the records cut in the studios. It also owed a lot to the musicians' insistence on making their instruments really audible, and on the very new, attention-grabbing style of the singers. Whether on stage or in the studio, this emphasis on raw performance and emotional intensity generated an energy that had never been seen or heard before.

Saxophonists were one of the driving forces of rhythm and blues. Among the star performers in the big bands, which could have as many as five, they now energized the sound of the combos. Known as "honkers," they employed the riff-based style of gospel. In many rhythm and blues recordings, sax riffs took the place of the old vocal harmonies and created a new kind of "musical egocentrism." Illinois Jacquet was one of the pioneers of this new style of expression in his tenor solo on "Flying Home," recorded with Lionel Hampton and His Orchestra in 1942. A few years later Jay McNeely, a Jacquet disciple, even started playing his instrument on his knees and writhing on the floor. His audiences trembled in ecstasy upon hearing his acrobatic riffs driven along by incredible physical energy, helping to popularize sax solos. Pianists could be just as eccentric. They modernized boogie-woogie by emphasizing the left-hand notes that established tempo and performed the bass and drum parts. In Los Angeles the young pianist Amos Milburn had a huge hit with "Chicken Shack Boogie," which was #1 on the rhythm and blues charts in November 1948, and had a string of five hits the following year. Named "Rhythm And Blues Artist Of The Year" by *Billboard*, he toured nationwide under the joke name Chicken Shack Boogie Man and His Aladdin Chicken Shackers. He frequently played with Joe Liggins who was one of the first pianists to exceed the volume of big band music with his rhythm and blues combo on the phenomenally successful instrumental "The Honeydripper (Parts 1&2)" in 1945.

Big Joe Turner, a singer from Kansas City, was another example of a successful transition from big band to rhythm and blues. Far from moaning about the new trends, he asserted his independence and embraced the arrival of the irresistible "blues shouter" style.
Two of his disciples, Roy Brown in New Orleans and Wynonie Harris in Kansas City, became uncontested stars of the rhythm and blues scene. "Have you heard the news?" challenged Roy Brown, a former boxer, in his provocative hit "Good Rockin' Tonight" in 1948. As for Wynonie Harris, also known as "Mr. Blues," he summed up the essence of postwar rhythm and blues, his famous raucous voice celebrating good times with sex and alcohol aplenty. He, too, sang "Good Rockin' Tonight" in 1948, and performed it swinging his hips and sticking out his chest, as if he sensed the imminence of the coming of rock 'n' roll.
As the 1950s approached, rhythm and blues gained acceptance. Vocal groups were all the rage. Racial segregation was still in effect, but rhythm and blues lifted black music out of the humiliating "race records" category to which it had been confined since the 1920s. The most popular vocal group on the black circuit was the "5" Royales. Not only did they feature bewitching harmonies and epic exchanges between Johnny and Eugene Tanner, but also the guitar of Lowman Pauling, who was inspired by T-Bone Walker and, like him, played his instrument between his legs.
Almost as elegant and less rough around the edges, the vocal harmonies of the Dominoes, led by Clyde McPhatter, exemplify this golden age of rhythm and blues. "Sixty Minute Man" was the first song by a black group to appear on the white charts. Topping the rhythm and blues hit parade for fourteen weeks, it was one of the most daring songs of the whole decade. In the same regard, Hank Ballard's Midnighters excitedly sang to hypnotic rhythms with a prominent electric guitar and gospel choir sound in "Work With Me Annie." The lewd double meaning of the lyrics was hard to miss: "Annie, please don't cheat, Give me all my meat, ooo!" In July 1954 their follow-up single "Sexy Ways" boasted what was to be the most frequently copied guitar riff of the decade, played by Arthur Porter. Rhythm and blues just kept getting raunchier and raunchier.

A few months earlier, Big Joe Turner established the black rhythm and blues style that we now know as rock 'n' roll with "Shake, Rattle And Roll," a hard, swinging rhythm, tinkling piano, lively sax, enthusiastic clapping, and belted vocals.
This version was supplanted by a more restrained Bill Haley version.
Where Turner sang:
  Way you wear those dresses, the sun comes shinin' through
  I can't believe my eyes, all that mess belongs to you,
Haley sang:
  Wearin' those dresses, your hair done up so nice
  You look so warm, but your heart is cold as ice.
Still, relations between the races had begun to thaw and the two musical worlds of rhythm and blues and rock 'n' roll would soon come together in Memphis, and then all over America in the summer of 1954.

TRANSLATED FROM FRENCH BY CHARLES PENWARDEN

Rhythm and Blues revue on the midway at the Cotton Makers Jubilee in the Beale Street Auditorium Park, Memphis, Tennessee, early 1950s, by Ernest C. Withers.

"IN THE FIFTIES ROCK 'N' ROLL WAS OFTEN TAKEN TO BE SIMPLY A NEW NAME FOR '<u>RHYTHM AND BLUES</u>,' OR 'R&B,' THE MUSIC INDUSTRY'S GENERIC TERM FOR ANY POPULAR MUSIC PRIMARILY PRODUCED AND CONSUMED BY AFRICAN AMERICANS."

BARRY HANSEN, MUSIC HISTORIAN, 1992

Joe Liggins (on piano) and His Honey Drippers, c.1945.

Roy Milton (on drums) and His Solid Senders, c.1945.

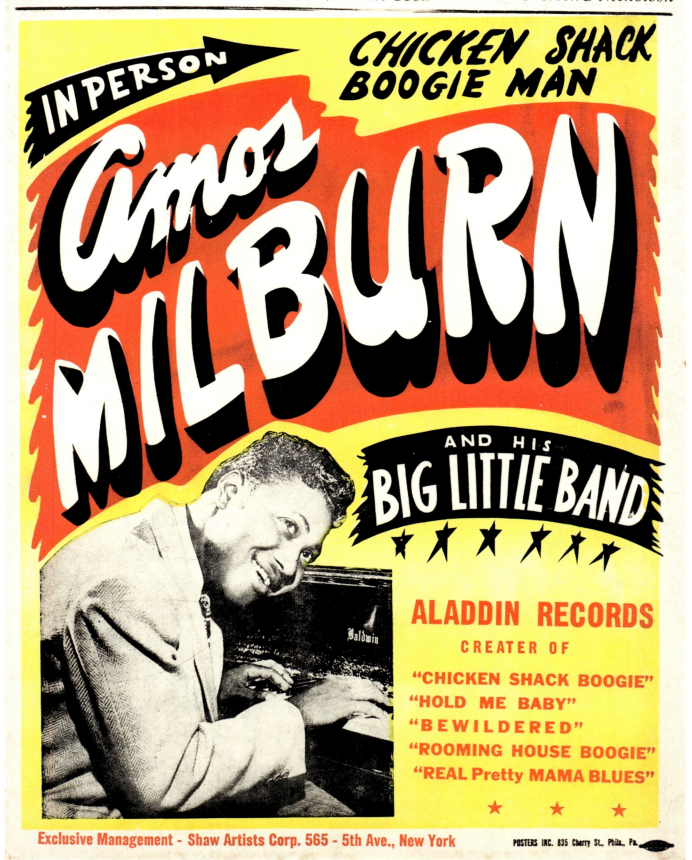

Amos Milburn concert poster, February 17, 1952, Wichita, Kansas.

Johnny Otis concert poster, July 27, 1951, Elk, Pennsylvania.

Joe Turner, c.1942.
Amos Milburn, c.1946 (opposite).

Roy Brown and Wynonie Harris, *Battle Of The Blues*, King, LP, 1959 (recordings from the late 1940s).

Roy Brown and Wynonie Harris, *Battle Of The Blues*, volume 2, King, LP, 1959 (recordings from the late 1940s).

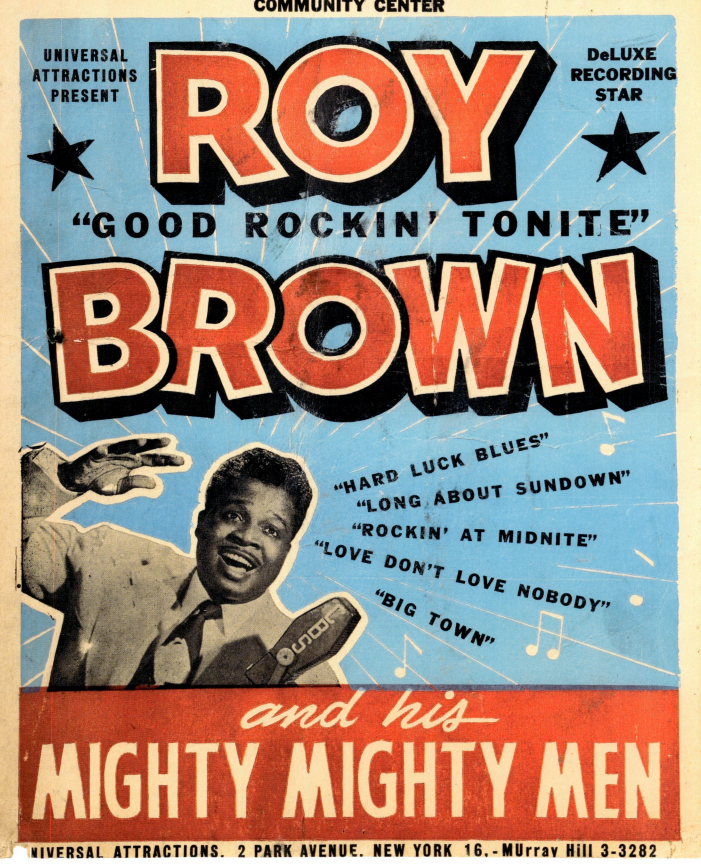

Roy Brown concert poster, December 3, 1952, Gadsden, Alabama.

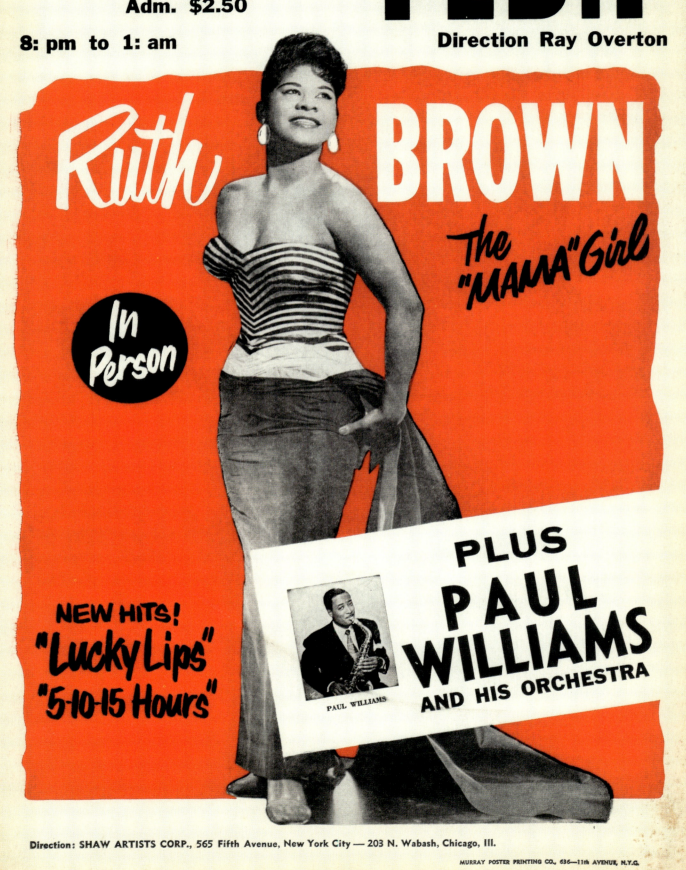

Ruth Brown concert poster, February 1, 1958, Wichita, Kansas.

Illinois Jacquet concert poster, January 3, 1948, New Britain, Connecticut.

Big Jay McNeely concert poster, May 3, 1957, Louisville, Kentucky.

The Robins, 1953. The Midnighters, 1953.
The "5" Royales, 1953. The Orioles, 1950.

Billy Ward and The Dominoes, 1953.

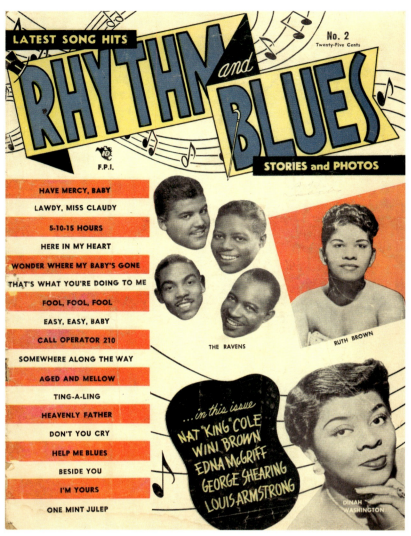
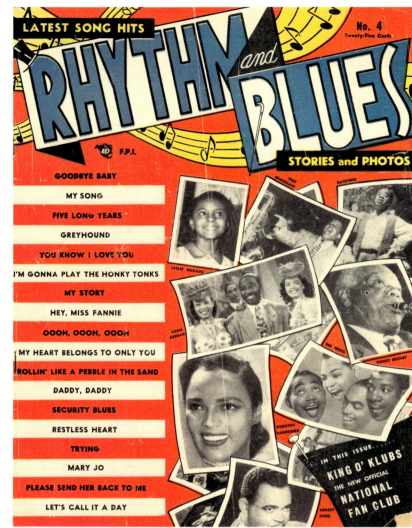
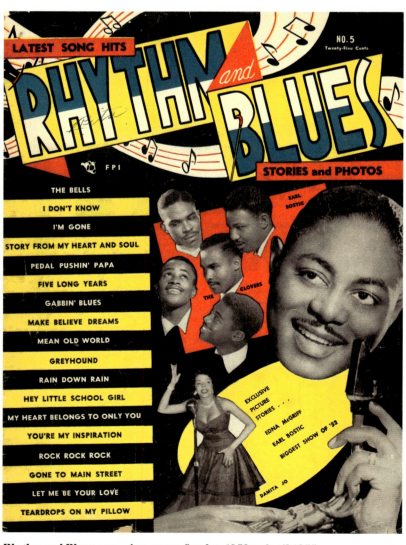
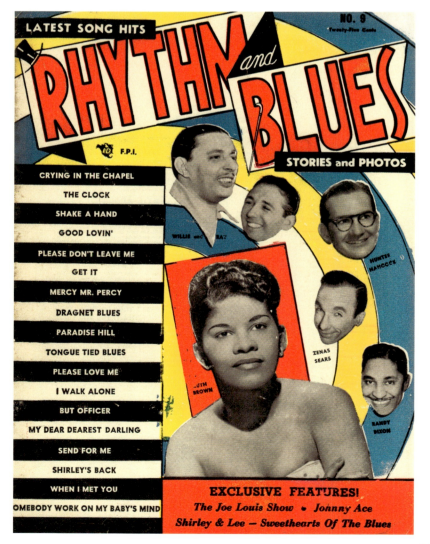

Rhythm and Blues, magazine covers, October 1952 to April 1955.

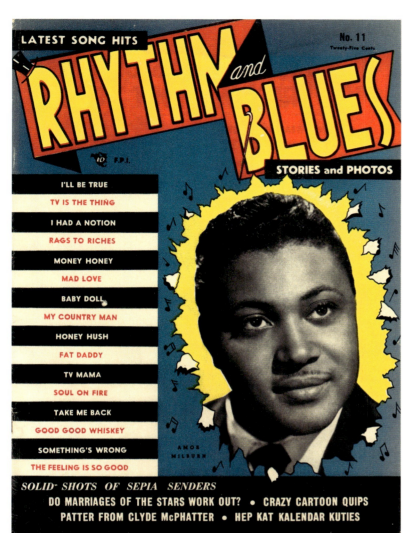
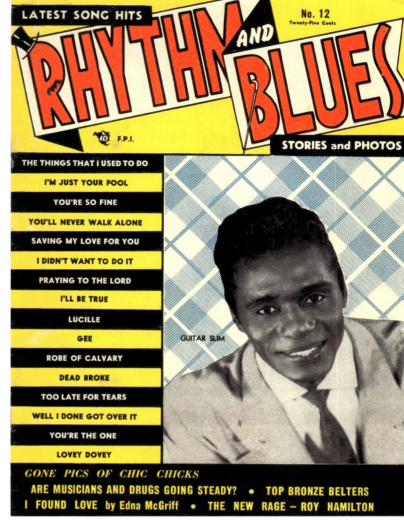
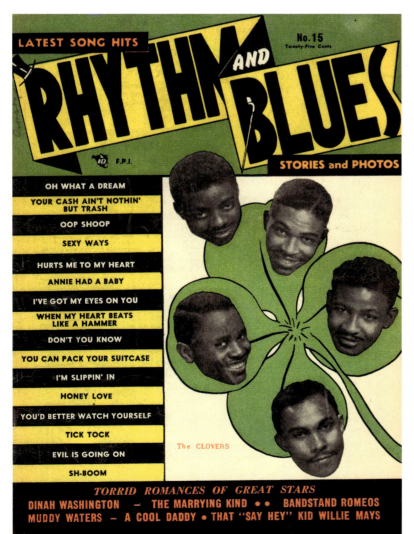
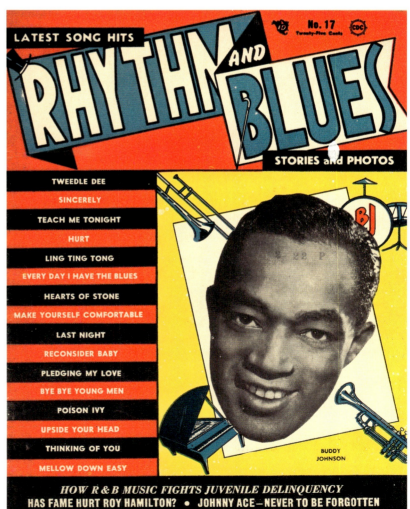

LOUIS JORDAN:
"WITH MY LITTLE BAND, I DID EVERYTHING THEY DID WITH A BIG BAND. I MADE THE BLUES JUMP."

Louis Jordan, Chicago, Illinois, 1948, by Wayne Miller.

Louis Jordan and His Tympany Five, c.1945.

Louis Jordan, *Caldonia*, Decca, 78 rpm, 1945.

112

Louis Jordan, *Choo Choo Ch'Boogie*, Decca, 78 rpm, 1946.

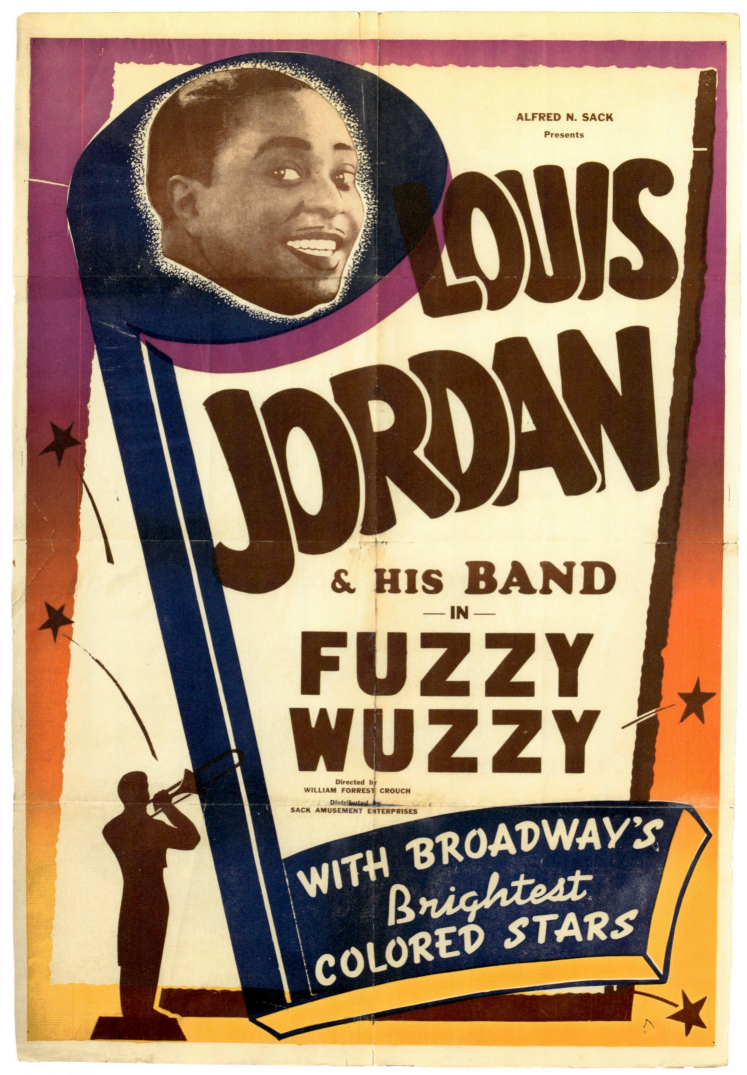

Louis Jordan concert poster, 1946.

Louis Jordan. Lobby cards for the film *Look-Out Sister* by Bud Pollar, 1947, starring Louis Jordan and for *Reet-Petite and Gone* by William Forest Crouch, 1947 with Louis Jordan and His Tympany Five.

"WE CONCLUDE THAT IN THE FIELD OF PUBLIC EDUCATION THE DOCTRINE OF 'SEPARATE BUT EQUAL' HAS NO PLACE. SEPARATE EDUCATIONAL FACILITIES ARE INHERENTLY UNEQUAL."

BROWN V. BOARD OF EDUCATION
DECISION OF THE U.S. SUPREME COURT, 1954

May 1954: Sitting on the steps of the U.S. Supreme Court in Washington D.C., a mother explains to her daughter the meaning of the high court's ruling in the *Brown* v. *Board of Education* case. The decision declares that segregation in public schools is unconstitutional, ending the "seperate but equal" doctrine, in place in the South since 1896.

MONTGOMERY LINE ENDS SEATING BIAS

Official of Boycotted Buses Says He Has 'No Choice'

By The Associated Press.

MONTGOMERY, Ala., April 23— The Montgomery City Lines tonight ordered an end to segregated seating on buses effective tomorrow.

A notice on the company bulletin board said the desegregation order was the result of the United States Supreme Court's ruling today, which said that segregated seating was unconstitutional.

The notice was signed by J. H. Bagley, the manager of the bus company. Mr. Bagley's family said he was not available to confirm the desegregation decree.

Mayor W. A. Gayle said he had not studied the court case as yet. However, he said he would continue to enforce state and city ordinances in regard to segregation on buses.

"We are going ahead and enforce segregation on buses just as we have been doing," he said.

Mr. Gayle's statement was made before the bus company's notice was posted. He was not available for comment on the bus company's action. The manager's letter "to all employes" said:

"We have been advised that today the Supreme Court of the United States rendered a decision, the effect of which is to hold unconstitutional segrega-

Continued on Page 22, Column 4

MONTGOMERY LINE ENDS SEATING BIAS

Continued From Page 1

tion of the races on buses.

"Under the circumstances, the company has no choice except to discontinue the practice of segregation on passengers on account of races, and drivers will no longer assign seats to passengers by reason of their race."

Copies of the order were sent to K. E. Totten and B. W. Franklin, officials of the National City Lines in Chicago, the parent company.

A suit attacking the constitutionality of city and state segregation laws already is on file in United States District Court. A hearing is scheduled May 11 before a three-judge panel.

Jack Crenshaw, attorney for Montgomery City Lines whose buses have been boycotted by Negroes for nearly five months, said, "Offhand it sounds like the Supreme Court said Alabama's statues are unconstitutional.

"It indicates the court has adopted the same rule as that for schools," he continued, "and if so, I would anticipate that a court order will be entered here (May 11) along the same line."

'Calm Reasonableness'

Alabama was not directly affected by today's court ruling, but an order from the three-judge panel next month could apply the decision to this state.

Meanwhile, a leader in the Montgomery boycott, the Rev. M. L. King Jr., appealed to members of both white and Negro races to use "calm reasonableness."

Mr. King said the desegregation order would not immediately end the boycott.

The bus company order apparently satisfies the complaint about segregated seating and discourtesy to Negro patrons from bus drivers, he said, but the protesting group also has asked the company to hire Negro bus drivers on predominantly Negro routes.

Mr. King said the strategy committee of the Montgomery Improvement Association would meet tomorrow afternoon to make recommendations to its executive board. A mass meeting will be held later to decide whether to continue the protest movement, he said.

seamstress, refused to surrender her seat to a white man.

It developed quickly and, some of the Negro leaders contended, almost spontaneously, from a one-day protest showing into a Ghandi-like resistance movement.

Mrs. Parks refused a bus driver's order to leave her seat on Dec. 1. The driver was acting under law. She was arrested, jailed briefly and released on bond. She is appealing her conviction for violating the state's segregation law.

Her day in court—Dec. 5— was chosen for a mass protest by fifty leaders of the Negro community, meeting in the church of Mr. King. The next day, from somewhere, came mimeographed appeals to Negroes to stay off the buses and to attend a mass meeting "for further instructions."

This second meeting promulgated the full-scale boycott. Its leaders, many of them Protestant ministers, insist that the demand for it had grown to such an extent that they were forced to take charge less the animosity turn into open racial hatred and violence.

The protest proved effective. The city transit line lost about 65 per cent of its pre-boycott income. To some extent, too, it hurt the city, which collected fewer taxes.

A new bitterness was reflected in the arrests in February of ninety-three Negro leaders. They were charged with having violated a 1921 Alabama law that bars organized boycotts "without just cause or legal excuse."

In March Mr. King was the first of this group to be tried. He was convicted and fined $500 and $500 court costs. This was changed to 386 days in jail because he chose to appeal the verdict, but the sentence was suspended pending outcome of the appeal. The case was expected to go to the Supreme Court.

On December 1, 1955 Rosa Parks refuses to give her seat to a white person on a Montgomery bus. By December 5 the black community has organized protests and a bus boycott to oppose segregation, which eventually receives the support of the Supreme Court. *The New York Times*, April 24, 1956.

A black woman walks home during the bus boycott, Montgomery, Alabama, December 1955, by Don Cravens.

Rosa Parks (center, with hat) at the end of the Montgomery bus boycott, which forced an end to segregation in public transportation, December 26, 1956, by Don Cravens.

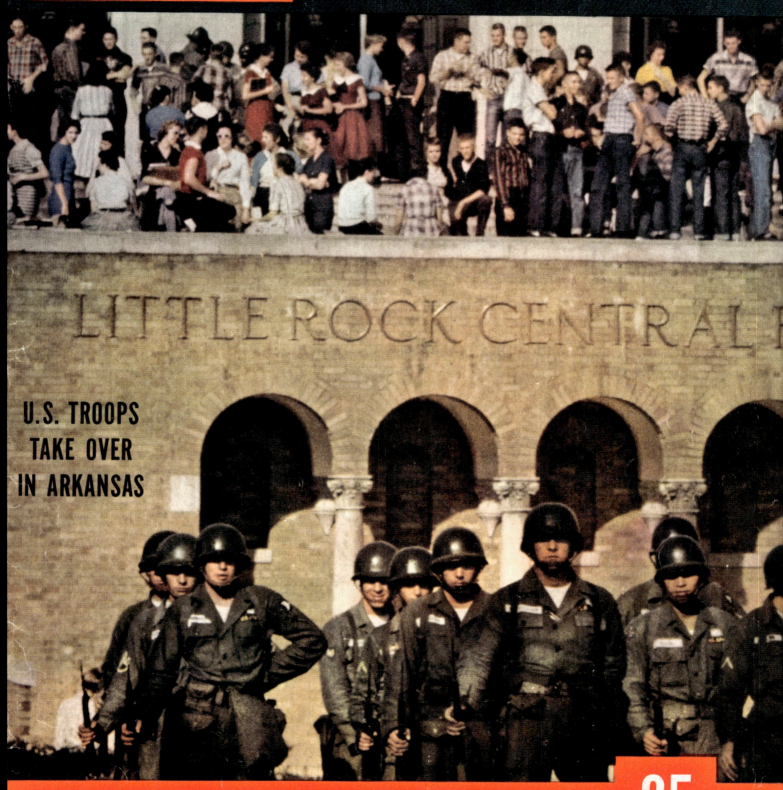

Despite the Brown ruling in 1954, certain states in the South continue segregation in schools. On September 3, 1957 in Little Rock, Arkansas Governor Orval Faubus blocks black students from entering the high school. After 18 days of media pressure, President Dwight D. Eisenhower finally decides to send in National Guard troops to protect the students in what is coined, the "Battle of Little Rock," which lasted until the end of November 1957. *Life*, magazine cover, October 7, 1957.

Historic Week CONTINUED

FIGHT STARTED BY CIVILIAN brings the soldiers into action. C. E. Blake, a railroad employe, tries to grab the rifle away from a 101st Division paratrooper.

GRAPPLING WITH SOLDIER, Blake keeps his grip on the rifle and falls, pulling the soldier after him. Another trooper stepped in and hit Blake with his rifle butt.

BEING INTEGRATED, the Negro pupils with their paratroop escort walk up steps into Central High on Thursday as white children watch quietly. By Thursday only five white children walked out in protest.

THE BATTLE OF LITTLE ROCK

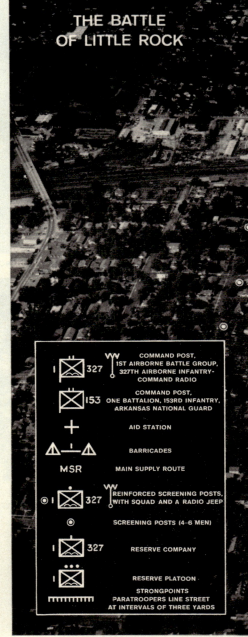

THE MILITARY DISPOSITIONS around Central High deployed the 1st Airborne Battle Group, 327th

DRIVING BACK CROWD that tried to reach Blake as he rolled, bleeding, on the ground, the paratroop line advances at master sergeant's command, "Bayonets at the back of their heads, move 'em fast."

END OF SCUFFLE comes as Blake rises to his feet. He was treated at the hospital, but was not arrested.

WHAT FAUBUS SAID— AND WHAT HAPPENED

The paratroopers fanned out to their stations (*map, left*) and checked the crowd. For two days they brought the Negroes into Central High (*opposite page*). Then Faubus took to TV to reconstruct the battle of Little Rock.

The governor bewailed "the use of sharpened naked bayonets on schoolgirls . . . the bludgeoning of others with rifle butts and the wholesale arrests" made by the paratroopers. He dramatically brandished a picture (*below*) of C. E. Blake to support his charges.

Actually, as the pictures at the top of these pages show, Blake had assaulted a paratrooper. As for Faubus' bayoneting charge, not a schoolgirl had been touched but one man had been pinked when he accidentally swung his arm lightly against a bayonet. The "wholesale arrests" totaled eight, mostly of people who refused to move on. They were turned over to civil authorities.

Faubus also claimed that "teen-age schoolgirls have been taken by the FBI and held incommunicado for hours of questioning." In Washington, FBI Chief J. Edgar Hoover had tougher words. He called Orval Faubus a liar.

Airborne Infantry of the 101st Airborne Division at barricades, screening posts and lined before school. Reserves stood by. Battalion from Arkansas National Guard that President had federalized shared duty.

DEFIANT FAUBUS in TV speech attacking the use of federal troops shows picture of clubbed Blake.

Historic Week CONTINUED
STUDENTS, PEACEFUL SO FAR, PLAYING AND CHEERING TOGETHER

EATING AMID WHITES, Negro student Terrence Roberts sits in Central High cafeteria during lunch.

CHEERING WITH WHITES, Minnie Brown helps practice school yells. This was Wednesday when school turned out, ostensibly for fire drill, actually because of unfounded report bomb had been planted.

PITCHER IN GYM CLASS SOFTBALL GAME, MINNIE BROWN (CENTER) RUNS WITH HER SCHOOLMATES DURING CHANGE OF SIDES WHILE TROOPS (RIGHT) LOOK ON

HAPPY BIRTHDAY of Gloria Ray (*second from right*) is celebrated by Central High schoolmates, (*from left*) Thelma Mothershed, Minnie Brown, Melba Pattillo.

FRIENDLY RELATIONS prevail between Linda Cook, 16, who refused to attend school, and Lieutenant Snodgrass even though he would not let her in for a visit.

"WHEN OPPRESSED PEOPLE RISE UP AGAINST OPPRESSION THERE IS NO STOPPING POINT SHORT OF FULL FREEDOM."

MARTIN LUTHER KING JR., "NON VIOLENCE AND RACIAL JUSTICE," *THE CHRISTIAN CENTURY*, FEBRUARY 6, 1957.

THE ROC
EXPLO

ELVIS AND THE FIFTIES 128
BY DAVID HALBERSTAM

ELVIS PRESLEY PORTFOLIO 172
BY ALFRED WERTHEIMER

SAM PHILLIPS 249
BY PETER GURALNICK

DEWEY PHILLIPS 251
BY PETER GURALNICK

ELVIS IN PARIS 277
BY LINE RENAUD

ELVIS, T
ROCK'N'ROL

K'N'ROLL
OSION

EENAGERS AND
L'ATTITUDE

ELVIS
AND THE FIFTIES

BY DAVID HALBERSTAM

The Supreme Court ruling on *Brown* v. *Board of Education*, which occurred in the middle of the decade, was the first important break between the older, more staid America that existed at the start of the era and the new, fast-paced, tumultuous America that saw the decade's end. The second was Elvis Presley. In cultural terms, his coming was nothing less than the start of a revolution. Once, in the late 1960s, Leonard Bernstein, the distinguished American composer and conductor, turned to a friend of his named Dick Clurman, an editor at *Time* magazine. They were by chance discussing political and social trends. "Elvis Presley," said Bernstein, "is the greatest cultural force in the twentieth century." Clurman thought of the sultry-faced young man from the South in tight clothes and an excessive haircut who wiggled his body while he sang about hound dogs. Bernstein's statement seemed a bit much. "What about Picasso?" he began, trying at the same time to think of other major cultural forces of the century. "No," Bernstein insisted, and Clurman could tell that he was deadly serious, "it's Elvis. He introduced the beat to everything and he changed everything—music, language, clothes, it's a whole new social revolution—the Sixties comes from it. Because of him a man like me barely knows his musical grammar anymore." Or, as John Lennon, one of Elvis's admirers, once said, "Before Elvis there was nothing."

If he was a revolutionary, then he was an accidental one, an innately talented young man who arrived at the right place at the right time. He had no political interests at all, and though his music symbolized the coming together of black and white cultures into the mainstream in a way that had never happened before, that seemed to hold little interest for him. Though much of his music had its roots among blacks, he, unlike many young white musicians, seemed to have little interest in the black world and the dramatic changes then taking place there.

Indeed, he often seemed to have little interest in music at all. What he really wanted from the start was to go to Hollywood and be a movie star like James Dean or Marlon Brando, a rebel up on the screen. It was almost as if the music that shook the world was incidental. Brando and Dean were his role models, and when he finally got to Hollywood and met Nicholas Ray, who had directed Dean in *Rebel Without A Cause*, he got down on his knees and started reciting whole pages from the script. He had, Ray realized, seen *Rebel* at least a dozen times and memorized every line that Dean spoke. If he would never rival Brando and Dean as a movie actor, he learned from them one critical lesson: never to smile. That was the key to their success, he was sure. He was sure he could manage the same kind of sultry good looks they had. As a teenager he spent hours in front of a mirror working on that look, and he used it to maximum effect, later, in his own appearances.

Sam Phillips, Memphis recording man, enthusiast of black music, had been looking for years for someone like Elvis—a white boy who could sing like a black boy and catch the beat of black music. Elvis, Phillips later said, "knew I was there a long time before he finally walked into my studio. I saw that Crown Electric Company truck that he was driving pull up a number of times outside the studio. He would sit in it and try to get his courage up. I saw him waiting there long before he got the nerve to come in. "Elvis Presley walked into that studio in the summer of 1953. He had been sent there by another talent scout, who wanted nothing to do with him—and those awful pegged pants, the pink and black clothes.

He was an odd mixture of a hood—the haircut, the clothes, the sullen, alienated look—and a sweet little boy—curiously gentle and respectful, indeed willing and anxious to try whatever anyone wanted. Everyone was sir or ma'am. Few young Americans, before or after, have looked so rebellious and been so polite.

Sam Phillips immediately liked Presley's early greaser style. The clothes came from Lansky's, a store more likely to be visited by flashy black men about town than by young white males. "And the sideburns, I liked that too. Everyone in town thought *I* was weird, and here was this kid and he was as weird as I was," Phillips recalled. "What do you sing?" Phillips' secretary Marion Kreisker asked. "I sing all kinds," she remembered him answering. "Well, who do you sound like?" she prodded. "I don't sound like nobody," he replied. He told her he wanted to cut a record for his mother's birthday, which was still several months away.

So he sang into Sam Phillips' little record machine, getting his three dollars' worth. He sang two Ink Spots songs: "My Happiness" and "That's When Your Heartaches Begin." Presley himself was disappointed with the results. "Sounded like someone beating on a bucket lid," he said years later. Sam Phillips later said that he heard Elvis sing and thought to himself, "Oh man, that is distinctive. There is something there, something original and different."

Sam Phillips listened to Presley a few times and was sure that Elvis had some kind of special talent, but he just wasn't sure what it was. He was not a particularly good guitar picker, but there was a sound almost buried in there that was distinctive. Part of it was Elvis' musical promiscuity: he did not really know who he was. After one frustrating session, Phillips asked him what he could do. "I can do anything," he said. He sang everything: white, black, gospel, country, crooners. If anything, thought Phillips, he seemed to see himself as a country Dean Martin. "Do you have any friends you woodshed with?" Phillips asked him. Woodshedding was a term to mean musicians going off and working together. Elvis replied, "No." Phillips said he had two friends, and he called Scotty Moore at his brother's drycleaning shop. Moore was an electric guitar player and Phillips suggested he and Bill Black, a bassist, work with Elvis.

They were to try to bring forth whatever it was that was there. Elvis—Moore thought—that's a science fiction name. After a few weeks of working together, the three of them went to Phillips' studio to record. Phillips by chance entered the date in his log: July 5, 1954. For a time the session did not go particularly well. Elvis' voice was good, but it was too sweet, thought Phillips. Then Elvis started picking on a piece by a famed black bluesman named Arthur Crudup called "That's All Right." Crudup was a Mississippi blues singer who had made his way to Chicago with an electric guitar. He was well known within the narrow audience for black blues.

He had recorded this particular song seven years earlier, and nothing had happened with it. Suddenly, Elvis Presley let go: he was playing and jumping around in the studio like all the gospel singers, black and white, he had watched onstage. Soon his two sidemen joined him. "What the hell are you doing?" Phillips asked. Scotty Moore said he didn't know. "Well, find out real quick and don't lose it. Run through it again and let's put it on tape," Phillips said. They turned it into a record. Having covered a black blues singer for one side, it seemed only fitting to use Presley's version of bluegrass singer Bill Monroe's "Blue Moon Of Kentucky" on the other.

Country blended with black blues was a strain that some would come to call rockabilly, something so powerful that it would go right to the center of American popular culture. Crudup, one of the legendary pure black blues singers of his time, was not thrilled by the number of white singers who seemed to make so much money off work he had pioneered. "I was makin' everybody rich and I was poor," he once said. "I was born poor, I live poor, and I'm going to die poor." Bo Diddley, the great black rocker, was more philosophical. Someone later asked Diddley if he thought Presley had copied his style. "If he copied me, I don't care—more power to him," Diddley said. "I'm not starving."

Phillips was sure the record was a winner and he sent it to a local disc jockey named Dewey Phillips (no relation), who had a show called *Red, Hot And Blue*, on WHBQ. He was very big with the young white kids—Elvis himself had listened faithfully to him almost every night since he was fourteen years old. Dewey Phillips played traditional white artists all the time, but just as regularly, he played the great black singers, blues and gospel. "Dewey was not white," the black blues singer Rufus Thomas once said in the ultimate accolade. "Dewey *had* no color." Dewey and Sam, spiritually at least, were kin. If Sam was a man who subscribed to very few local conventions, then Dewey openly liked to flaunt them. He had ended up at WHBQ, as much as anything else, by being very unsuccessful at anything else he tried. At the time Memphis had a radio show called *Red, Hot And Blue*, which consisted of fifteen minutes of popular music on WHBQ. Dewey Phillips often told friends that he would do the show for nothing if they would let him try. He went down to WHBQ, asked for a job, and miraculously got it. He was so different, so original, that the management did not know at first whether to fire him or expand the show; within a year he had three hours to himself. He was, in the words of his friend Stanley Booth, both brilliant and terrible as a disc jockey. He could not read a line of copy and he could not put a record on without scratching it. But he had perfect taste in the music that young people wanted to hear. Soon he was the conduit that hip young white Memphis kids used to hear black music with its powerful beat. Political boss Ed Crump might have kept the streets and schools and public buildings segregated, but at night Dewey Phillips integrated the airwaves. Daddy-O-Dewey, he was soon called. Phrases he tossed away casually at night on his show became part of the teenage slang of Memphis the next day. Stumble he might while doing the commercials (and he might even do commercials for people who had not bothered to buy time—he was always suggesting that his listeners go out and buy a fur-lined Lincoln, even if Lincoln was not an advertiser), but he was wildly inventive.

Dewey Phillips had, in his friend Sam Phillips' words, "a platinum ear" and was connected to young listeners like no other adult. Therefore, he was the first person Sam Phillips thought of when he had Elvis' first disc. Dewey agreed to play it. The night he did, Elvis was so nervous that he went to a movie by himself. The two songs were such a success that all Dewey Phillips did that night was flip the record back and forth. The switchboard started lighting up immediately. Finally the disc jockey decided he wanted to interview Elvis on the air, and he called Sam Phillips and told him to bring the boy in. The Presleys did not have a phone, but Sam called over to their neighbors and they got Elvis' mother. Gladys and Vernon Presley had to go looking for their elusive son in the movie theater. "Mama, what's happening?" he asked. "Plenty, son," she answered, "but it's all good." Off they went to the station, where he was introduced to Dewey Phillips, who was going to interview him. "Mr. Phillips," he said, "I don't know nothin' about being interviewed." "Just don't say nothin' dirty," Phillips said. So they talked. Among other things, Phillips deftly asked Elvis where he had gone to high school, and Elvis answered Humes, which proved to the entire audience that yes, he was white. At the end Phillips thanked him. "Aren't you going to interview me?" Presley asked. "I already have," Phillips said.

Elvis Aron Presley was born in the hill country of northeast Mississippi in January 1935. It was a particularly poor part of a poor region in a nation still suffering through the Depression; in contrast to other parts of Mississippi, it was poor cotton land, far from the lush Delta 150 miles further west. Yet the local farmers still resolutely tried to bring cotton from it (only when, some thirty years later, they started planting soybeans did the land become valuable), and it was largely outside the reach of the industrial revolution. Presley's parents were typical country people fighting a daily struggle for survival. Gladys Smith, until her marriage and her pregnancy, operated a sewing machine and did piecework for a garment company, a rare factory job in the area. Vernon Presley—a man so poorly educated that he often misspelled his own name, signing it Virnon—was the child of a family of drifters and was employed irregularly, taking whatever work he was offered: perhaps a little farming, perhaps a little truck driving. He lived on the very fringes of the American economy; he was the kind of American who in the 1930s did not show up on government employment statistics. At the time of their marriage Gladys was twenty-one, four years older than Vernon. Because they were slightly embarrassed by the fact that she was older, they switched ages on their marriage certificate. Elvis was one of twins, but his brother, Jessie Garon Presley, was stillborn, a death that weighed heavily on both mother and son.

When Gladys became pregnant, Vernon Presley borrowed $180 from Orville Bean, a dairy farmer he worked for, and bought the lumber to build his family a two-room cabin. The cabin was known as a shotgun shack—because a man could stand at the front door and fire a shotgun and the pellets would go straight out the back door. When Elvis was two years old, Vernon Presley was picked up for doctoring a check from Bean.

It had been an ill-conceived, pathetic attempt to get a few more dollars, at most. Friends of Vernon's pleaded with Bean not to press charges. They would make up the difference. But Bean was nothing if not rigid and he held firm against their pleas. Vernon Presley could not make bail, and he waited seven months in the local jail before the trial even took place. He was convicted and sent to Parchman prison in the middle of the Depression for two and a half years. It was a considerable sentence for a small crime, but those were hard times. When he came out times were still hard; he worked in a lumberyard and then for one of the New Deal aid programs for the unemployed, the WPA.

During World War II he got a job doing defense work in Memphis, eighty miles away. That at least was steady work, even if he was away from home much of the time. After the war, returning veterans had priority for any jobs. Vernon had no skills and was soon out of work again. In the late 1940s the new affluence rolling quickly across much of the country barely touched people like Vernon and Gladys Presley. They were poor whites. Their possibilities had always been limited. They were people who lived on the margin. Religion was important to them, and when Elvis was nine he was baptized in the Pentecostal church. As a symbol of Christian charity he was supposed to give away some of his prized possessions, so he gave his comic books to other children.

Because a city like Memphis held out more hope of employment, Vernon Presley moved his family to Memphis in the late 1940s, where he took a job in a paint factory for $38.50 a week. They had made the move, Elvis said later, because "we were broke, man, broke." The family was still so poor that it had to live in federal housing—the projects, as they were known. The Presleys paid thirty-five dollars a month for rent, the equivalent of a week's salary. To some whites, living in the projects was an unspeakable idea, for it was housing that placed them at the same level as blacks; for the Presleys, the projects were the best housing they had ever had.

Even in a high school of his peers, Elvis Presley was something of a misfit. He went to Humes, an all-white high school where he majored in shop. There was no thought of college for him. Not surprisingly, he was shy and unsure of himself. He was bothered by the way his teeth looked. He worried that he was too short. As an adult he always wore lifts in his shoes. He did, however, have a sense that his hair worked for him. Soon he started using pomade; his style, black clothes, shirt collar up in back, hair pomaded into a major wave, was an early form of American punk. His heroes—Brando and Dean—were narcissistic, so too by nature was he. His social life was so limited that he did not know how to slowdance with a girl; rather, in the new more modern style, he knew how to dance only by himself. His peers deemed him effeminate and different. Everyone, it seemed, wanted a shot at him, particularly the football players. Years later he would tell a Las Vegas audience, "They would see me coming down the street and they'd say, 'Hot dog! Let's get him! He's a squirrel! He just come down outta the trees!'" His one friend was Red West, a more popular Humes student and a football player. West stopped about five other boys from cutting off Elvis' hair in the boys' room one day. "He looked like a frightened little animal," West said.

The one thing he had was his music. He could play a guitar and play it well. He could not read a note of music, but he had an ear that, in the words of Chet Atkins, the guitarist who supervised many of his early RCA recordings, was not only pure but had almost perfect pitch. He could imitate any other voice he chose. That was his great gift. Some of the other kids suggested he play his guitar at a school picnic, and he did, with surprising success. His homeroom teacher asked him to play it at the school variety show. He did, playing the Red Foley country favorite "Old Shep," about a boy and his dog. When the dog dies and goes to heaven, the boy does not feel too badly, for "old Shep has a wonderful friend." For the first time he gained some popularity.

On the surface, the Mississippi he grew up in was a completely segregated world. That was seemingly true even in music. Among the many musical subcultures that flowed across the Mississippi Delta were black rhythm and blues music (called race music in the trade), black gospel, and white gospel, which in no small part was imitative of black gospel and country or hillbilly music. Because whites were more influential and affluent than blacks, the latter was the dominant strain in the region.

For Elvis Presley, who lived in a completely segregated world, the one thing that was not segregated was the radio dial. There was WDIA ("the Mother Station of the Negroes," run, of course, by white executives), which was the "black" station on which a young white boy could listen to, among other people, the Rev. Herbert Brewster, a powerful figure in the world of Memphis black churches. A songwriter of note, he composed "Move On Up A Little Higher," the first black gospel song to sell over a million copies. What was clear about the black gospel music was that it had a power of its own, missing from the tamer white church music, and that power seemed to come as much as anything else from the beat. In addition there was the immensely popular Dewey Phillips. When Elvis listened to the black radio station at home, his family was not pleased. "Sinful music," it was called, he once noted. But even as Elvis Presley was coming on the scene, the musical world was changing. Certainly, whites had traditionally exploited the work of black musicians, taking their music, softening and sweetening it, and making it theirs. The trade phrase for that was "covering" a black record. It was thievery in broad daylight, but black musicians had no power to protect themselves or their music.

As the decade began, there were signs that young white kids were buying black rhythm and blues records. This had been happening in pockets throughout the country, but no one sensed it as a trend until early 1951. In that year a man named Leo Mintz who owned a record store in Cleveland told a local disc jockey named Alan Freed about this dramatic new trend. Young white kids with more money than one might expect were coming into his store and buying what had been considered exclusively Negro music just a year or two before. Freed, something of a disc jockey and vagabond, had a late-night classical music show, and Mintz was pushing him to switch over to a new show catering exclusively to these wayward kids. Mintz told Freed he knew the reason why the taste was changing: it was all about the beat. The beat was so strong in black music, he said, that anyone could dance to it without a lesson. Mintz promised he would advertise himself on Freed's new program and that he would help find other advertisers if Freed would switch.

In the summer of 1951, Freed inaugurated *The Moondog Show* on a 50,000-watt clear channel station in Cleveland, a station so powerful it reached a vast area of the Midwest. His success was immediate. It was as if an entire generation of young white kids in that area had been waiting for someone to catch up with them. For Freed it was what he had been waiting for; he seemed to come alive as a new hip personality. He was the Moondog. He kept the beat himself in his live chamber, adding to it by hitting on a Cleveland phone book. He became one of them, the kids, on their side as opposed to that of their parents, the first grown-up who understood them and what they wanted. By his choice of music alone, the Moondog had instantly earned their trust. Soon he was doing live rock shows. The response was remarkable. No one in the local music business had ever seen anything like it before: Two or three thousand kids would buy tickets, and sometimes, depending on the level of talent, thousands of others would be turned away—all for performers that adults had never even heard of.

At virtually the same time, Elvis Presley began to hang out at all-night white gospel shows. White gospel singing reflected the region's schizophrenia: it allowed white fundamentalist groups, whose members were often hard-core segregationists who wanted nothing to do with black culture, to co-opt the black beat into their white music. Presley gradually got to know some of the gospel singers and, by the time he graduated from high school in 1953, he had decided to become one himself. He was eighteen, with extremely limited options. For a country boy with his background, the possibilities were few: he could drive a truck or hope for a job in a nearby plant—and he could dream of being a singer. Soon he was singing with a local group from his church called the Songfellows. But a few random singing dates were hardly a career, so he was also working at a small plant in Memphis where artillery shell casings were made. By the standards of the time and the region, the pay was not bad—$1.65 an hour—and he made about sixty dollars a week with overtime. Soon he left that job for another that excited him more—driving a truck for Crown Electric. Driving a truck seemed infinitely freer than working in a defense factory. It seemed at that moment that he would be driving a truck for the rest of his life. In September 1956, a year after he had exploded into the consciousness of his fellow Americans, he tried to explain the secret of his success to a writer for the *Saturday Evening Post*. "I don't know what it is. . . . I just fell into it, really. My daddy and I were laughing about it the other day. He looked at me and said, 'What happened, E? The last thing I can remember is I was working in a can factory and you were drivin' a truck.' . . . It just caught us up."

The Memphis of 1954 was a strictly segregated city. Its officials were white and its juries were white, and as late as 1947 there had been no black police in the city (when the first few were finally hired in 1948, they could not arrest white people). In 1947 *Annie Get Your Gun* was banned from Memphis because it included a black railroad conductor, and as the local censor Lloyd Binford said, "We don't have any Negro conductors in the South." That same year the American Heritage Foundation, which sponsored the Freedom Train, a traveling exhibition filled with historic documents about American history, took Memphis off its itinerary because local officials there insisted that the train be segregated.

Sam Phillips thought the city's segregation was absurd. He was not a liberal in the traditional sense and he was not interested in social issues, as many of the activists of the period were. He was a raw, rough man with an eleventh-grade education, a pure redneck in all outward manifestations, such as his love of used Cadillacs. A good country boy, Sam saw Cadillacs as the surest sign of status and comfort. But he was different in one sense: his love of the blues. He had been drawn to Memphis in the first place because he *knew* it was a great center for black music, and he intended to capture some of it on record. Sam Phillips hated the hypocrisy of a city that denied the richness of its own heritage. Sam Phillips, thought his friend Stanley Booth, a talented music writer, was drawn to what he was doing not because he was a liberal and felt that the social order ought to be changed: "It wasn't a humanitarian gesture, and people like Sam weren't social activists," Booth said. "You did it because of the power of the music—you were drawn to the music. It made you hip and a little different, and in addition, in a life which was often very hard, it was the one thing which gave you a little grace." What others thought about his passion mattered little to him. He held a job as an engineer at the Peabody Hotel, working on a radio show broadcast from there; at the same time he began to record some of the region's black singers in a small studio he had created. He generally did this on the weekends, and it was great sport among his colleagues at the Peabody to tease him on Monday mornings, "Well, Sam, I guess you didn't spend the weekend recording all those niggers of yours like you usually do because you don't smell so bad today."

He never for a second doubted his own ear. Nor, for that matter, did he doubt his purpose. He wanted to be a pioneer and an explorer. "I have my faults in the world, a lot of faults, I guess," he once said, "but I have one real gift and that gift is to look another person in the eye and be able to tell if he has anything to contribute, and if he does, I have the additional gift to free him from whatever is restraining him." It was a description, his friends thought, that was remarkably accurate.

He had grown up poor in northern Alabama, aware of the tensions between blacks and whites. Every Sunday Sam Phillips went to a white Baptist church in town. About a block and a half away was a black Methodist church. In those days before air conditioning, the windows of both churches were open during the summer, and the power of the music in the black church was transcendent. "There was something there I had never heard before or since," he said years later. "Those men and women singing the *Amen*. Not the choir singing it. I mean the congregation. It was a heaven on earth to hear it. A Jubilation. The Amen and the rhythm. They never missed a downbeat." There was, he thought, so much more power in their music than his own, so much more feeling and so much more love. He felt pulled toward it, and he would leave his own church and linger outside the black church to listen.

As he came to adulthood, he began to follow the music, to ever bigger cities, working as a disc jockey. He finally made it to a big, powerful station in Nashville, but he was still restless. Nashville was the capital of white country music, but that music cast no spell on him. He knew he had to go to Memphis. It seemed to be his destiny. Phillips knew that the best and richest soil was in the bend of the Tennessee River near where he grew up and that where there was a rich soil, the people were also rich—in sorrow and joy and, above all, in music. Fertile land somehow produced fertile people as well, he believed. "There was going to be no stopping something as big as Memphis and the Mississippi River. I always knew that, *knew that*. I'd driven to Memphis, and the closer I'd gotten to the Mississippi, I knew that there was something rich ahead, this totally untamed place, all those people who had these hard hard lives, and the only way they could express themselves was through their music. You had to be a dunce not to know that."

He reached Memphis in 1945, and he was not disappointed. "I'd never seen such a gulf between two worlds. One side white, the other side black. One world all white, the other world, a few blocks away, all black. There was no street like Beale Street, no street I'd ever seen. It had a flavor all its own, entirely black. Lined with clubs and dives and pawnshops. Lord there were pawnshops! All these black people, some of them rich and some of them poor, they'd come from Mississippi and Arkansas and Tennessee, saved up all their money, determined to spend every bit of it there. No one tried to save money when they came to Beale Street. It was wonderful, all that energy, all those men and women dressed in their best, the country people from those hamlets, black hicks a lot of them trying to pretend that they're not hicks, that they're men of the street. It was amazing, there were these people who were rich, and who had saved all their money and were celebrating, and the people who had nothing, who were down and out, they were celebrating, too, and the one thing that was different from white folks was that it was impossible to tell who was rich and who was poor on Beale Street."

He built his own studio, a small storefront out at 706 Union Street. He laid the tile on the floor and on the walls himself, to maximize the acoustics, and created a raised control room so he could see the musicians who were recording, and finally installed an air conditioner, which always dripped. It cost about $1,000 to fix the place up and he was paying about $75 a month rent.

In January 1950 he quit his job at the Peabody to record full-time himself. Almost all his white friends thought he was crazy, giving up a good solid job at the grandest hotel in the entire region to go off and record black music. "Hell, Sam," one friend told him. "You're not only recording them, you're going to shake hands with them, too." As a white man recording black singers he offended local mores. Phillips himself, however, was absolutely sure of his mission. In Memphis there was all kinds of talent around: B.B. King, Phineas Newborn, Howlin' Wolf. B.B. King was typical of the music and the region: His real name was Riley B. King and he came from Indianola, in the Delta. He had grown up picking cotton (he once noted that he could pick four hundred pounds a day and make as much as thirty-five cents a hundred pounds—no one, he thought, could pick more cotton than he could). He had driven tractors, sung spirituals, and had finally ended up in Memphis in 1947, where he had worked his way up and down Beale Street playing in different clubs. He was good, authentic; everyone knew it—no one had to be told. It was even in his nickname—Beale Street Blues Boy, which eventually was shortened to B.B. There was nothing smooth about his sound: it was raw and harsh, almost angry. Eventually, he got a job on WDIA. It was not an auspicious beginning.

He started by singing commercials for Peptikon, a patent medicine guaranteed to cure all the things that ailed you plus a few things that did not. Soon he got his own half hour in the midafternoon, the *Sepia Swing Club*, and his popularity began to grow. In those days B.B. King was young and shy, particularly around white people. The first time he recorded for Sam Phillips, he revealed that he could not play the guitar and sing at the same time, which made him different from most singers. "Can't you sing and play at the same time?" Phillips asked him. "Mr. Phillips, that's the only way I every played," he answered. "Whatever you do," Phillips told him, "don't change it. Just keep it natural."

The last thing Phillips wanted was sweeteners: "I didn't build that studio to record a big band. The big bands didn't need me. I wanted to record the local talent. I knew the talent was there. I didn't have to look it up to know B.B. King was talented. And I knew what I wanted. I wanted something *ugly*. Ugly and honest. I knew that these people were disenfranchised. They were politically disenfranchised and economically disenfranchised, and to tell the truth they were musically disenfranchised. . . . The big trouble in those days, if you were recording black musicians, was that they would start changing what they were doing for you because you were white. They did it unconsciously. They were adapting to you and to the people they thought were going to be their audience. They'd look up in the recording booth and see a white man and they'd start trying to be like Billy Eckstine and Nat King Cole. I didn't want that. The things that RCA and Capitol winced at, I loved. I didn't want anyone who had ever recorded before, and I didn't want to do what other recording studios did."

So word got out that there was this slightly crazy man who had set up his own studio and was taping black people. It was a simple operation. He called it the Memphis Record Service. The studio was so small that Phillips did not even have a real office. His office, his friends like to point out, was the simple cafe next door, Miss Taylor's, third table back. That's where he'd meet someone who wanted to do a business deal. When he recorded black musicians he could not take them to Miss Taylor's, so he would take the food out himself and bring it back for them. To make enough money to survive, he also advertised that he recorded weddings, banquets, bar mitzvahs. "We Record Anything–Anytime–Anywhere" was his motto.

He also hired out his studio to any person who wanted to record. It was a good way of hearing new talent and making a little money on the side. The price was three dollars a shot. He sensed, long before the major record companies located far away in New York did, that the traditional musical barriers that had always separated the musician constituencies no longer held. He often told his assistant, Marion Kreisker, "If I could find a white man with a Negro sound I could make a billion dollars." In addition, he said, "I knew that for black music to come to its rightful place in this country we had to have some white singers come over and do black music—not copy it, not change, not sweeten it. Just *do* it."

It would turn out that he would engineer an entire musical migration of whites into black music. In addition to Elvis, he discovered Johnny Cash, Carl Perkins, Roy Orbison, and Jerry Lee Lewis, all major talents and all, in different ways, American originals.

Even as Sam Phillips was inventing himself as a producer, the musical world was changing dramatically.

The old order was fragmenting. The traditional giants, RCA, Columbia, and Decca, had dominated in the past. They had the big names, the crooners. But they were hardly entrepreneurial; the bigger they were, the more conservative they inevitably were as well. They watched the world of country and western and rhythm and blues with disdain, bordering on disapproval. It was music that came from the wrong side of the tracks. Some companies in fact even referred to black music as the "sepia market." It was not an important slice of the market, obviously, because sepia people did not have very much money. Recorded music, in fact, until the 1950s bore the label of class. People from the upper middle class and upper class had the money for phonographs with which they listened to classical and high pop, the crooners and the big bands. The people who liked country and black music listened to the radio. But the forces of change were far more powerful than anyone at the big companies realized. Technology was democratizing the business of music—phonographs and records alike were becoming much cheaper. It was only a matter of time before the artists began to cross over on the traditionally racially segregated charts. In 1954 a white musician named Bill Haley did a version of "Shake, Rattle And Roll." By February 1955 it sold one million copies; by the summer of 1955 it was #1 on the white chart and #4 on the rhythm and blues (or black) chart. In that same year Chuck Berry brought out "Maybellene," which was the first successful assault on the main chart by a black musician; "Maybellene" went to the top of the rhythm and blues chart and went to #5 on the white chart. Soon there was "Tutti Frutti" by Little Richard.

After Elvis Presley's sensational debut on Dewey Phillips' show, his career skyrocketed. He was what first the region and then the nation wanted: a white boy to explode into the beat, to capture it for the whites. The success spread steadily: DJs in Texas soon picked up on it, and soon after that Elvis was making regular appearances on the *Louisiana Hayride*, which was second only to the *Grand Ole Opry* as a showcase of country white talent. He began traveling the South with a company of country musicians, headlined by Hank Snow. But almost overnight he became the star of the touring group, something that did not escape the attention of Snow's manager, Colonel Tom Parker. Parker, it appeared, though he did not own Presley's contract, was encouraging the large companies to move in and buy it from Sam Phillips. In the beginning, Phillips probably would have sold it for $5,000 or $10,000, for he lacked the resources to promote and sustain a major success. But interest constantly escalated. Mitch Miller at Columbia called. Phillips asked $20,000. Miller replied, "Forget it. No artist is worth that kind of money." Ahmet Ertegun, the head of Atlantic, a label that was coming on quickly because of its owners' exceptional early awareness of rock 'n' roll, was probably the one record executive who personally knew how valuable Presley was. He made an offer of $25,000, which, as Ertegun told Phillips, was everything Atlantic had, including the desk he was using. It was too low, said Phillips. By then Colonel Parker was in on the game, and the Colonel had friends at RCA, the traditional recording powerhouse. Phillips was fairly sure he ought to sell Elvis' contract, but just to be sure he was doing the right thing, he called his friend Kemmons Wilson, the local contractor who was just beginning to enjoy success in his own amazing career as the builder of America's first great motel chain, Holiday Inn. Sam Phillips had been smart enough to be an early investor, and he would eventually become a millionaire from his investments with Wilson. Phillips asked whether he should sell Elvis' contract. "I wouldn't hesitate," Wilson said. "That boy isn't even a professional." So Phillips went ahead. When the negotiations were over, Sam Phillips had $35,000 and Elvis was the property of RCA.

Presley's timing was nearly perfect. The crossover, led by Bill Haley, Chuck Berry, and Little Richard, was in full force. Parents might disapprove of the beat and of their children listening to what they *knew* was black music. But their disapproval only added to Presley's popularity and made him more of a hero among the young. Local ministers might get up in their churches (almost always well covered by local newspapers) and attack demon rock as jungle music and threaten to lead a crusade to have this Presley boy arrested if he dared set foot in their community (generally, there was no problem, their towns were too small for him to play). It did not matter: Elvis Presley and rock music were *happening*.

A new young generation of Americans was breaking away from the habits of its parents and defining itself by its music. There was nothing the parents could do: This new generation was armed with both money and the new inexpensive appliances with which to listen to it. This was the new, wealthier America. Elvis Presley began to make it in 1955, after ten years of rare broad-based middle-class prosperity. Among the principal beneficiaries of that prosperity were the teenagers. They had almost no memory of the Depression and the great war that followed it. There was no instinct on their part to save money. In the past when American teenagers had made money, their earnings, more often than not, had gone to help support their parents, or had been saved for one treasured and long-desired purchase, like a baseball glove or a bike, or it had been set aside for college.

But now, as the new middle class emerged in the country, it was creating as a byproduct a brand new consuming class: the young. *Scholastic* magazine's Institute of Student Opinion showed that by early 1956 there were thirteen million teenagers in the country, with a total income of $7 billion a year, which was twenty-six percent more than only three years earlier. The average teenager, the magazine said, had an income of $10.55 a week. That figure seemed remarkable at the time; it was close to what the average American family had in disposable income, after all essential bills were paid, fifteen years earlier.

In addition, technology favored the young. The only possible family control was over a home's one radio or record player. There, parental rule and edicts could still be exercised. But the young no longer needed to depend on the family's appliances. In the early 1950s a series of technological breakthroughs brought small transistorized radios that sold for $25 to $50. Soon an Elvis Presley model record player was selling for $47.95. Teenagers were asked to put $1 down and pay only $1 a week. Credit buying had reached the young. By the late 1950s, American companies sold ten million portable record players a year.

In this new subculture of rock 'n' roll the important figures of authority were no longer mayors and selectmen or parents; they were disc jockeys, who reaffirmed the right to youthful independence and guided teenagers to their new rock heroes. The young formed their own community. For the first time in American life they were becoming a separate, defined part of the culture: As they had money, they were a market, and as they were a market they were listened to and catered to. Elvis was the first beneficiary. In effect, he was entering millions of American homes on the sly; if the parents had had their way, he would most assuredly have been barred.

Certainly, Ed Sullivan would have liked to have kept him out. Ed Sullivan, in 1955 and 1956, hosted the most successful variety show in America on this strange new piece of turf called network television. The official title of his show was *The Toast Of The Town*. Sullivan made his way to television from the world of print, where he'd worked as a Broadway gossip columnist, first on the old *New York Graphic* and eventually making his way to the *New York Daily News*. His column, in the city's largest paper, was one of considerable influence. In 1947 he had served as master of ceremonies for an annual amateur dance contest sponsored by the *News* called the "Harvest Moon Ball." Unbeknownst to Sullivan, CBS was televising the show. A CBS executive was impressed at how graciously Sullivan treated everyone he dealt with that evening and how natural his skills as an MC were. He seemed completely comfortable with himself despite the fact that the show was being televised; the reason he was so comfortable was that he didn't realize it was going out on television: He thought all those cameras around the hall were simply movie cameras. CBS was in the process of putting together a Sunday night variety program, and Sullivan was offered the show. The show opened a year later, and much to everyone's surprise, it was a stunning success. Certainly, part of the reason was the leverage of Sullivan's column. Those who went on his show were likely to get plugs in the column, and it was for that reason that on his opening broadcast, Dean Martin and Jerry Lewis clowned, Eugene List played the piano, and Rodgers and Hammerstein happened to drop in just to say hello.

Eight years later, Ed Sullivan was the unofficial Minister of Culture in America. His was the great national variety theater where one could find the famous. Broadcast at 8 p.m. on Sundays—an hour when families were likely to have gathered together—Sullivan's show provided a pleasant, safe blend of acts, including some performers of exceptional talent. In addition there seemed to be a guarantee that nothing would happen that was at all threatening. Sullivan was, after all, involved in the most delicate business imaginable: selecting acts to perform live in millions of American living rooms, a place where no one had ever performed before. There was something there for everyone, and Sullivan made sure that there was always one act for the children. He stressed the importance of variety, and few acts got more than a couple of minutes. The popularity of Sullivan's show was remarkable because the master of ceremonies was, on the screen and in real life, a stiff—a staid, humorless, rather puritanical man.

CBS, on whose network the show was carried and for whom he made a great deal of money, was never entirely happy with him. Yet miraculously, despite what the critics said, the show worked. Why, no one really knew. Perhaps it was the perfect hour for a variety show: 8 p.m. on Sunday. Perhaps it was the sheer quality of the entertainers, since almost every entertainer in the world was desperate to be showcased on so prominent a platform. Perhaps it was the fact that television was still new and there was something comforting for ordinary Americans, tuning in their first television sets, to take this adventure with so stolid and careful a man. For his taste was conservative, cautious, and traditional. When some of the blacklisting groups criticized some of the performers he put on in the late 1940s, Sullivan backed down immediately and gave the blacklisters a veto power over any acts or performers who might have political liabilities.

In 1956, he was at the height of his power. He was making about $200,000 a year from CBS and another $50,000 from the *News*. He was most assuredly not a man to cross. His show was at the exact center of American mass culture. And he wanted no part of Elvis Presley, who was now in the process of enraging endless ministers and parent groups by dint of his onstage gyrations and the overt sexuality of his music.

Earlier, as Elvis conquered the South with regional appearances, he had begun to perfect his act. Some of it was natural instinct—he had to carry a beat, and it was hard to carry a beat while standing still. So he began to gyrate as he had seen endless gospel singers gyrate. The first time he had done it, he had been driven by pure instinct and the crowd began to shout. Later he asked a friend what had happened. The friend explained that Elvis had started jumping around on the stage and using his body and the crowd had loved it. From then on it became part of his act; if you were going to do a live show, he explained, you had to have an act. That's what people came to see. Otherwise, they could just as well stay at home and play records. A country singer named Bob Luman once said of an early Elvis concert: "This cat came out in a coat and a pink shirt and socks and he had this sneer on his face and he stood behind the mike for five minutes, I'll bet, before he made a move. Then he hit his guitar a lick and he broke two strings. I'd been playing for ten years and I hadn't broken a total of two strings. So there he was, these two strings dangling, and he hadn't done anything yet, and these high school girls were screaming and fainting and running up to the stage and then he started to move his hips real slow like he had a thing for his guitar. . . ."

The teenyboppers started to maul him. They did not mean him any harm, he explained. What they wanted "was pieces of you for souvenirs." By the end of 1955 RCA was ready to push his records nationally, and he had signed to do six Saturday night shows on a show produced by Jackie Gleason called *Stage Show*. He got $1,250 a show for the Gleason appearances plus, of course, national exposure. Gleason knew exactly what was happening. "He's a guitar-playing Marlon Brando," he said. Only part of what worked for Elvis was the music, Gleason knew. Certainly, that was important, but it was more than just the music. It was also the movement and the style. And a great deal of it was the look: sultry, alienated, a little misunderstood, the rebel who wanted to rebel without ever leaving home. He was perfect because he was the safe rebel. He never intended to cause trouble. He was a classic mama's boy, and Gladys Presley had barely let him out of her sight until he was in high school; now finally on the threshold of great success, he used his royalties in that first year to buy three new homes, each larger than the last, for his parents. He also gave each of his parents a new Cadillac, though the one he gave his mother never got license plates since she did not drive.

By 1956 he had become both a national celebrity and a national issue. His success, amplified as it was by the newfound wealth of the nation and the new technology of radio, record players and, finally, television, defied the imagination. He quickly made a three-picture deal with Hal Wallis for $450,000. "Hound Dog" sold two million copies and "Don't Be Cruel" sold three million. His singles were not merely taking off, they were defying traditional musical categories: "Heartbreak Hotel" was #1 on the white chart, #1 on the country chart, and #5 on the rhythm and blues chart; "Don't Be Cruel" and "Hound Dog" became #1 on all three charts. In April 1956 he already had six of RCA's all-time top twenty-five records and was selling $75,000 worth of records a day.

That month he made a rather sedate appearance on *The Milton Berle Show* and in June Berle had him back. This time he cut loose, causing an immense number of protests about the vulgarity of his act. Now Elvis Presley was working the American home, and suddenly the American home was a house divided. At this point Ed Sullivan lashed out against Presley. He announced that Presley's act was so suggestive that it would never go on his show. This was Sullivan as a guardian of public morals, a man born in 1902, fifty-four years old that summer. Within three weeks Sullivan had to change his mind. His competition, *The Steve Allen Show*, immediately called Colonel Parker and booked Presley for July 1. The problem for Allen, of course, was that, like everyone else, he wanted it both ways. He wanted Elvis on board, but he did not want a big protest on the part of the traditional segment of his audience. So he and his staff compromised: They would go high Elvis rather than low Elvis. They dressed Elvis in a tux, and they got him to limit his body movement. He did a dim-witted sketch with Allen, Imogene Coca, and Andy Griffith, in which he played a cowboy named Tumbleweed, and he sang "Hound Dog" to a live basset hound. The Presley fans hated it. After the show, Dewey Phillips called Elvis long distance in New York: "You better call home and get straight, boy. What you doing in that monkey suit? Where's your guitar?" When Elvis returned to Memphis for a concert in Phillips' honor, he cut loose with a pure rockabilly performance. It was Presley at his best, and when he finished, he told the audience, "I just want to tell y'all not to worry—them people in New York and Hollywood are not going to change me none."

But *The Steve Allen Show* had worked in one sense; it was the first time Steve Allen had beaten Ed Sullivan in the ratings. Sullivan surrendered almost immediately. His people called Colonel Parker and signed Elvis for $50,000 to do three shows. It was a figure then unheard of. It was one thing to guard public morals for the good of the nation and the good of your career; it was another thing to guard public morals at the cost of your career.

The battle was over: Ed Sullivan had conceded and the new music had entered the mainstream of American culture. Sullivan was not there for the first show; he was recuperating from an auto accident, and Charles Laughton was the host. The producers deliberately shot Elvis from the waist up. But soon he would be singing and dancing in full sweep. Sullivan was pleased; his ratings were extraordinary. He also wanted to make clear that he had not lowered America's morals.

"I want to say to Elvis Presley and the country that this is a real decent, fine boy," Sullivan told his audience after the third show. "We've never had a pleasanter experience on our show with a big name than we've had with you. You're thoroughly all right." It was the deftest of surrenders; it appeared to be the generous speech of a man receiving a surrender while in fact it was the speech of a man who had just surrendered himself. Market economics had won. It augured a profound change in American taste: In the past whites had picked up on black jazz but that had largely been done by the elite. This was different; this was a visceral, democratic response by the masses. It was also a critical moment for the whole society: The old order had been challenged and had not held. New forces were at work, driven by technology. The young did not have to listen to their parents anymore.

FIRST PUBLISHED IN DAVID HALBERSTAM, *THE FIFTIES*. NEW YORK: VILLARD BOOKS, 1993.

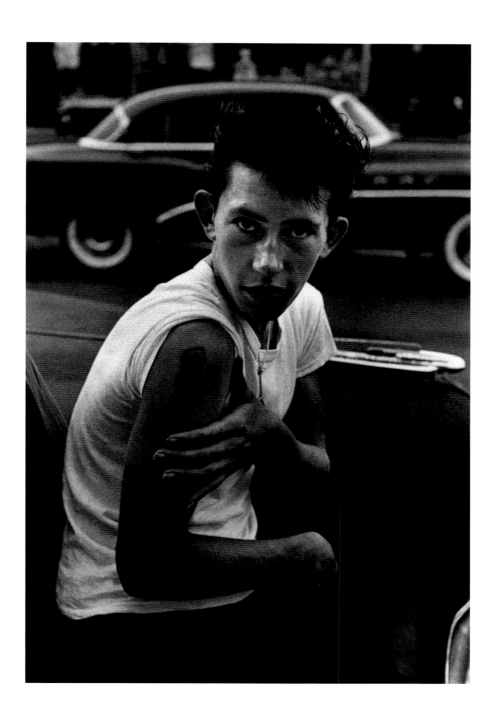

Brooklyn Gang, New York City, 1959, by Bruce Davidson.
High school student at the local coffee shop after school, Port Jefferson, Long Island, 1956, by Eve Arnold (opposite).

Brooklyn Gang, New York City, 1959, by Bruce Davidson.

School Dance, 1956, by Wayne Miller (above). *Jivin' Joint*: a teen imitates Elvis Presley's dance moves in a record store in Jacksonville, Florida, 1956, by Robert W. Kelley (below).

High school students in a coffee shop dating after school, Long Island, New York, 1956, by Eve Arnold.

Brooklyn Gang, Coney Island, New York, 1959, by Bruce Davidson.

Brooklyn Gang, New York City, 1959, by Bruce Davidson.

Brooklyn Gang, New York City, 1959, by Bruce Davidson.

Brooklyn Gang, New York City, 1959, by Bruce Davidson.

Dancing, 1950s.

"WHAT IS THIS THING CALLED ROCK 'N' ROLL? WHAT IS IT THAT MAKES TEENAGERS—MOSTLY CHILDREN BETWEEN THE AGES OF 12 AND 16—THROW OFF THEIR INHIBITIONS AS THOUGH AT A REVIVALIST MEETING? WHAT—WHO—IS RESPONSIBLE FOR THESE SORTIES? AND IS THIS GENERATION OF TEENAGERS GOING TO HELL?" GERTRUDE SAMUELS, *NEW YORK TIMES MAGAZINE*, JANUARY 12, 1958

Teenagers waiting in line for Alan Freed's *Rock and Roll Stage Show*, Times Square, Manhattan, New York, July 3, 1957.

MUSIC OR MADNESS? *A jangling, jumping musical craze has infected U. S. teen-agers—and stirred up a whirlwind of adult protest*

Disgusted Adults Battling Music of Delinquents

(The first cracks are appearing in the records of rock 'n' roll. Within the past month steps have been taken to curb the explosive effects of these teener-tunes. First of two articles on a musical revolt.)

By JESS STEARN

WHILE rock 'n' roll is apparently growing in popularity with teen-agers, long-suffering adults are beginning

A TENOR SAXOPHONE tilts backward and throws insistent, brutal notes into the air. The melody is simple and repetitious. More important is the beat; it is so firm and strong you can practically walk on it. Bill Haley (left, below) and his Comets are playing *Rock Around the Clock* at the Sports Arena in Hershey, Pa., to an audience that wails, screeches and sometimes dances in the aisle (right).

This scene is being repeated all over the nation as teen-agers rock and roll to a new musical craze that has frightened parents, turned the music-publishing business upside down and sent psychiatrists to their textbooks for new ways to say "adolescent rebellion."

While music critics moan and newspapers complain (left), a hard core of supporters insists that this music is a victim of a "vicious conspiracy," started by old-timers in the music business who have been hurt by the fad, and perpetuated by parents and others seeking a scapegoat for their failures with youth.

Meanwhile, Benny Goodman, whose swing music started "riots" 20 years ago, says, "I guess it's O.K.., man. At least, it has a beat."

continued

Produced by GEORGE B. LEONARD, Jr.   Photographed by ED FEINGERSH

1 o'clock...

The great Rock'n'Roll

40

Look, magazine. June 26, 1956.

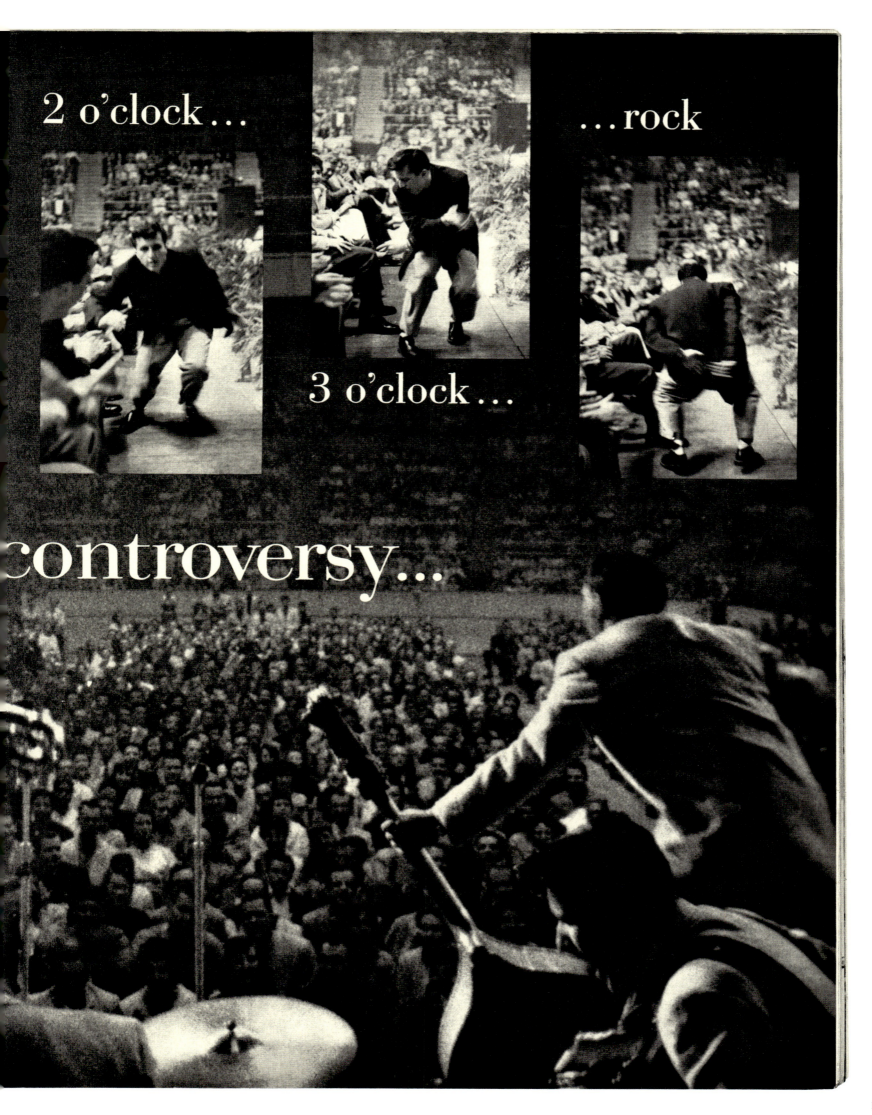

2 o'clock... ...rock

3 o'clock...

controversy...

ROCK 'N ROLL

COP IN CONTROVERSY, Police Chief Francis McManus of New Haven, Conn., banned rock 'n roll.

A frenzied teen-age music craze kicks up a big fuss

The nation's teen-agers are dancing their way into an enlarging controversy over rock 'n roll. In New Haven, Conn. the police chief has put a damper on rock 'n roll parties and other towns are following suit. Radio networks are worried over questionable lyrics in rock 'n roll. And some American parents, without quite knowing what it is their kids are up to, are worried that it's something they shouldn't be.

Rock 'n roll is both music and dance. The music has a rhythm often heavily accented on the second and fourth beat. The dance combines the Lindy and Charleston, and almost anything else. In performing it, hollering helps and a boot banging the floor makes it even better. The over-all result, frequently, is frenzy.

ORIGINATOR of craze, Disk Jockey Alan Freed of New York's WINS, has fans with lettered jackets.

A CROWD OF 1,500 GUESTS OF DISK JOCKEY AL JARVIS

JUMPER, shoeless girl of Boston's famous Totem Pole, hops up to swing across floor to *Ko Ko Mo*.

CLAP HANDS TO KEEP THE BEAT BOTH HEAVY AND HAPPY AS TWO JIVING COUPLES ROCK 'N ROLL IN THE PARKING LOT OF A SUBURBAN LOS ANGELES SUPERMARKET

ROCKING couples demonstrate dance craze in San Francisco TV studio with an ice cream parlor set.

ROLLING, Herbert Hardesty lies on floor honking out a sax solo of *Don't You Know* as rhythm section of Fats Domino's band beats out accompaniment at 54 Ballroom in Los Angeles. The fans loved it.

CONTINUED ON NEXT PAGE 167

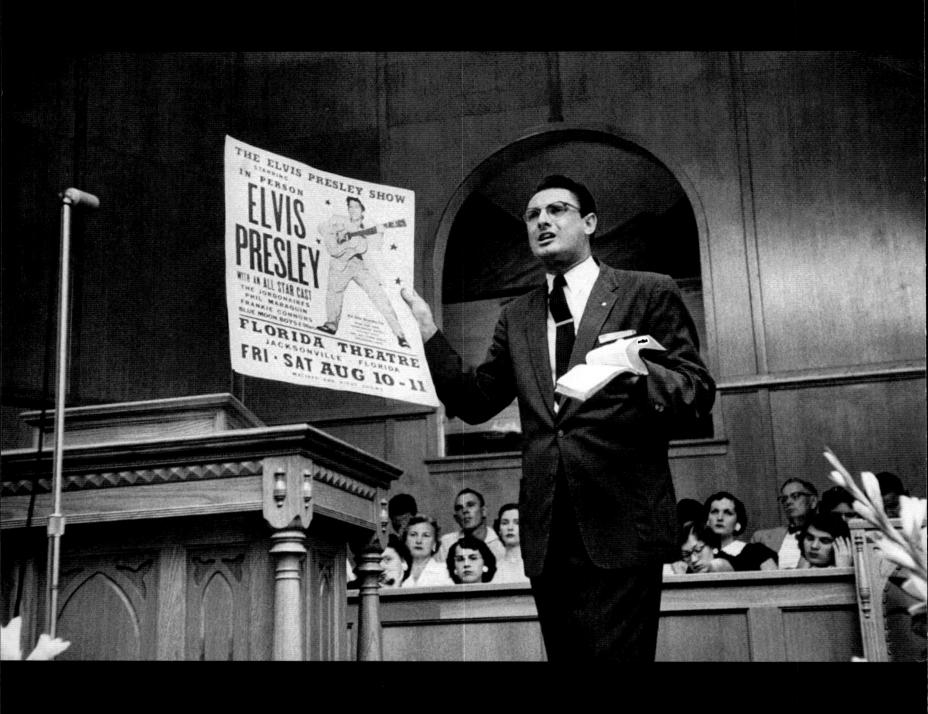

Fire and Brimstone. The preacher Robert Gray compares an Elvis Presley concert poster and a Bible. The reverend declares that the singer has "achieved a new low in spriritual degeneracy." Jacksonville, Florida, 1956, by Robert W. Kelley.

"ROCK 'N' ROLL SMELLS PHONY AND FALSE. IT IS SUNG, PLAYED, AND WRITTEN FOR THE MOST PART BY CRETINOUS GOONS AND BY MEANS OF ITS ALMOST IMBECILIC REITERATION, AND SLY, LEWD, IN PLAIN FACT, DIRTY LYRICS . . . IT MANAGES TO BE THE MARTIAL MUSIC OF EVERY SIDEBURNED DELINQUENT ON THE FACE OF THE EARTH." FRANK SINATRA, 1957

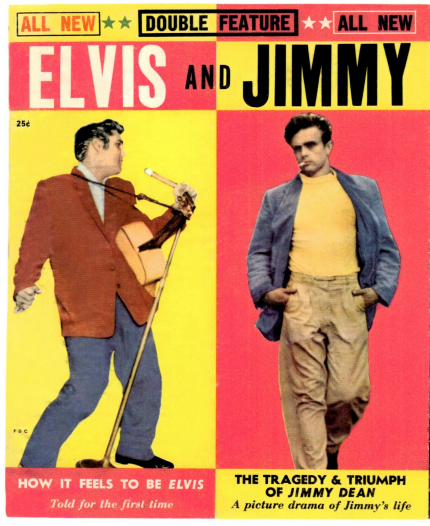
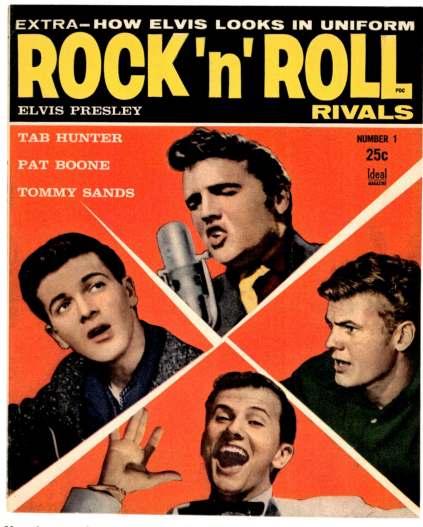
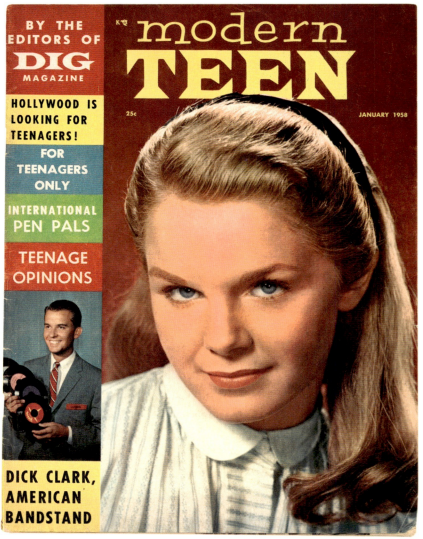

Magazine covers for teenagers, December 1956 to January 1958.

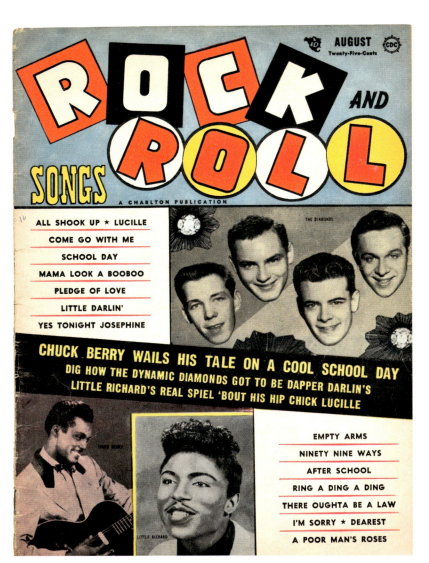
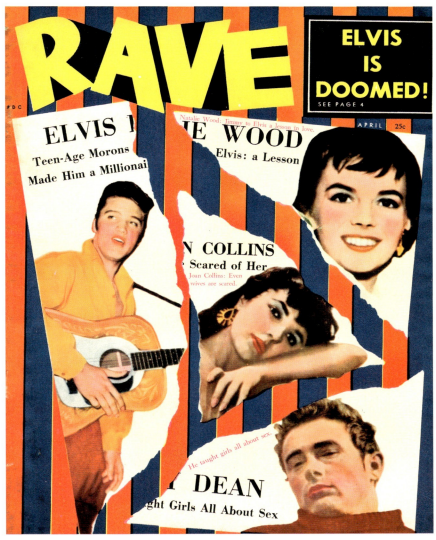

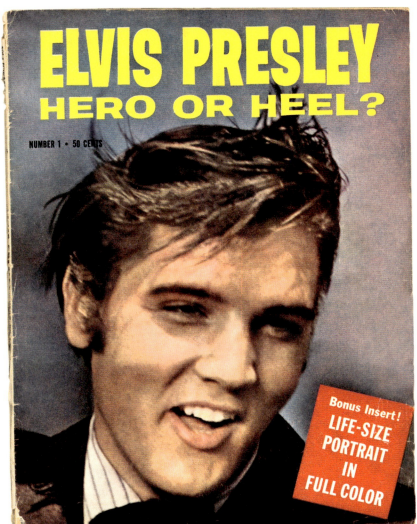

A teenager sits in her bedroom among her collection of James Dean memorabilia, Haverhill, Massachusetts, January 29, 1957.

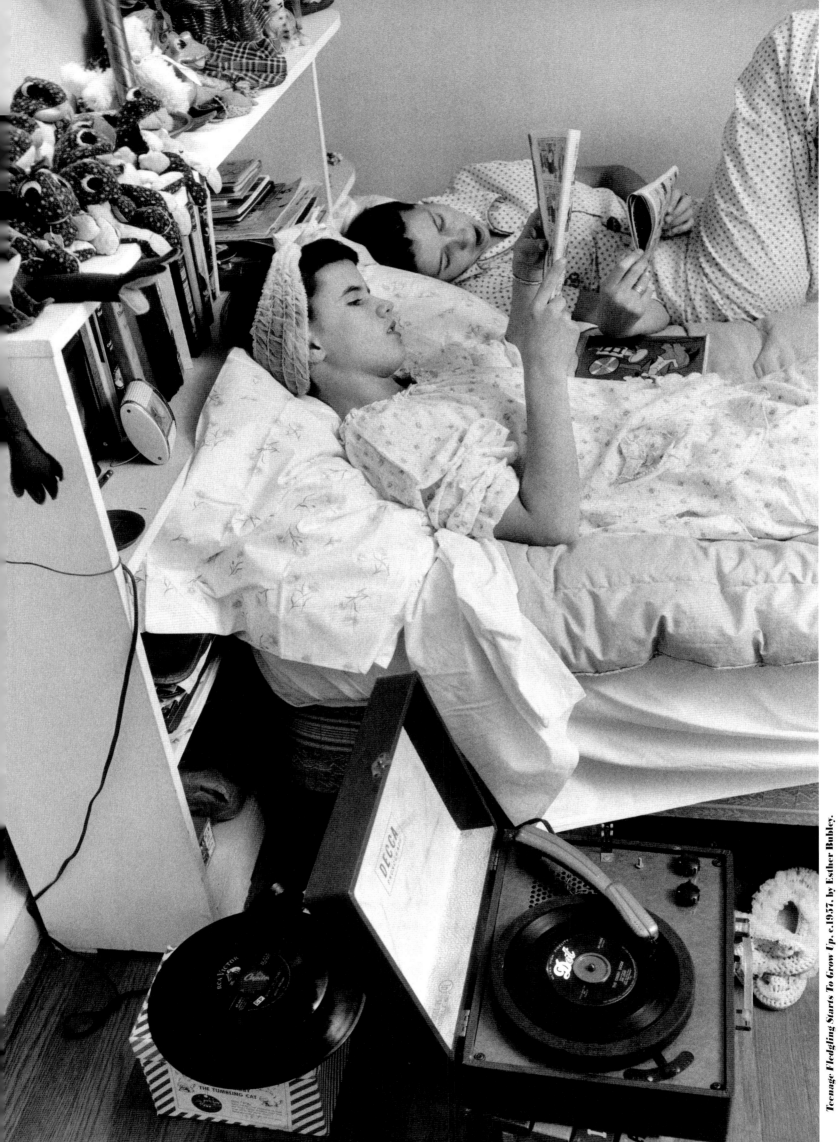

Teenage Fledgling Starts To Grow Up, c.1957, by Esther Bubley.

Record Stores, Los Angeles, early 1950s.

Teenage Fledgling, 1957, by Esther Bubley.

"WHO PUTS THE MOST DIMES IN THE JUKEBOX? AND WHO GETS UP AT EVERY RECORD COUNTER ACROSS THE LAND, DAY AFTER DAY, WEEK AFTER WEEK, MONTH AFTER MONTH? TEENAGERS, MY FAVORITE AUDIENCE."

— ALAN FREED, 1956

Ami A Jukebox, 1946–1947.

Wurlitzer Jukebox 1015, 1946–1947.

Wurlitzer Jukebox 1100, 1948.

Wurlitzer Jukebox 1900, 1956.

Seeburg V 200 Jukebox, 1955.

ELV

MARCH 1956: ELVIS PRESLEY HAS JUST BEGUN HIS CAREER. ALFRED WERTHEIMER, A YOUNG PHOTOGRAPHER IN NEW YORK, IS ASKED BY THE SINGER'S RECORD LABEL TO FOLLOW HIM DURING A TELEVISION APPEARANCE AND A RECORDING SESSION. IN THE MONTHS THAT FOLLOW, ALFRED WERTHEIMER DECIDES TO ACCOMPANY HIM ON OTHER EVENTS, NOTABLY ON HIS RETURN TO MEMPHIS. THE PHOTOGRAPHER WAS ABLE TO CAPTURE, IN ONLY A FEW DAYS OF SHOOTING, THE CHARISMA AND SPONTANEITY THAT MADE ELVIS KING.

BY ALFRED W

"Elvis always needed an excuse to get away from the conversation. Whether it was an accordion, guitar, or piano, he would pick up whatever musical instrument happened to be there. It was his way of calming himself down and letting people know that he was absorbed in his music. The agents and others were impressed by the fact that Elvis could even sing gospel. Everyone always thought of him as a rock 'n' roll singer."

Previous pages: Rehearsal of *The Steve Allen Show*, New York, June 29, 1956.
Opposite: Backstage at the Mosque Theater, Richmond, Virginia, June 30, 1956.

"Elvis didn't like the idea of singing to a hound dog but had enough good humor to go along with it since he was a guest on Steve Allen's show. Moreover, Elvis was a twenty-one-year-old singer being introduced to the American public. He didn't have much weight to throw around . . . yet."

Following pages: *The Steve Allen Show*, New York, July 1, 1956.

"Passing a newspaper stand, Elvis saw a headline about 127 people killed in an airplane crash. . . . [He] picked up a copy of the *Sunday Mirror*, which had pictures of two of the stewardesses on the cover, and was completely preoccupied with this story. He walked through the station totally oblivious to everything else that was going on around him."

"A box full of fan mail was left for him on the couch, so he flopped down and threw his feet up. Taking a fistful of letters, he began opening and seriously reading them. . . . Once Elvis finished reading, he tore each letter up into little shreds and put them on the coffee table. 'Why are you doing that Elvis?' 'I'm not going to carry them with me. I've read them and seen what's in them. It's nobody else's business.' "

Opposite: New York, July 1, 1956.
Following pages: Warwick Hotel, New York, March 17, 1956.

"The last guy anyone wanted in the recording studio was the photographer because of the noise, so I had to grab my chances to shoot during the rehearsals in between recordings. . . . That day, three songs, 'Hound Dog,' 'Don't Be Cruel,' and 'Any Way You Want Me,' were recorded. The first two became Elvis' third and fourth gold records, respectively. 'Hound Dog' was already very popular, so the recording was going to be released as a single with 'Don't Be Cruel' on the b-side. But 'Don't Be Cruel' also became a number-one hit so they reissued it with 'Hound Dog' as the b-side."

"The studio had Neumann condenser microphones that stood about six inches high. They weren't the most modern microphones, but they gave the music a certain sound quality that Elvis liked. . . . Elvis, however, still was not used to the idea of stationary microphones. He used his body when singing and preferred holding the microphone in his hand or dragging the stand wherever he was going onstage. Even in the sound booth, he had a tendency to move about, causing parts of the song to drop out of the recording. The engineers frequently would say, 'Elvis, could we do it one more time? Try to stay on mike.' There couldn't be any patching or splicing, so the songs had to be recorded straight through."

Opposite and following pages: The Recording Session, Studio One, New York, July 2, 1956.

"What was so different about Elvis? First of all, he made the girls cry and second, he permitted closeness."

Opposite: New York, July 1, 1956.

"Apart from the crowds on the lawn, it really was just a pleasant day with a regular family whose son had just returned home for a summer holiday. Through my camera, I joined a neighborhood full of friendly folk. I saw a mother happy to see her boy and a boy giving his mother a kiss. Elvis had come home."

Previous page, opposite, and following pages: Audubon Drive, Memphis, Tennessee, July 4, 1956.

"Elvis was preoccupied with the recording session. Finding an electric outlet in his compartment, he put a record player on his lap and repeatedly played the three tunes, 'Hound Dog,' 'Don't Be Cruel,' and 'Any Way You Want Me.' . . . Watching him with his record player, I had to ask him, 'Why do you keep playing them on this tiny little player?' It obviously wasn't very good quality, especially when just the day before we'd heard them on large speakers in a sound studio. He pointed out, 'This might only be a twenty-dollar record player, but that's the way my fans will hear it.' He wanted to know how he sounded to them."

Opposite and following pages: On the train from New York to Memphis, July 3 and 4, 1956.

"White, Tennessee was a small town right outside of Memphis. That stop was closer to Elvis' home on Audubon Drive than the main train terminal in Memphis. With only the records, no luggage or instruments, he hopped off the train and headed down a grassy knoll towards the sidewalk of this little town. Between telephone poles and Cadillacs, Elvis stopped to ask a black woman on the street for directions and then turned to wave to us on the train. . . . That was probably one of the last times he could just walk down the street like an ordinary guy."

Opposite and following pages: White, Tennessee, July 4, 1956.

"Elvis just naturally knew how to get to the ladies. . . . He had with him the script for *The Steve Allen Show* featuring Tumbleweed Presley. Flipping through some of the pages, he was trying to impress this young lady whose name I forgot to get. But she remained cool, not wanting to look too impressed. Elvis continued to try to loosen her up with conversation. At one point, he came in close, within three inches of her face, and just shouted, 'Ahhh!' "

"Elvis continued to be at turns debonair and playful, or stern and wrapping both his hands around her neck in a mock ceremony of choking her, trying to get her to loosen up. He had style, you had to admit that. Junior, on the other hand, was scowling in the backseat and paying no attention to the lovebirds."

" 'I'll bet you can't kiss me, Elvis,' she said and stuck out her tongue mocking him. Finally, she was letting her guard (and her pocketbook) down. 'I'll bet ya I can,' he said and stuck out his tongue. On his first try, he overshot the mark and bent her nose."

Opposite and following pages: Richmond, Virginia, June 30, 1956.

"Since Elvis had been seen just three days earlier on *The Steve Allen Show*, where he was tightly scripted into a tuxedo singing to a hound dog, he started this night's performance off with a statement. 'Tonight, you're going to see what the real Elvis Presley is all about.' Before you knew it, he was gyrating all over the stage in his signature way. The audience loved it. Thousands of people screamed and hollered for their hometown boy who had made it in the big time. Elvis felt good that night, and so did I."

"Gladys and Vernon, Elvis's Uncle Travis, his grandmother Minnie May, and Barbara had been escorted already to a special VIP area near the stage."

Opposite and following pages: Russwood Park Concert, Memphis, Tennessee, July 4, 1956.
Two last double pages: Studio 50, New York, March 17, 1956.

"BEFORE ELVIS THERE WAS NOTHING."

JOHN LENNON

Elvis Presley with his parents, Gladys and Vernon, Tupelo, Mississippi, 1937.

Elvis Presley with B.B. King backstage at the WDIA Goodwill Revue, Memphis, Tennessee, 1957, by Ernest C. Withers.

Elvis Presley and his tailor Nudie Cohen at Nudie's Rodeo Tailors, Los Angeles, California, c.1957.

Elvis Presley, Scotty and Bill, "Good Rockin' Tonight," Sun, single, 1954.
Elvis Presley, Scotty and Bill, "That's All Right," Sun, single, 1954.

Elvis Presley, Scotty and Bill, "Mystery Train," Sun, single, 1955.
Elvis Presley, Scotty and Bill, "Baby Let's Play House", Sun, single, 1955.
Elvis Presley, Scotty and Bill, "Milkcow Blues Boogie", Sun, single, 1955.

"IF I COULD FIND A WHITE MAN WITH THE NEGRO SOUND AND THE NEGRO FEEL, I COULD MAKE A MILLION DOLLARS."

**SAM PHILLIPS
EARLY 1950s**

Sam Phillips (center) with Elvis Presley, Robert Johnson, and Leo Soroka, Sun Studio, Memphis, Tennessee, December 4, 1956

SAM PHILLIPS

BY PETER GURALNICK

Sam Phillips could be said to be the man who invented rock 'n' roll.

Born on a farm outside of Florence, Alabama, on January 5, 1923, his two primary role models were an old blind black man named Silas Payne whom his family took in when he was eight, and his deaf-mute Aunt Emma, from whom as a child he learned to sign and whom he would take care of until her death in 1965.

From Silas Payne he learned the gift of imagination, "that you must have a belief," as Sam always insisted, "in things that are unknown to you." From his deaf-mute aunt, whom he considered, even with her handicap, to be one of the most brilliant and accomplished people he knew, "I just thought, 'Man, alive, me with a couple of pretty good ears and a couple of eyeballs, there shouldn't be any limit to what I try—*if* I set my mind to it.'"

The fundamental lesson was communication, and that was what Sam brought to his work first in radio, then in the recording studio. Sound was the vehicle. Anyone who ever listened to Sam expound upon his boyhood knows that it was sound that carried him away. The sound of a whippoorwill. The sound of a mockingbird's song. The sound of the sharecroppers working and singing in the fields. The sound of a hoe striking the ground. And the sound of the silences in between. As Sam said, "I would hear somebody speak to a mule harshly—I heard that. Nothing passed my ears."

He started in radio in his hometown, migrated to Nashville, then Memphis, where he took a job at the city's most sophisticated station, WREC, in 1945, at the age of twenty-two. There he engineered the big band broadcasts on a national hookup from the roof of the Peabody Hotel every night, but in the end, much as he loved the sound of the bands, he tired of their lack of spontaneity: "They might have played the damned song four thousand times, and they were *still* turning the pages." To Sam if you weren't doing something different, then you weren't really doing anything and, in furtherance of that principle, in January of 1950 he opened up a little studio, the Memphis Recording Service, for the avowed purpose of "mak[ing] records with some of the great Negro artists in the South who just had no place to go."

He did this, as he often pointed out, at the risk of his job, at the risk of his health, at the risk of his young family's future. When he showed up for his work as an engineer at the radio station, he was greeted with sarcastic comments and racial jibes and advised on more than one occasion that maybe he ought to start thinking about giving up his eccentric little experiment and start focusing on his own professional future. Instead he quit his job because, he said, "with the belief that I had in this music, in these people, I would have been the biggest damn coward on God's green earth if I had not."

In 1951 he made what is widely considered to be the first rock 'n' roll record, Ike Turner and Jackie Brenston's "Rocket '88'," and he recorded the artist he still considers the greatest talent with whom he ever worked, Howlin' Wolf. He recorded B.B. King, Bobby "Blue" Bland, Little Junior Parker, and Rufus Thomas as well, all at the outset of their careers, until, in the summer of 1953, a shy eighteen-year-old kid with sideburns, just graduated from high school, wandered into his studio to make a record "for his mother"—and in hopes that somehow he might get noticed. "He tried not to show it," said Sam Phillips, "but he felt so *inferior*. Elvis Presley probably innately was the most introverted person that [ever] came into that studio."

This Elvis Presley considered himself a ballad singer almost exclusively, but Sam heard something different in his voice. He didn't discover what it was until almost a year later when he finally summoned Elvis back for a studio tryout with guitarist Scotty Moore and bass player Bill Black. After running through a series of ballads with little success, the three musicians were taking a break when Elvis, perhaps sensing that his opportunity was slipping away, picked up a guitar and started fooling around with an old blues song called "That's All Right Mama." That was when Sam Phillips' ears perked up. "What are you doing?" he said. "I don't know," said Elvis, somewhat abashed. "Well, back up, try to find a place to start, and do it again."

After that Phillips recorded, in short order, Carl Perkins, Johnny Cash, Roy Orbison, Jerry Lee Lewis, and Charlie Rich, not to mention such rockabilly notables as Sonny Burgess and Billy Lee Riley. Memphis became the spearhead of a musical movement, the Memphis Recording Service at 706 Union Avenue became its epicenter, and Sam Phillips was seen, both then as now, as the avatar of a revolution, whose vision gave birth to a moment of freedom and individuation. He scorned copy artists and imitators. The individuals that he championed had only one thing in common: a commitment to expressing themselves each in his own way—what Sam liked to call *individualism in the extreme*.

Like other great American creative geniuses—like Walt Whitman, who sought to encompass the full range of the American experience in his poetry; like William Faulkner, who could see past prejudice to individual distinctions; like Mark Twain, who celebrated the freedom of the river and a refusal to be civilized—Sam Phillips had a democratic vision of his own. In *his* vision, categories of every sort would be broken down, and people would be free to express themselves as they liked, make any kind of damn fool of themselves that they wanted to—and be judged solely on the individual results.

He himself got out of the music business at an early age—after 1960, for all intents and purposes, he devoted himself to other interests, radio in particular—but he never wavered in his belief in giving voice to those who had no voice, in his commitment to the kind of freedom that he believed rock 'n' roll in its first flowering represented, not just in musical but in social, racial, and political terms.

"If it could be worked," he said presciently, "to where just a few like Elvis could break out again, then I would preach, I would become an evangelist if I were alive, saying, 'For God's sake, don't let's become conformists. Just do your thing in your own way. Don't ever let fame and fortune or recognition or anything interfere with what you feel is here.' And I'll tell you, I hope it's not too long coming, because of the fact that as we go longer and longer into the lack of individual expression, as we go along, if we get too far we're going to get away from some of the real basic things. All of us damn cats that appreciate not the Fifties necessarily but that freedom are gonna forget about the feel. We gonna be in jail, and not even know it."

Roscoe Gordon and Sam Phillips, Sun Studio, Memphis, Tennessee, early 1950s, by Ernest C. Withers.

Dewey Phillips, Hippodrome, Beale Street, Memphis, Tennessee, early 1950s, by Ernest C. Withers.

DEWEY PHILLIPS

BY PETER GURALNICK

For a brief moment, in Memphis in the 1950s, Dewey Phillips was at the center of the musical universe.

He got his first fifteen-minute radio slot in 1949, leaping into it from his job managing the record department at the W.T. Grant five-and-dime, where he spun an eclectic mix of the latest records—hillbilly and "race" music, sacred and profane, Frank Sinatra and Wynonie "Mr. Blues" Harris—over the store's PA. From the start he drew an equally mixed, equally eclectic in-house audience—as many young as old, as many black as white—in a strictly segregated store, in strictly segregated Memphis, in the heart of the Deep South. His listeners were clearly drawn not just by the music but by the irrepressible enthusiasm of the twenty-three-year-old white man who was playing it, singing it, sometimes even competing with it, with a deliberately mangled range of verbal inventiveness that knew no race but was delivered in the rawest, most disarming of hillbilly accents.

The radio show was a hit from the start. It was called *Red, Hot And Blue*, and the name stuck, suggesting as much as anything the untrammeled feeling that Dewey Phillips brought to the music. There was no medium in Dewey's world, no cool, everything was red-hot and rocking even when the music was blue, if only because, from Dewey Phillips' point of view, with music this earthshakingly important, it was essential that every man stand up and be counted.

Within a year he was on the air six nights a week, two hours a night, reaching a previously undreamt-of audience that seemingly rejected categories, musical or otherwise, as much as he did. Rock 'n' roll would not be acknowledged, or named for that matter, for another four or five years, but Dewey had discovered the new world as surely as Columbus (or *someone*) discovered America. Frankie Laine's "Mule Train" might lead in to a hot gospel number by Sister Rosetta Tharpe, a lowdown Muddy Waters blues could be followed by a pretty ballad from Nat "King" Cole or Larry Darnell, and it would scarcely come as a shock if a Hank Williams "heart song" were thrown in for good measure. The one constant, the one element that held it all together was Dewey's impassioned advocacy, his mad, manic patter. "If you can't drink it," he extemporized, singing the praises of his sponsor, locally brewed Falstaff Beer, "freeze it and eat it. If you can't do that, open up a cotton-picking rib and POUR it in." Above all, he advised his listeners, whatever business they might be about, "Tell 'em Phillips sentcha." And they did, one even going so far as to deliver that message to a startled emergency room staff at a local hospital.

He captivated Memphis ("Dewey had no color," said rhythm and blues singer Rufus Thomas admiringly), and he captivated Sam Phillips, who had just opened up a little studio at 706 Union Avenue to record some of the same sounds that Dewey was showcasing on the air. Recognizing from the start how much they had in common—not just the music but a belief, as Sam would articulate it, in *individualism in the extreme*—Sam persuaded Dewey to join him in a new record label that would be called the Phillips, in tribute to their mutual interests and shared last name. The Phillips, billed a little optimistically as "The Hottest Thing In The Country," lasted for only one release, but their friendship (they were, Sam said, closer than brothers) lasted until Dewey's death in 1968 at the age of forty-two. Each man pursued his own path, with Dewey achieving the kind of regional celebrity and universal recognition (he was, said Sam, a genuine *superstar*) almost unimaginable in a present-day climate of monopoly, commodification, and international conglomeratization. Memphis may have been a small town, but it was perched right at the crossroads of history, and Dewey was in the thick of it, shouting, gesticulating, to all intents and purposes directing traffic for a world that had yet to settle on a handbook of musical rules and assumptions.

Dewey was the first to play Elvis. Sam, decidedly not a man given to reticence, was reticent about submitting "That's All Right" to Dewey because he was afraid he might not like it. As it turned out, Sam said, "he loved the damn record," and the next night he played it over and over again on the air, as the phones lit up and he called in the nineteen-year-old singer himself for an interview. "He said, 'Mr. Phillips, I don't know nothing about being interviewed.' I told him, 'Just don't say nothing dirty.'"

Dewey didn't simply introduce Elvis to his audience, he introduced Elvis to his world. He carried Elvis to Beale Street, where he had long since taken out citizenship papers and where he vouched for this strange-looking young white boy to skeptical black club owners and stars like Lowell Fulson, Calvin Newborn, and B.B. King. It was a curriculum, of course, that Elvis had already embarked upon and, together with Sam Phillips, Dewey helped complete Elvis's musical education.

Dewey was courted by virtually every record label, the majors as well as the independents, not just because he played their records but because he imparted to their success a certain indefinable spirit. "Call Sam!" he shouted at each and every juncture, musical or otherwise. One evening, to conduct an unscientific survey of his own popularity, he urged his listeners to blow their car horns at ten o'clock, and the entire city erupted in a cacophony of sound. When the police called to remind Dewey of Memphis's antinoise ordinance, imploring him not to do it again, he announced on the air, "Well, good people, Chief Macdonald just called and said we can't do that any more. Now I was going to have you do it at eleven o'clock, but the chief told me we couldn't, so whatever you do, at eleven o'clock don't blow your car horns." The results were predictable.

His television show, *Pop Shop*, went on the air in 1957, an unsanitized version of *American Bandstand*, and for a time was the biggest thing going in Memphis. Then, four days after he had been forced into a late night time slot by the network syndication of *Bandstand*, Dewey, according to the station manager, "embarrassed the station, and he embarrassed me personally," when he encouraged his sidekick, a noted young abstract painter who dressed in an ape suit on the air, to fondle a life-size cutout of Jayne Mansfield. That pretty much ended Dewey's television career, and he lost his radio show a few months later due to the same combination of originality, impetuosity, and unpredictability that had first catapulted him to stardom.

He lived another ten years. He had other radio shows and called everyone "Elvis" long after he had ceased to see much of his one-time protégé. As his rapid-fire speech grew garbled to the point of impenetrability, it was said that he had simply burned out on pills and alcohol, but he never lost his love for the music.

"Dewey could convince you that if you missed what he did, you missed something good," said Sam Phillips. "And [if you failed to stay with him], you were going to miss the best because the next record coming up was going to be even better than the last—and that was the best!" And yet, said Sam of a man he considered not just his closest friend but "a genius—and I don't call many people geniuses—when he got off the air at night, there was something about Dewey that kind of left him a little bit, because of the actual feeling of spirituality that he put into his program. He never liked to see the clock say midnight and he had to play his theme and go off the air. Now can you imagine that, a man who for nearly ten years was on the air and never wished for a night off?"

There were black jocks, said Memphis musician Jim Dickinson, who grew up listening to Dewey's show, who played black music for black people, "and white radio stations were playing white music for white people, but Dewey called his audience 'good people'—he was playing good music for good people. And it got across."

August 10, 1954

Mr. Marvin Leiber
Pan American Distributing Company
P. O. Box 37 Biscayne Annex
Miami 52, Florida

Dear Mr. Leiber:

In answer to your recent request for our complete catalogue, and since we do not yet have a formal catalogue ready for release, we enclose herewith a list of the SUN releases to date. We are also sending a copy to your Jacksonville branch.

We note your request to send samples on future releases direct to Jacksonville, and we will certainly do that.

We were happy to receive your initial order on Sun 209, and to know you are getting on it down there. We are confident that this is going to be one of the biggest records of the year, provided we can line up a little extra help from you and your staff.

Now here are the points we would appreciate your help on: because the record is going ALL THREE WAYS - Pop, Country and R&B - we want you to please make sure that all the R&B and Hillbilly Jockeys have a copy of the record ... also all the pop boys that cater somewhat to the "cat" trend on their pop shows. Make sure they are exposed to the THAT'S ALL RIGHT side. Music Sales, our Memphis distributor, reports that it is being bought by operators for ALL locations, white and colored, and as evidenced by the outstanding retail sales and by what the owner of one of the leading retail stores here called to tell us, everybody from white teenagers to old colored people are buying it with equal zest.

Again, our point is to make sure in your territory that the record is in the hands of all three types of DJ's .... this is very, very important. Of course, we will certainly reimburse you on all the records you use in promotion on the number.

Excerpt of a letter from Sam Phillips to Marvin Lieber, a distributor in Miami, August 10, 1954.

September 24, 1954

Mr. Sam C. Phillips
Sun Record Company
706 Union
Memphis, Tennessee

Dear Sam:

      Although I have never met you, I feel that we are friends enough that I can call you by your first name. In answering your letter of September 22nd, I am sorry our shipping clerks made the error of shipping you back some of the sample records. First of all to explain, for the quantity of sample records I receive, I am only able to give them out to one or two radio stations, or at the most, three stations here in Miami, to see if there is any reaction to them. If a record has good results, I cover every single station and give them to every disc jockey that comes into the office. Consequently, if a record shows no promise whatever, the remaining samples I have get placed in a pile. There would be no point in giving a jockey samples of merchandise that don't cause any reaction in the retail outlets or through the operators. You can, of course, deduct this amount from my return, and that goes as well for the freight as I am fully aware of the distributor's return set-up.

      Your record 209 is giving me a little problem in that certain locales throughout the State have operators which have them on every machine and in other locales, they won't even touch it. That is one of the strange things about the record business. I think it is a great record, my immediate reaction in Miami was good but in the northern part of Florida, they won't touch it as they consider it too racy. As you say, we are looking forward to a better Fall season.

Respectfully yours,

PAN AMERICAN DISTRIBUTING CORP.

Marvin Lieber

ML/pr

Distributing the Tops in Music — — Popular, Race, Hillbilly, L. P.'s, 45's, Albums, etc.

A letter from Marvin Lieber to Sam Phillips, September 24, 1954.

A poster for a festival featuring Hank Snow with Elvis as an opening act, December 4 to 7, 1955, Indianapolis, Indiana.

Elvis Presley concert poster, August 10 to 11, 1956, Jacksonville, Florida.

255

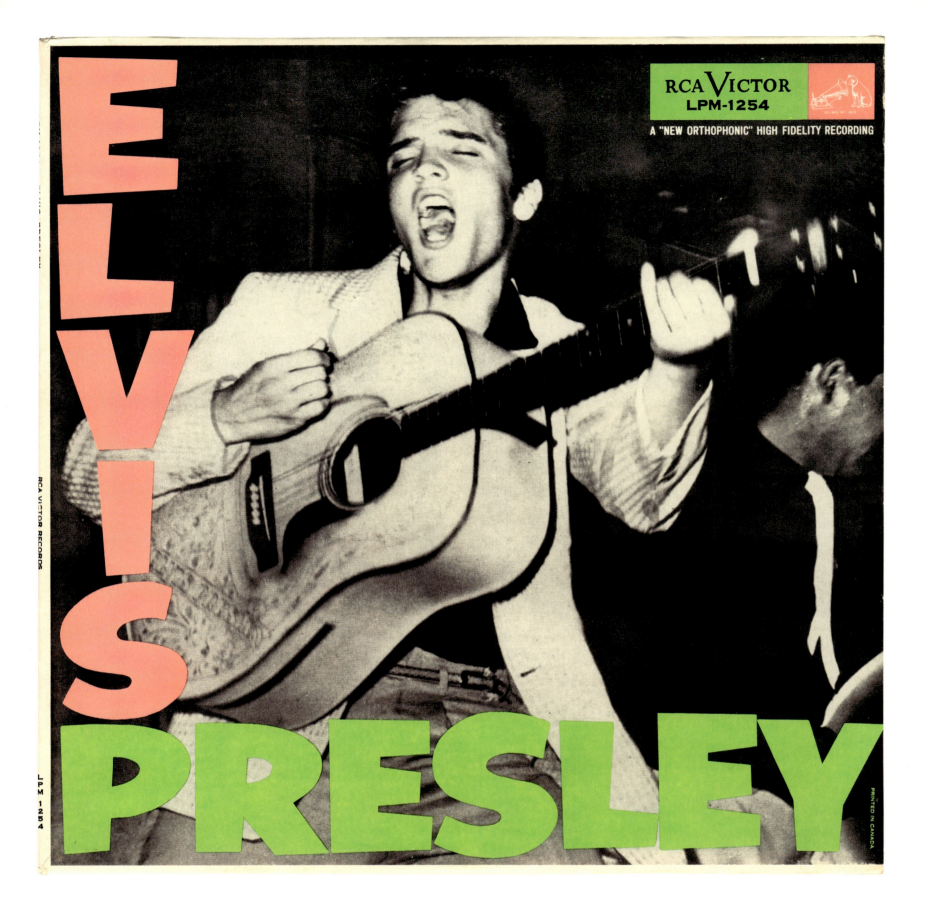

Elvis Presley, *Elvis Presley*, RCA Victor, LP, 1956.

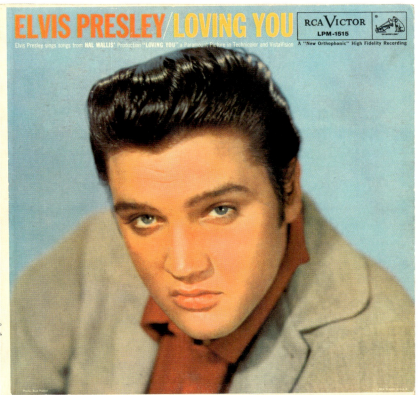
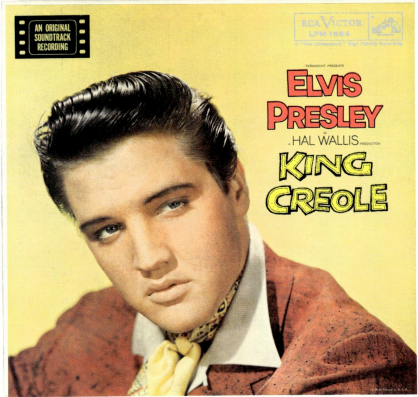
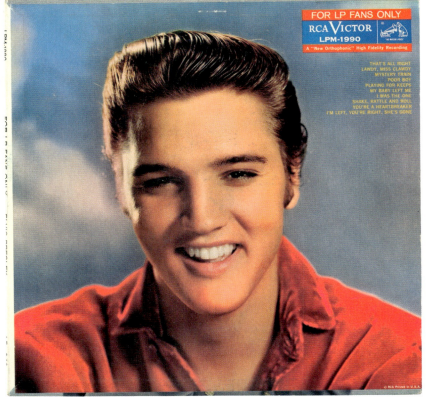

Elvis Presley, *Elvis*, RCA Victor, LP, 1956. Elvis Presley, *Loving You*, RCA Victor, LP, 1957.
Elvis Presley, *King Creole*, RCA Victor, LP, 1958. Elvis Presley, *For LP Fans Only*, RCA Victor, LP, 1959.

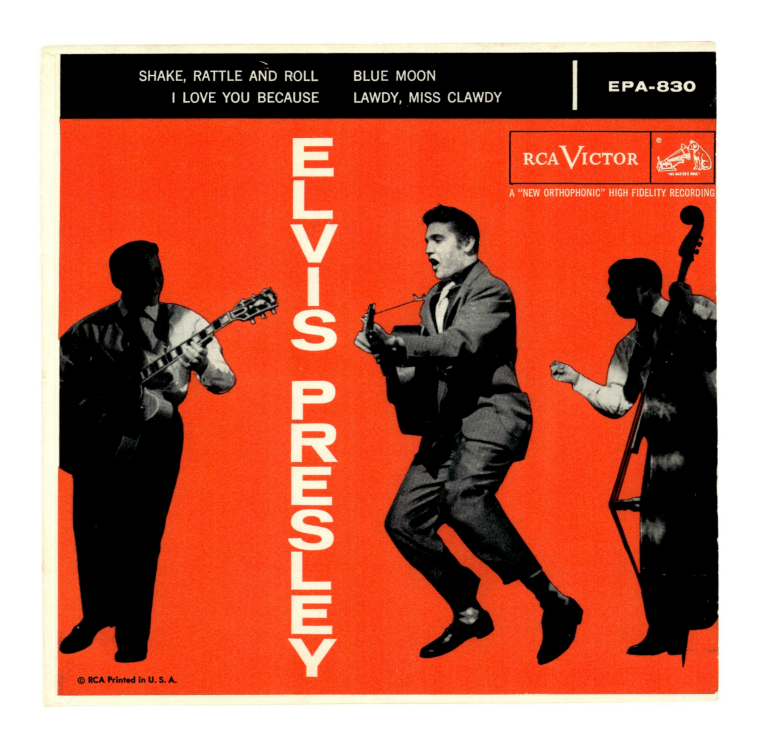

Elvis Presley, *Elvis Presley*, RCA Victor, 45 EP, 1956.

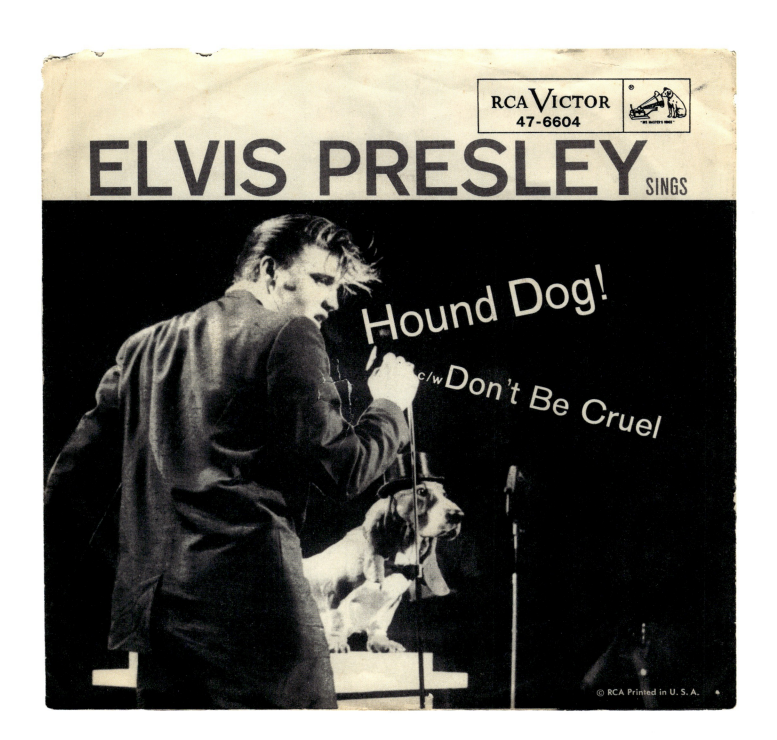

Elvis Presley, "Hound Dog," RCA Victor, single, 1956.

Rock 'n Roll Jamboree, magazine, Fall 1956.

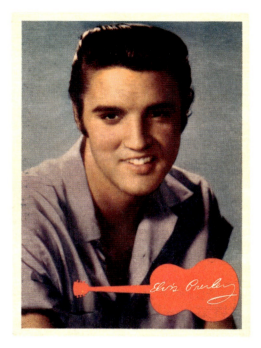
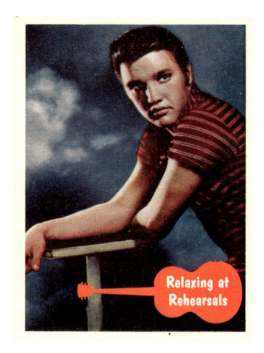
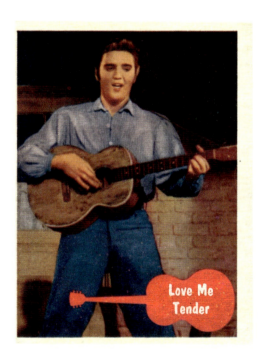
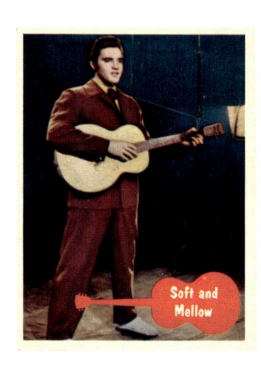

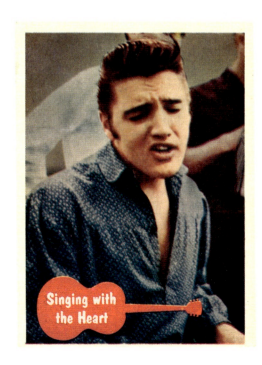
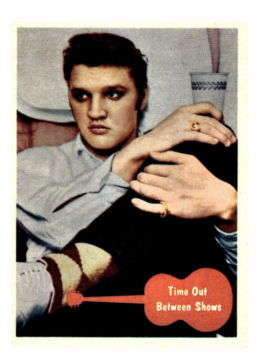

Elvis Presley collector's cards, 1956.

3 — ask Elvis
DO YOU GET MUCH FAN MAIL?

Yes, I get a lot of swell letters from folks all over the world and there's nothing I like better than taking time off and reading them. Most of the letters tell me how the fans feel about me, sometimes there's a fellow or girl who wants advice. When I come across a fan with a problem, I usually tell them to talk things over with their folks — they're sure to understand and help them out.

Elvis
©BUBBLES INC. PRINTED IN U.S.A.
©1956 ELVIS PRESLEY ENTERPRISES — ALL RIGHTS RESERVED

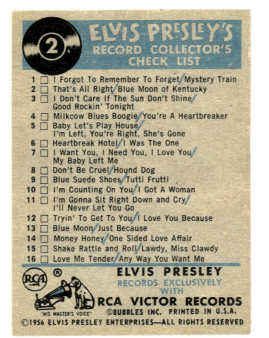
2 — ELVIS PRESLEY'S RECORD COLLECTOR'S CHECK LIST

1. ☐ I Forgot To Remember To Forget / Mystery Train
2. ☐ That's All Right / Blue Moon of Kentucky
3. ☐ I Don't Care If The Sun Don't Shine / Good Rockin' Tonight
4. ☐ Milkcow Blues Boogie / You're A Heartbreaker
5. ☐ Baby Let's Play House / I'm Left, You're Right, She's Gone
6. ☐ Heartbreak Hotel / I Was The One
7. ☐ I Want You, I Need You, I Love You / My Baby Left Me
8. ☐ Don't Be Cruel / Hound Dog
9. ☐ Blue Suede Shoes / Tutti Frutti
10. ☐ I'm Counting On You / I Got A Woman
11. ☐ I'm Gonna Sit Right Down and Cry / I'll Never Let You Go
12. ☐ Tryin' To Get To You / I Love You Because
13. ☐ Blue Moon / Just Because
14. ☐ Money Honey / One Sided Love Affair
15. ☐ Shake Rattle and Roll / Lawdy, Miss Clawdy
16. ☐ Love Me Tender / Any Way You Want Me

ELVIS PRESLEY RECORDS EXCLUSIVELY WITH **RCA VICTOR RECORDS**
©BUBBLES INC. PRINTED IN U.S.A.
©1956 ELVIS PRESLEY ENTERPRISES — ALL RIGHTS RESERVED

1 — ask Elvis
HOW DID YOU GET YOUR FIRST START?

A couple of years ago, I was at a picnic back home in Memphis. On the stage was a Hillbilly singer who had lots of rhythm. I just naturally began to sing along and people turned around to watch me instead of the performer. He was kind of mad, and dared me to come on the stage and try my luck. I took him up on it and it seemed the folks liked me. From there I got club dates and one night stands and my career began.

Elvis
©BUBBLES INC. PRINTED IN U.S.A.
©1956 ELVIS PRESLEY ENTERPRISES — ALL RIGHTS RESERVED

6 — ask Elvis
WHAT KIND OF GIRL DO YOU LIKE BEST?

It might sound corny, but that old song about wanting a girl just like the girl that married dad, goes for me. The girl I want has to love to do the things I do. She's got to be natural — not all made up to be something she's not. She doesn't have to be a movie queen or beauty contest winner. She should be able to cook — that's real important. And she must learn how to make my favorite dishes.

Elvis
©BUBBLES INC. PRINTED IN U.S.A.
©1956 ELVIS PRESLEY ENTERPRISES — ALL RIGHTS RESERVED

5 — ask Elvis
SHOULD PEOPLE GO INTO SHOW BUSINESS?

It's no secret that show business has been great to me. But let's not forget that I'm lucky — and I mean *lucky*. There are plenty of kids with talent who are having their hearts broken in the entertainment business. Success depends on having a certain talent recognized and then getting the right breaks. If you are willing to work hard and give your 'all' you probably can make a success in show business.

Elvis
©BUBBLES INC. PRINTED IN U.S.A.
©1956 ELVIS PRESLEY ENTERPRISES — ALL RIGHTS RESERVED

4 — ask Elvis
WHO IS YOUR FAVORITE ACTOR?

Someone I thought was going to be one of the all-time great actors was Jimmy Dean. I'd say that Jimmy was the actor I admired most. As far as one favorite actor, I couldn't say. You go to a dramatic movie and see great acting and next time you're splitting your sides laughing at a comedian — or a musical with a fine singers or or dancers. See what I mean — it's awfully tough to say for sure who I like best.

Elvis
©BUBBLES INC. PRINTED IN U.S.A.
©1956 ELVIS PRESLEY ENTERPRISES — ALL RIGHTS RESERVED

9 — ask Elvis
WOULD YOU RATHER DRIVE A CYCLE OR CAR?

Both cars and motorcycles can be a lot of fun. I guess I'm partial to cars though, and I bought a couple for myself. Then I began to wonder what the kick was with a motorcycle — so I got one for myself. Well, it's a thrill! The wind snaps at you and you can maneuver very easily. For greater comfort and safety, there's nothing like a car — but it's nice to hop on my 'cycle every now and then and take off.

Elvis
PRTD. IN U.S.A.
©BUBBLES INC.
©1956 ELVIS PRESLEY ENTERPRISES — ALL RIGHTS RESERVED

8 — ask Elvis
DO YOU SMOKE?

No, I don't and I don't drink either. Why? 'Cause I just don't like to. I tried pipes and cirarettes but I get no kick from them. Some people smoke because they tense up, but when that happens to me I just try to relax or else do some exercise like swimming or calisthenics. My folks didn't object to my smoking when they thought I was old enough, but it's a matter of taste — I just don't like it.

Elvis
©BUBBLES INC. PRINTED IN U.S.A.
©1956 ELVIS PRESLEY ENTERPRISES — ALL RIGHTS RESERVED

7 — ask Elvis
DO YOU LIKE TO TRAVEL?

Sure I like travelling, who wouldn't? You get to see every part of this great country of ours and really begin to appreciate what makes the good old U.S.A. tick. I've seen the farmlands, central plains, the Far West and the South. I feel very lucky to be able to see America and to meet my fellow citizens from all over — it gives you a real feeling of pride to be an American. I wish everyone could travel.

Elvis
PRTD. IN U.S.A.
©BUBBLES INC.
©1956 ELVIS PRESLEY ENTERPRISES — ALL RIGHTS RESERVED

FILMS · RADIO · VIDEO · MUSIC · STAGE

Variety

Published Weekly at 154 West 46th Street, New York 36, N. Y., by Variety, Inc. Annual subscription, $10. Single copies, 25 cents.
Entered as second-class matter December 22, 1905, at the Post Office at New York, N. Y., under the act of March 3, 1879.
COPYRIGHT, 1956, BY VARIETY, INC. ALL RIGHTS RESERVED

Vol. 204 No. 8   NEW YORK, WEDNESDAY, OCTOBER 24, 1956   PRICE 25 CENTS

ELVIS A MILLIONAIRE IN 1 YEAR

20th Would Share in NTA Film Web In Backlog Deal as New Diversification

Diversification by motion picture studios into television is taking a new form. First, Metro moved into the field of station ownership through the sale of its backlog. Now, 20th-Fox is reported to be dickering for a substantial interest in the new NTA Film Network Inc. as one of the terms of a deal under which it would sell its backlog to the film web.

Understood that if all the wrinkles in the NTA-20th discussions, which have been going for mon'hs now, are smoothed out, the studio would get more than a third ownership in the new network, which is now a wholly-owned National Telefilm Associates subsidiary. The deal for the 20th backlog, which would be turned over at a staggered rate covering several years, would involve heavy cash payments as well.

Such an ownership stake in the new web, if consummated, could lead to many new avenues through which 20th could expand its television activities and extend its diversification in day-to-day operations. Studio is currently producing only two regular network series, despite a major studio investment in revamping its lot for tv. But if it were to have an ownership stake in the film network, conceivably it could turn out new series for the film network at an unprecedented ra<e.

Such an approach makes the basic assumption that the film network project will be a success—and up to now, efforts in that direction have failed. But NTA is on the air with the network already, a oint nobody else reached, and
(Continued on page 78)

Havana's Booming 3 R's; ^um, Rhumba & Roulette

By JAY MALLIN

Havana, Oct. 23.

Cuban tourism will get one of the biggest boosts ever within a year or so when three big new hotels are completed. All three hotels will add three casinos to the country's already-thriving gambling circle.

The new Habana Hilton, costing $11,000,000, 600 rooms, is being built by the Gastronomic Workers Union of Cuba, and will be managed by the Hilton Corp.

Havana Riviera. Cost: $12,000,000, 400 rooms. To be built by the Riviera Hotel Co. Those interested include Harry and Ben Smith, of Toronto (former owns Toronto's Prince George Hotel) and, reportedly, the gentlemen from Las Vegas who now run the Hotel Nacional's Casino Internacional (including Wilbur Clark and Meyer and Dave Lansky).

Unnamed hotel. Cost: $5,000,000, 300 rooms. To be built by the Shepard Hotel Co. Those interested include J. J. Shepard, owner of Miami's Leamington Ho-
(Continued on page 79)

Webster & His Words

Hollywood, Oct. 23.

For the first time in the history of the Academy Awards, a lyricist faces the possibility of having three songs, from as many productions, competing for an Oscar nomination in the best song department.

Writer is Paul Francis Webster, who teamed with Dimitri Tiomkin for tunes in "Giant" and "Friendly Persuasion," both of which have been released and are being touted as contenders. Webster also lyricized Alfred Newman's title tune for "Anastasia," a 20th-Fox release, which is also figured as a possible nominee.

Symph Conductors A Hardy Breed; Range Into 80's

New York Philharmonic-Symphony, which last week contracted Leonard Bernstein as co-musical director with Dimitri Mitropoulos for 1957-58 season, will now have to find a replacement for Bruno Walter, who wants to retire after current season. Walter, who was 80 last month, does annual guest stints with the Philharmonic and, though these are limited to a few weeks, they are always regarded as artistic high spots and the box-office generally is good.

Last season, Walter directed the principal Philharmonic celebration of the Mozart bicentennial and also conducted the Metropolitan Opera's production of "The Magic Flute." He's to do a few perform-
(Continued on page 67)

LITERATE JOCKEY'S BIOPIC

Huston May Extol His Pal, Billy Pearson

Hollywood, Oct. 23.

John Huston is after film rights to "The Billy Pearson Story," book about the jockey who won "The $64,000 Question" on CBS-TV. Stephen Longstreet wrote the tome, being published by Simon & Schuster next spring. The jockey, longtime pal of the producer-director, rode horses in Huston's stable, when he had one a few years ago.

Huston is dickering with Pearson and Longstreet for pix rights, and it's likely if the deal goes through he would include it on his agenda at Allied Artists.

Meanwhile, Huston has cast Pearson in the role of Gregory Peck's friend in "Typee," which he is producing and directing for AA.

MDSE. SWELLS RECORD TAKE

By MIKE KAPLAN

Hollywood, Oct. 23.

Controversy has always meant cash in show business and the latest proof is Elvis Presley, whose jet-propelled career will reach stratospheric heights in his first full year in the bigtime with an indicated gross income of at least $1,000,000. Tally is an underestimation, based on what he has done in the first nine months of 1956.

Despite the carping critics who contend he can't last, reasonable projections of future income indicate he'll do at least as well in 1957, with the tally possibly bouncing even higher as result of his share of an unprecedented $40,000,000 retail sales volume of Elvis Presley merchandise during the next 15 months.

Presley's entry into the bigtime usually is dated from his appearance on the Milton Berle show last midsummer. Actually, he had been a rising performer for some months prior to that, as witness hefty disk sales and personal appearances that drew door-busting crowds. Since the Berle show, however, Presley has been a true atomic-ag phenomenon.

Estimate of $1,000,000 for his 1956 earnings is based solely on the known factors, which include unprecedented heights in some departments. The near-1,000,000 advance sale of his "Love Me Tender" disking for RCA Victor is an indication of the pace of his platters. For the 1956 calendar year, Presley figures to wind up with a total of at least 10,000,000 records
(Continued on page 78)

Odor Accents Art; 'Smellies' Loom

The film jokes about the "smellies" will get another realistic try if Dragoco, a German dye and essential oils outfit, goes through with its experiments to link pleasant odors with cinematic entertainment. Dragoco, in Holzminden, near Hannover, Germany, has been experimenting with "smell-mixing," much as sound-mixing is now an acoustical quality in the present-day form of celluloid entertainment.

Ambition is to go beyond the elementary accent of the senses, such as the audience sniffing a rose odor if the heroine receives a bouquet; or to achieve a bower-of-flowers' scent in, say, a woodlands set.

Dragoco's experiments with travelog films of many lands have been along the lines of creating a literal atmospheric aura so that the realistic "smell" of the locale
(Continued on page 78)

30,000 Legit Plane-Train Tourists Add Up to $8,000,000 Gotham Spree

Byliners' TV Binge

At a farewell party last week for publicist Eli Lloyd Hoffman, who's packing in the Gotham beat for Miami Beach, a Broadway pressagent commented on the flock of byliners on video.

"I spend so much time watching the columnists on tv," he said, "I don't have any time left to write copy."

Jr. Davis Carves 'Turkey' Into B. O. Winner Vs. Critics

"Mr. Wonderful," having already beaten the critical rap by getting a Broadway run, is about to parlay the achievement by earning a modest profit. It could presumably make a cleanup, except that star Sammy Davis Jr. is due to exit the cast in mid-February, upon completion of his contract. He's already committed for nitery dates, and since he's figured irreplaceable, the musical will have to fold.

On the basis of the last auditor's statement, for the four-week period ending Sept. 29, the show needed only $64,121 to recoup the balance of its $225,000 investment. At its current rate of operating profit, the Jule Styne-George Gilbert production is due to get into the black by about the end of November. Thus far, $90,000 of the capital has been returned to the backers.

Although Davis' contract is for a year from the date of the opening of the tryout in Philadelphia, ast Feb. 20, it had been understood that he would extend the deal if the show were to click. However, when "Wonderful" was panned by the New York critics, a Broadway run seemed out of the question, so the young star signed for cabaret appearances to start not later than next February.

Figuring that the musical might get a following among the devoted Davis following, Styne and Gilbert
(Continued on page 67)

AT SEVEN, BEETHOVEN'S FIFTH

Another Cradle Alumnus Will Show Adult Conductors

Seven-year-old Joey Alfidi will make his conducting debut at New York's Carnegie Hall Nov. 18. The juve batoneer will conduct the Symphony of the Air in Beethoven's Fifth Symphony, Haydn's Symphony No. 94, Mozart's "Marriage of Figaro" Overture and Rossini's "William Tell Overture."

By JESSE GROSS

Hinterland-to-Broadway theatre tours have snowballed into a major source of revenue for New York. This season the show trains and planes, transporting around 30,000 passengers, are expected to bring an estimated $8,000,000 into the city.

Pioneered in 1952 by the Columbus (O.) Citizen, the tours have progressively spread in the ensuing four years and are now originating from numerous other U. S. cities, Canada and in some instances Europe. Contributing most to the present bullish situation is Theatre Tours & Planes, the busiest of the legit travel operations.

TT&P, which brought in its first theatre group in August, 1955, carries the bulk of the show plane and train trade. During its first six months of the operation, the outfit brought in about 600 people. Since then the number has rocketed to an anticipated 20,000 for the present legit season, beginning last June and ending next May.

On the basis of figures supplied by TT&P, it's estimated that those out-of-towners will pour approximately $5,880,000 into New York legit, hotels, niteries, restaurants, depart-
(Continued on page 78)

3,750,000 R&H Albums Sold Since World War II

The album boom since the advent of LP eight years ago has resulted in a tremendous payoff for the Richard Rodgers-Oscar Hammertsein 2d combine. Counting sales of their original cast legit albums, and more recently, the film soundtrack packages of their shows, it's figured that some 3,750,000 R&H albums have been sold since the end of the last war. "Oklahoma" started the R&H cycle on wax and the Decca set is now way over the 1,000,000 mark. The "South Pacific" set, on Columbia Records, is at around the same figure.

In addition, there are the single sales on the individual songs, the remakes of several shows written by Rodgers with Larry Hart and the latest set of Rodgers & Hammerstein songs packaged for kiddies by Golden Records. These sales are estimated at around 10,000,000 singles.

Elsa's Vegas Bow at 5G

Elsa Maxwell makes her nitery bow at El Rancho Vegas, Las Vegas, Jan. 3 for two weeks at $5,000 a week. She played the Versailles Club, N. Y., about 20 years ago with George Jessel, her only other cafe date.

She will be paired with the $15,000-a-week Joe E. Lewis, a regular fixture at this Beldon Katleman spot.

ELVIS PRESLEY

Can Fifty Million Americans Be Wrong?

By Les Brown

DO WHAT YOU WILL to Elvis Presley—slander him, mock him, step on his blue suede shoes—he'll still be king to his insuppressible army of fans.

Recently, in three successive *Record Whirl Blindfold Tests* by Leonard Feather, and in varying degrees of intensity, Jeri Southern, Mel Torme, and Dick Haymes each scorned the recorded work of young Presley.

The teenage readership responded with a howl. "I use to think Jeri Southern and Mel Torme were pretty good singers," reads a typical letter, "but now I wouldn't have their records if they gave them away free." And another, ". . . They should have deported Haymes."

Not two letters, but hundreds.

To hear some of the kids tell it, Mel, Jeri, and Dick never could sing a proper note in their lives, and all had better hurry pronto for some voice lessons—maybe from Carl Perkins.

There is another kind of letter which argues, "How can they dare say Elvis is bad? If he isn't a good singer, how come everybody buys his records? I don't see Jeri Southern or Mel Torme selling even a half million."

THIS RAISES AN interesting point—shall criticism be aesthetic or democratic?

Can 50,000,000 Americans possibly be wrong?

The answer, it seems to us, is that it's not really a problem of right and wrong. Except in clear-cut matters of fact and morality, it's presumptuous for any man to declare another right or wrong.

It can be said, however, that 50,000,000 Americans have shallow or undeveloped tastes. And indeed, it should be said.

It's a bandwagon-conscious public, and most persons, perhaps for reasons of personal insecurity, feel a compulsion to get aboard every time. A small number—either because they are naturally iconoclastic, refined in their tastes, or otherwise aberrated—become the snipers.

Curiously, it's harder to make the people swallow sound, adverse criticism than it is to enlist them as adoring fans. Intellectual reasoning rarely succeeds in opening an emotional or anti-intellectual vise, but we are always in need of heroes.

IMMEDIATELY AS ELVIS came into popular renown, the intimate side of his life was revealed, accurately or not. From correspondence and personal conversations I have had with Presley's staunchest teenage supporters, it has become clear that they favor him as much for his looks, his reputed kindnesses, his concern for his parents, and for the Horatio Alger character of his climb as they do for his vocal and physical gyrations.

Pure aesthetics have almost nothing to do with it, but that must have been obvious the first time you heard Presley perform.

Presley's miracle came easier than, say, Liberace's; and Libby was adored similarly, but mainly by a matronly element of the public. Yet, only a month before Libby's popularity began to lather by way of his television film series, you couldn't give him away to the press. Once lionized, however, Libby's life was serialized from Atlantic to Pacific on the front pages of the dailies.

Elvis never wanted for press, even from the first. The critics gave it to him with both barrels. Today, in a bid for the circulation nickel, the press is less reproachful, and Elvis continues to get plenty of space.

THERE HAVE BEEN WORSE SINGERS than Elvis Presley but few as "heroic." If he satisfies some ineffable universal need of the moment in 50,000,000 Americans, there seems to be no wrong or right about it. As long as they don't pretend to like him for artistic reasons.

What is deplorable is that so many Presley admirers have *wronged*, or are oblivious to, the fine talents of Jeri Southern, Mel Torme, Dick Haymes, and other serious vocal artists. They're not buying quality as yet, and before they do, they'll have to learn to distinguish between high quality and low quality.

That educational responsibility seems to fall mainly on the disc jockey, who still has the greatest proximity to, and the greatest influence over, the record-buying public. Fifty million Americans can easily be misled.

Advertisement for RCA Victor, *The Cash Box*, magazine, November 28, 1959.

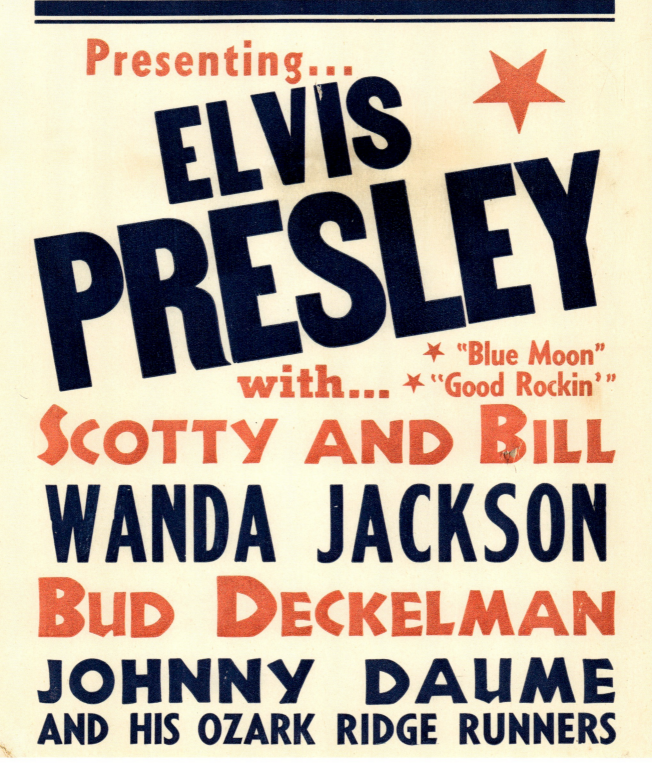

Elvis Presley with Scotty and Bill concert poster, Wednesday, July 20, 1955, Cape Girardeau, Missouri.
Elvis Presley's guitar, a Martin D-18, 1942 that he used for all of his Sun Studio recording sessions as well as in public performances from 1954 to 1956 (opposite and following page).

"I CAN'T FIGURE OUT WHAT I'M DOING WRONG. I KNOW MY MOTHER APPROVES."

ELVIS PRESLEY, AUGUST 10, 1958

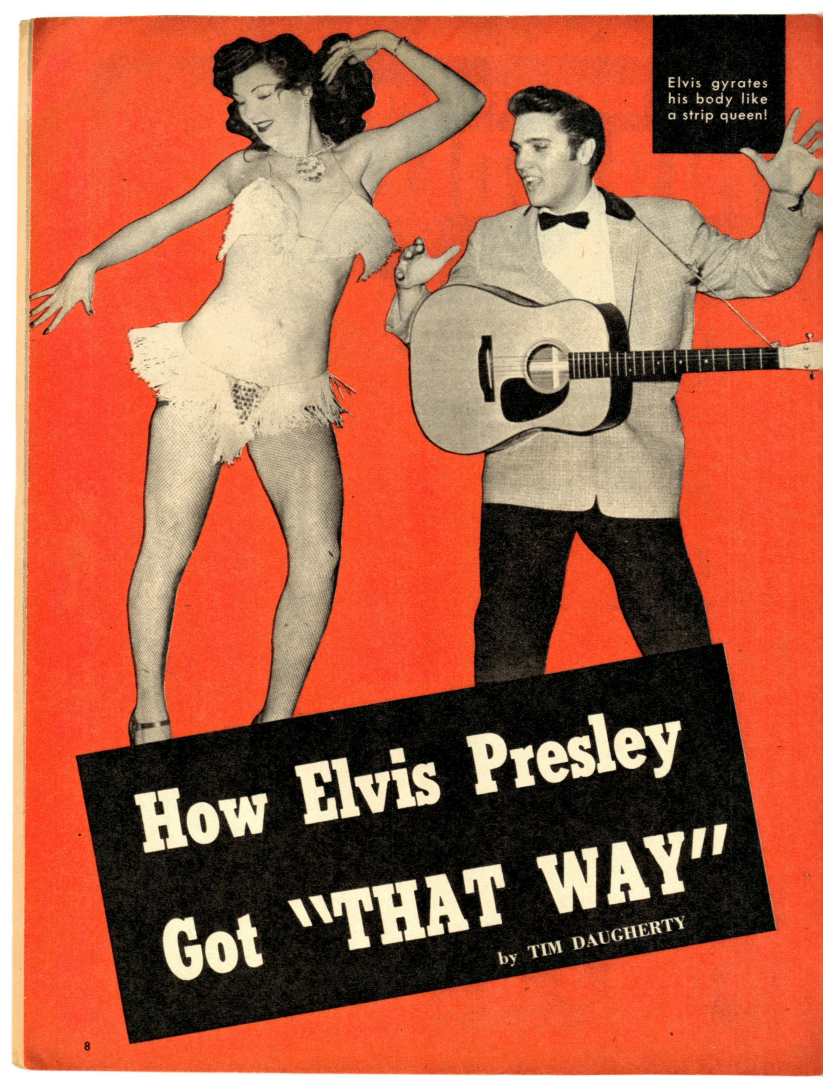

Elvis gyrates his body like a strip queen!

How Elvis Presley Got "THAT WAY"

by TIM DAUGHERTY

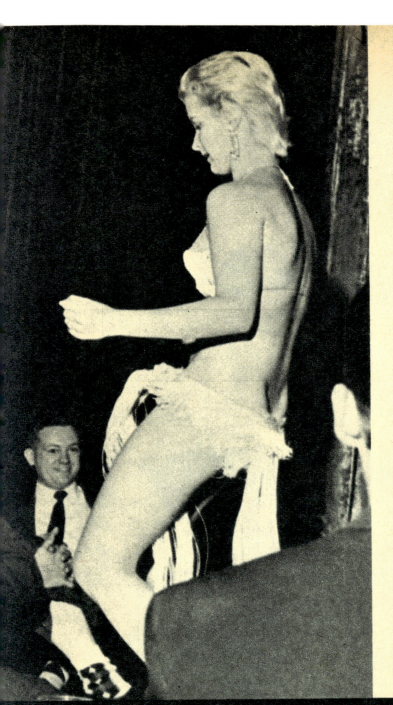
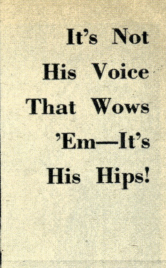

It's Not His Voice That Wows 'Em—It's His Hips!

There's more to stripping than taking clothes off! Elvis studies techniques like this and uses them!

Presley doesn't look much like a truck driver now, but twisting a wheel inspired those twisting hips!

AND WHEN that high beat kept rolling and rolling, boring like some live thing that wouldn't stop, the slim figure with the flailing arms began making with the hips. Wilder and wilder, the hips bucked and swirled; more and more those hips rocked and rolled; faster and faster until with one convulsive motion, the hips relaxed and the song was over.

Was this in an African jungle? No. Was this on the grimy boards of some cheap burlesque house? No. Was this a woman and were those hips womanly hips? No.

They were the vaunted hips of a kid known far and wide as Elvis (The Pelvis) Presley, who makes up for lack of singing talent with hips that speak a language all their own. He has put Johnny Ray in the shadow and his followers are legion. As a matter of fact, in certain areas a bad word about Elvis will meet with the crack of a beer bottle on the noggin.

The young rock 'n roll set is just wild about Elvis because, with his hips, he sends them a message. It is a message of sex that reflects all their adolescent dreams; it is a feverish sending that tells its own tale.

This wriggling, squirming, yowling, former Memphis truck driver reportedly got his ideas on how to put over a song while driving in the cab of his truck. As he went up and down the highways and made left and right turns, his body swayed and twisted with the song that was in his head. That's how he later developed his famous "I'm Left, You're Right," number that rocks and rolls them in the aisles.

UNCENSORED teenage opinions . . .

Elvis Presley, Memphis: If you marry Dottie, I'll squeal. *Kim, Duluth*

IVY LEAGUE

You guys who write that magazine are way, way behind the time. Not only in styles but in manner of speech. And some of those jokes are really sickening. This guy Vander of Fresno says "*Boys and girls like to keep up with the styles.*" Then in the next breath he says "*When we kids go down the street with our sleeves rolled and our collars turned up*" . . . Let me clue you in buddie, I hope to tell you that's about 6 years behind time. Here in San Francisco about 70% of the guys dress conservatively and Ivy League, which I really eat up.

A regular guy wears a short hair cut or flat top—a sweater, shirt or pendleton, a McGregor with tan or blue peggers—desert boots or bucks or saddles. An Ivy Leaguer (which I am) wears Ivy League shirts with a button on the back of the collar, buckle back pants, Ceasar hair cut, bucks or saddles. None of these "grubby" Levis or long duck-tail haircuts. Ugh! Let's get cool and go Ivy League, huh?

E. B.
San Francisco

P.S. I'm no paddy, or sissy either.

Why didn't you sign your name?—Trajen

HINDER HUMANITY?

Here's a load of complaints for your magazine. I agree with Garry Fisher in saying the normal teenager, or, as slobs like "Lee Vander Las" might put it in the ugh way of "cool cats," don't use the undignified language as cool, cat, crazy, or dig.

If you come to any city and check with school or police records, you will find that only the trouble-makers, juvenile delinquents, or slobs use language such as that. Guys who wear ducktails and Levis around their hips are as bad as the girls with D.A.'s and their bluejeans in giving the American society a "bad" name.

I believe that all teenagers can have fun

DIGS IVY LEAGUE

Guys who wear duck-tails and pegged-pants (I used to wear them 2 years ago) are mostly immature, uneducated and behind the times. The well-dressed, smart teen-ager is going "Ivy League." Of course there are guys who live in areas where pegged-pants are still in style, but if they wore anything conservative they'd be laughed at and many times "beat up." These "Kats" think they're so tough too. The only way they're tough is in gangs. They can't be tough because they never do anything clean, healthful or whole-some. In our neighborhood a stranger is welcomed, not beat up as these "greasers" would do.

I like your magazine very much and I'd like to tell you the only reason you received 233 letters blasting Gary Fisher and only four agreeing with him is that your magazine started out aimed at the "Kat population" of teenagers by using a title such as "Dig" and also by using "hep talk." Around here "hep talk" like "dig, crazy, cool, square, and the most" was definitely out two years ago.

As you can see there are two definite groups of teenagers in America and I think the "Ivy Leaguers" are the better. One thing all teen-agers agree on is rock n' roll. Those who do not like it are real "homebodies" or "sissies."

PETER HABERMANN
Buffalo, N.Y.

THE TEENS TALK

(*Continued from Page* 19)

IS FIFTEEN AND HAS ULCERS

Maybe I'm wrong, and maybe I'm right, but I think Elvis Presley is taking the fun out of my teen-age life. Before I discovered him, I was a happy, healthy 13-year-old girl. I am now 15 and have ulcers. I have read in the newspapers and in magagine articles of several cases where formerly happy girls murder their friends or family, commit suicide, lose their good sense and make people ashamed of them . . . all because they have liked Elvis too long and have not thought of anything else. I have liked him for two years . . . and for two years my life slowly became what it is now. I am not saying this is Elvis' fault. It may be a phase that some teens pass through . . . a time when they let their emotions run away with them. At any rate, he must be a phenomenon. He's a strange force that affects the teen-age world. I know this and I still like him.

A nut (?)
Santa Cruz, Calif.

HIPSTERS DICTIONARY

Rusty

By Elaine Coffin & Rusty Minute

Elaine

Here's the latest and most complete dictionary of words and phrases used by hipsters. If any additional ones can be added, jot them down on a postcard and mail them to either Elaine Coffin, 144 Harrison Drive, Lido Beach, Sarasota, Fla., or Rusty Minute, 3947 Lee Heights Blvd., Cleveland 28, Ohio.

Our thanks go out to Bernie Grieb, Orange, Conn.; Carol Kumhall, Cleveland, Ohio; Sharon Dooley, Excelsior Springs, Mo.; Gail Stewart, Goodman, Mo.; Barb Long, Chase, Kansas; Carol Mayzer, Chicago, Ill.; Leana Hoeline, Forest Park, Ill.; Gail Stivale, Bloomfied, N. J.; A Hipster from Columbus, Ohio; Sheran Kelley, Creswell, Oregon; Rarmona Robertson, Veronica, Ore.; Sandi Shepperd, Aurora, Colorado; Trina Tottka, Bellaire, Ohio; Marlene Stuva, Bridgewater, Iowa; Wayne Holloran, Cleveland, Ohio; Roslyn Braun, Sidney, Australia; K. Rayher, Mt. Prospect, Ill.; Sue Baker, Pubeblo, Colorado . . . plus many others to be mentioned in the next issue.

A.B.C. — Means "Always Be Cool".
ABES CABE — A five ($5) bill.
ACE — Has two meanings. A dollar bill. An important cat.
AIR — Answer.
ALL SHOOK — Really excited about something.
ALL WASTED — It's not right. Not with it.
APE — Cool. Crazy. Terrif.
APPLE — A square.
BAD — Means good fitting, suitable.
BAD-DAD — A cat who thinks he's so rough and tough . . . but only he, nobody else does.
BAIL OUT — To peel out from a traffic light or around a corner.
BALL — Same as Bash.
BALLET DANCER — A person who dances on their (or your) toes.
BARGAIN — A square. Something cheap.
BARK — Money.
BASH — A ball. A real good time where you enjoyed, or will enjoy, yourself.
BATS — A creep.
BEAT — Tired.
BENDERS — Your arms, knees, elbows, legs.
BIG DADDY — Listen to me kat (or kitten)!
BIG GEORGE — A quarter. 25¢ piece.
BLAST — Another word meaning terrific. A good movie is a blast.
BLASTING — Real cool, terrific or crazy.
BLAZE — To go.
BLESSED EVENT — A party. A bash. A gig.
BLUE MAN — A policeman in uniform.
BOAST TOASTIE — A very conceited gal.
BOAT — A car.
BODO — A friend.
BOMB — A car.
BRAIN STORM — A smart kat or kitten.
BREAD — Money or loot.
BRICKS — Books, particularly schoolbooks.
BRIGHT — Day.
BROWN ABE — A penny.
BTO — An oldy that's still used. Means "Big Time Operator".
BUCKY — A person with buck teeth.
BUFFALO — A stick-in-the-mud square.
BUG — Driver of car.
BUG OUT — To leave or drive away fast.
BUGGED UP — To be talked into something.
BULLS — Cops or Highway Patrol.
BUR — Freeze treatment when a kat thinks a kitten is a creep.
BURY YOURSELF — Drop dead, dig a hole, crawl in and cover yourself up. Get lost.
BUST — Caught doing something wrong.
BUZZ — Squad car.
BYE THE SIDE — By the way. Also.
C.I.O. — Means "Cut It Out".
CAGE — The body. Your skeleton.
CAN — A hot rod.
CARTEL — Same gang of fellows or gals that pal out regularly.
CAT — A real cool and hip guy.
CELL BLOCK — Any room in a school.
CHAIN GANG — Group of pupils following a teacher. A bunch of squares.
CHALK — A weed. Cigarette.
CHANT — Home.
CHEATERS — Eyeglasses.
CHEESEATERS — A stool pigeon.
CHIC — A gal that's cool and hip.
CHLOROPHYL GEORGE — A dollar ($1) bill.
CHOP — To cut someone low; a very low and cutting remark.
CHOPPED ROD — Convertible.
CHOW CHOPPERS — Teeth.
CHROME-DOME — A bald cat.
CHROME-PLATED — A cat or kitten in their very best clothes. All dressed up.
CLAM — A talkative person.
CLAM UP — You talk too much.
CLEAN-CUT — A hip kat.
CLOWN — A goon. A real square.
CONTAINER — A car.
COOL — Terrific. Crazy. The best.
COOL BREW — A tasty drink. (Non-alcoholic)
COOL IT — Take it easy, slow down.
COOL JONAH — A great guy. A cool kat.
COOL THREADS — Nice clothes.
CRANIUM — Head.
CRAWLED THRU — Got in.
CRIB — House.
CUBE — A 3-D square.
CUE BALL — A cat or kitten that roams all over.
CUBIN' — A real 6-sided, 3-D square.
CULTURED — A cat or kitten who is a real hipster and knows this list of words and phrases by heart.
CURLY-LOCKS — A cat with a regular style haircut.
CUT — To tease or bother.
CUT OUT — To leave.
CUTTINGS — Records.
DADDY-O — A real cool friend who is hip to things.
DAP — Real cool, crazy, terrific.
DARKTIME — Night.
DEB — A girl.
DEEJAY (or DJ) — a disc jockey.
DESPAIR BARREL — A kitten's hope chest.
DETAILS — Expression used when reminded of something you forgot. A scolding from parents. A list of some kind.
DIG — To understand.
DISHY — Real smooth.
DOLL — A really chic girl.
DOUBLE-DOME — A real square.
DRAG — A dance, dancer, date, hot rod race. To feel bad. To worry about somthing.
DRAG IT — Hurry. Move yourself fast.
DRAGGIN WAGGIN — A car.

(*Continued on Page* 7)

THE LETTER

I have been thinking about the topic of segregation for some time now and I have decided to write to you about it. I hope it reaches the eyes, mind and conscience of many adults. Especially in the South.

When all the trouble started about school segregation in the South, I looked up the word "segregation" to see what it meant. The definition was "to set apart." The white race wanted to set the Negro apart from its schools. But why? Whose idea was this? Who could be this simple-minded?

This page is for teenage opinion, so I'm going to voice mine. I think the whole mess was started by a simple-minded prejudiced fool. Or else it was a lunatic. What other kind of a person could think he is any better than another person because his skin is white. In the Bible, it says, "God created man." That means he created the Negro as well as the white man. It was the devil who put the idea into some men's heads that they were better than the next ones because their skins were white and their neighbors' were dark. It also says in the Bible that we are all brothers and sisters. He made no favorites. So the Negroes are our brothers and sisters, for He loves the dark as well as the white.

A 14-year-old Negro boy was killed. And police who escorted Negroes to school have been beaten. Preachers have been badly beaten and others have had their homes bombed. Dark and light alike have suffered because of the ignorance of man. Adults have called teenagers hoodlums, idiots, sex-crazy, vulgar and many other names not fit to call a rat. I think it's about our turn to call some names. Any adult who would cause pain, both mental and physical to another human being, and even to small children, just because his skin is a different color, that person doesn't belong in our wonderful land of America. Such people teach their children to hate. And they set themselves up to judge other human beings! They seem to have forgotten it is the Lord who will be the Judge of all mankind on Judgment Day. And that they, too, will be judged by Him. And may He be merciful to them.

I am a white girl of 16. I have made up my own mind about what I will believe and not believe. I don't believe everything my parents do because on some things, I feel they are wrong. So teenagers, start believing as you think it is *right* to believe! Some day we will be the leaders of America. How to keep Communism out of America is a big problem. Keeping America free from racketeering and scandal are also big problems. And I hope you will wise up against some of the rank ideas some of our adults of today have. I hope you will not hold it against another man because God made his skin dark. And I hope for every white person, there will be a Negro. Because two heads are better than one, be they dark or light.

Sandy Crimeens
Monier, Illinois

Teenagers press clippings, November 1956 to May 1959, by Michel Aphesbero.

LETTERS TO THE JANITOR
TRAJEN X. WUNDERLEIGH

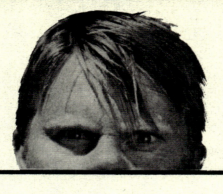

DISLIKES ELVIS

Do you believe that ALL teenagers like Elvis Presley? Well, we don't!

We cannot understand why adolescent girls become so vehement and violent in their reactions to Elvis' performances. There is no reason for hating him, but neither is there any reason for such fanatical outbursts on the part of his fans, who appear to be composed mostly of 12-15-year-old girls.

We believe, however, that a large portion of their actions is due to the fact that this age group knows next to nothing about sex and is curious about it. Elvis Presley's suggestive bodily movements excite their curiosity in a lamentable manner.

In our opinion, his vulgarity is inexcusable. He does not seem to be a very tactful young man. He certainly has no poise, no stage presence, and is uneducated, as his grammatical usage well proves. He assuredly does not conduct himself in the manner of a well-bred (and read) young man.

While we feel that his personal features are something he cannot help, we also agree that there are some handicaps he could overcome. His smile (?), that sort of smeary half-sneer, half-snarl, he turns on his audiences, appears to us like the look you might see on a dog who doesn't know whether to bite or just growl menacingly.

His extravagant vulgarity points to the fact that he is lacking some quality. He seems to get a thrill out of exciting young girls. Having heard all manner of rumors about him, from the fact that he collects teddy bears (at his age!) to the equally astounding note that he actually has the audacity to collect fees for the privilege of belonging to his fan club and being sent photos and registration cards, we think he should decidedly be psychoanalyzed.

While we do not know what percentage of the nation's teenagers are Elvis Presley FANATICS, we feel that the number is quite low compared to the percentage who are decidedly "anti-Elvis." The young people who are fans of his, however, are excessively entranced to the point of sensationalism, therefore, naturally being more noticeable than the girls (and boys) who quietly (or vehemently, as the case may be) denounce him and then go about their business. To put it mildly, if Elvis Presley provokes any emotion whatsoever in most of us, it is disgust and not the perturbed melodrama which his vulgarity seems to agitate in some teeners.

We feel that it is a shame that the wild turbulence of his fans should reflect on all teenagers. It is ruining our reputation as well as destroying in the minds of adults the confidence our parents have in us as responsible young people.

Collecting children's playthings. Bah! When is he going to grow up?

Whether or not the things we hear are all publicity, a large number of teenage boys and girls feel that Elvis Presley should take his guitar and his sideburns back to the hills and lose himself on the way.

The student body of Elyria District
Catholic High School
Elyria, Ohio

4. Square off back of hair. Straight line across bottom of hair is to be cut ½ inch below the ear lobe. Shave later.

8. This view will show you how flat the top of Jim's hair is. Photo at the right shows back of hair and crazy ducktail.

DECEMBER, 1956

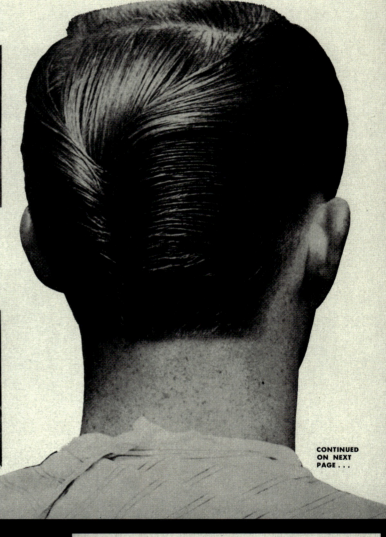

CONTINUED ON NEXT PAGE...

PRO-CAT?

If your magazine is pro-cat styles, why is all your advertising dominated by the Ivy League styles? On the inside cover, you have Sal Mineo wearing Taper Ivys. On the back, you usually feature Butch Wax for "all shortcuts . . . butches, crews, flattops, Ivy League." The clothing ads are dominated by nice-looking boys with crewcuts and "that Ivy look."

You say your mag is for all the teenagers, but I don't see any guys running around with their collars up and their levis low. Don't you think the "cats" should be given equal space?

F. Bietto
Park Forest, Illinois

● *We have no control over what type of teenager is displayed in the advertisements! We are not necessarily "pro-cat" . . . we are "pro-teenagers" . . . all of you.*

JUNE, 1957

Dear Elvis,

My parents were born in Poland and they don't like modern American music, such as Rock N Roll. They get mad when I play your records and try to make me buy classical records. I like classical music very much, but I like Rock N Roll better. My mom and dad say it doesn't even sound like music to them. They say that in Europe the people love good music and don't listen to Rock N Roll. I can't believe this. Are they right when they say that Rock N Roll isn't popular on the other side of the Atlantic?

Joe R.
Detroit, Mich.

ELVIS IN PARIS

BY LINE RENAUD

Elvis Presley never sang in France, except in my dressing room at the Casino de Paris. This was in December 1959 and I was heading my first revue, *Plaisir*, at the Casino de Paris, with the Golden Gate Quartet. One of the usherettes at the door thought she recognized him among the four American soldiers she had placed in the balcony seats. We couldn't believe it, but yes, it was him—on leave from the military service he was doing in Germany. During intermission, my husband Loulou Gasté went to see him. He told Elvis he had written the stage music, that the singer and dancer on stage was his wife, and that he would of course be welcome in my dressing room after the show.

After the curtain went down, Elvis came along with the three other American soldiers. When he saw Loulou's guitar, he asked, "Who plays the guitar?" "My husband, Loulou Gasté." "May I?" And so we gave him the famous Selmer guitar that Django had played. Loulou was very close to Django Reinhardt and when we told him that Django had played it, Elvis kissed the guitar. I thought that was wonderful. And then he asked, "Is the Golden Gates Quartet still here? You know, I grew up with their singing." So we went to get the Goldens from the *Colibri*, where they were playing table soccer. And there it was: Elvis Presley in shirtsleeves and the foursome from the Golden Gates gave a concert in my dressing room that lasted four hours, until six in the morning. I was sitting on the floor. My dresser was there, as were my hairdresser Michel and the Casino de Paris caretaker with his dog. There were five of us, plus the three American soldiers, listening to Elvis and the Golden Gates. Nothing but gospel and Negro spirituals. With, of course, "When The Saints," "Happy Days" . . . all the really great gospel songs that we all knew. It was incredible. He didn't sing any of his songs and we wouldn't have presumed to ask, because this was a real treat for him. This was his background, his childhood, his parents' childhood.

After that we stayed very close. I was going to sign for Las Vegas, so I knew I was going to be there in 1963. I told him, "I'm going to sing in Las Vegas, not right away, but in 1963." And when he said goodbye, he told me, "I will be at your opening." That's all. And, though we weren't in touch in between, Elvis really was there at my opening in October 1963, in a navy blue alpaca with his purple silk scarf: slim, warm, a great person. That was Elvis. Loyalty. Honesty. Tenderness. Kindness. Modesty. He was pure. Stunningly handsome. And such talent! I saw him sing in Las Vegas a number of times. There will never be anyone like Elvis Presley again.

What is really ridiculous is that at the time, in 1959, we had no camcorder, no tape recorder. I didn't even have a camera. Nothing. Today, I think the only person left who shares this wonderful memory with me is Clyde from the Golden Gates. However, I've been told that Elvis started recording an album that he never finished and that the song, the only song he really recorded was "Feeling," a song by Loulou Gasté! So we are doing some research in the United States to find out if that's true. That would be extraordinary for me, the climax of the story that has secretly been with me throughout my career.

PARIS, APRIL 2007
TRANSLATED FROM FRENCH BY CHARLES PENWARDEN

Elvis Presley and Line Renaud, Dunes Hotel, Las Vegas, Nevada, 1963.

THE GOLD[
ROCK'[
FROM BILL HAL[
TO BUDDY H[

EN AGE OF N' ROLL

FIVE STYLES OF ROCK 'N' ROLL 280
BY CHARLIE GILLETT

BUDDY HOLLY PORTFOLIO 350
BY WILLIAM EGGLESTON

RUFUS THOMAS 367
BY PETER GURALNICK

DOC AND OTIS 390
BY PETER GURALNICK

FIVE STYLES OF ROCK 'N' ROLL

BY CHARLIE GILLETT

Which came first, rock 'n' roll as a music or rock 'n' roll as a name? It's a chicken-and-egg question, but once the term was accepted as a description of the music that white teenagers liked so much, there was a rush to supply records to meet the new prescription. Eventually, the industry figured out some formulas, but from 1951 to the end of 1955, rock 'n' roll evolved more or less spontaneously in five parallel styles, four of which had local or regional associations.

Two types of bands started calling their music rock 'n' roll, each featuring seven or eight musicians: rhythm and blues combos like the New Orleans session teams which played on records by Fats Domino and Little Richard; and country boogie show bands in the north like Bill Haley and His Comets in Pennsylvania. Two other styles featured just a vocalist with a rhythm section of electric guitar, bass (initially a stand-up "bass fiddle," later electric bass guitar), and kit drum: country rock in Memphis, where Elvis Presley surfaced in 1954, and the black equivalent, the rocking blues of Chuck Berry and Bo Diddley in Chicago. The fifth style, by vocal groups, began in the Northeast but soon spread nationwide.

I. Country boogie show bands played a repertoire of country and western music, a broad category embracing the western swing of Bob Wills, Hollywood cowboy songs, and the ballads and dance tunes broadcast on the emerging country stations of the Southeast. As he recalled later, Bill Haley began experimenting by adding new ingredients: "... the style we played way back in 1947, 1948, and 1949 was a combination of country and western, Dixieland, and the old-style rhythm and blues."[1]

The "old-style rhythm and blues" he referred to was the roaring, riff-laden music with chanted vocals of bandleaders like Lionel Hampton, Paul Williams, and local bandleader Jimmy Preston, whose "Rock The Joint" (Gotham) was a national rhythm and blues hit in 1949. These mini-orchestras set out to entertain by creating as much excitement as possible, with musicians playing solos on one or two notes, lying on their backs or climbing on pianos or basses, or playing their instruments above their heads in search of thrilling visual effects. Contrasting the enjoyment of the audiences at this kind of dance with the staid reaction of audiences where white dance bands played, Haley saw the chance for change. "We decided to try for a new style, mostly using stringed instruments but somehow managing to get the same effect as brass and reeds."[2]

... Around the early 1950s the musical world was starved for something new ... the days of the solo vocalist and the big bands had gone. About the only thing in fact that was making any noise was progressive jazz but this was just above the heads of the average listener ... I felt then that if I could take, say, a Dixieland tune and drop the first and third beats, and accentuate the second and fourth, and add a beat the listeners could clap to as well as dance:

---

1. American Forces Network, September 1962. 2. *New Musical Express*, September 21, 1956.

this would be what they were after. From that the rest was easy … take everyday sayings like "Crazy Man Crazy," "See You Later, Alligator," "Shake, Rattle And Roll," and apply what I have just said.[3]

Haley sounded halfhearted on a cover of Jackie Brenston's "Rocket '88'" in 1951, but much more convincing on his revival of Jimmy Preston's "Rock The Joint" a year later. Preston's version had been used to end the radio show on Philadelphia's WPWA, which preceded Haley's "Country Store"; where Preston had yelled at his listeners to do the Jitterbug and Hucklebuck, Haley called for country dance steps like the Sugarfoot Rag and Western Reel. After a national top twenty hit in 1953 with "Crazy Man Crazy" (Essex), Haley switched to Decca, recording "Shake, Rattle And Roll" and "Rock Around The Clock" at the first session. The latter, with its slapped bass and a reprise of the guitar solo from "Rock The Joint," went on to become one of the biggest hits of all time.

II. One of the first of Haley's successors in covering rhythm and blues material for white audiences was Pat Boone, whose first big hit "Ain't That A Shame" (Dot) remained in the top ten for fourteen weeks through the summer of 1955. Whereas Haley had developed his style of rock 'n' roll himself, Boone had been surprised and rather shocked when he had been asked to record the uptempo "Two Hearts, Two Kisses" as his first release for Dot, a Southern independent company based in Gallatin, Tennessee. He had been accustomed to slow ballads, of the kind well established in the popular and country and western markets. With the rest of middle-class America, Boone regarded rhythm and blues material as being rather crude, musically and lyrically. Nonetheless, he went on to record "Ain't That A Shame," "Tutti Frutti," and a succession of cover versions of other rhythm and blues hits.

In contrast to Bill Haley, Boone was young and good looking and had a more expressive voice. But unlike Haley, he did not seem to be involved with the spirit of the musicians behind him, and he was important to rock 'n' roll only in the role he played bringing a little conservative respectability to the music's image. Although his early success delayed the mass public's awareness of real rock 'n' roll/rhythm and blues singers, it may also have indirectly generated interest in them. A few disc jockeys, for example, played the original versions of the Boone hits "Tutti Frutti" and "Ain't That A Shame," and when the original singers became better known, Boone retreated to the ballads he seemed from the start to have preferred to record.

"Ain't That A Shame" and "Tutti Frutti" were both first recorded in New Orleans with local rhythm and blues musicians, by Fats Domino and Little Richard respectively. Boone's cover versions were recorded in Chicago, but although his instrumentation was closely based on the New Orleans arrangements, there was a chasm between the two approaches: Boone sang with a crooner's detachment, with musicians who seemed to be reading their parts; Richard and Domino sang idiosyncratically, with musicians who *felt* what they were playing.

Fats Domino, working with Dave Bartholomew, a local big band leader and trumpeter, as his recording supervisor, cowriter, and session bandleader, helped to evolve the New Orleans dance blues through a remarkable series of records, which began with "The Fat Man" (for Imperial), a big hit in the rhythm and blues market in 1949 to 1950. At that time Domino sang in a high, exuberant tenor and played piano with a distinctive boogie-influenced style that featured chords with both hands. The effervescent good humor of his fast records was eventually discovered by the popular music audience, which in 1956, after he had achieved many hits in the black market, raised "I'm In Love Again" into *Billboard*'s top ten. Domino's follow-up to "I'm In Love Again" was a slow version of the standard "Blueberry Hill," sung with impressive control and apparently no effort at all. Domino's curious "creole" accent immediately identified his records, and he maintained a long string of hits, including both infectiously happy songs and plaintive appeals.

A feature of virtually all Domino's records was a tenor-sax solo, taken usually about two-thirds of the way through, often by either Lee Allen or Herb Hardesty. These solos were probably shortened versions of the solos that would have been played at dances, and they matched the relaxed control of Domino's voice. Like his singing, the sax tone was melodic, economical, warm, and slightly rough.

Although Little Richard came from Georgia and did not record for the same company as Domino, he often played with the same musicians. But in contrast to Domino's cool style, Little Richard was intensely involved in everything he sang, exhilarating his audiences with a frantic, sometimes hysterical performance, which was distinguished by pure-voiced swoops and whoops out of a raucous shouting style.

With Little Richard, the rock 'n' roll audience got the aggressive extrovert to enact their wilder fantasies, and his stage performance set precedents for anyone who followed him. Dressed in shimmering suits with long drape jackets and baggy pants, his hair grown long and slicked straight, white teeth and gold rings flashing in the spotlights, he stood up at, and sometimes on, the piano, hammering boogie chords as he screamed messages of celebration and self-centered pleasure. From "Long Tall Sally":

Well, Long Tall Sally,
She's built for speed,
She's got everything that Uncle John needs.

From "Rip It Up":

Well, it's Saturday night
And I just got paid,
A fool about my money,
Don't try to save …
Gonna rock it up,
Gonna rip it up,
Gonna shake it up,
Gonna ball it up,
Gonna rock it up,
At the ball tonight.

Both songs became standards in the repertoire of almost every rock 'n' roll singer, for the spirit of Little Richard affected and influenced most singers who followed him. Compared to Domino, Little Richard, musically and stylistically speaking, was coarse, uncultured, and uncontrolled, in every way harder for the music establishment to take. Among the white rock 'n' roll singers, Elvis Presley was similarly outrageous compared with his predecessors Bill Haley and Pat Boone.

III. Presley was the most commercially successful of a number of Memphis singers who evolved what they themselves called "country rock" and what others, record collectors and people in the industry, have called "rockabilly." Country rock was basically a Southern white version of the twelve-bar boogie blues, shouted with a minimum of subtlety by ex-hillbilly singers over an accompaniment featuring electric guitar, stand-up bass, and—from 1956—drums, still taboo in Nashville. The style evolved partly from the imaginative guidance of a Memphis radio station engineer, Sam Phillips, who entered the recording business by supervising sessions with local blues singers and leasing the masters to a number of independent companies (Chess in Chicago, owned by the Chess brothers, or Modern/RPM in Los Angeles, owned by the Bihari brothers). The success of some of these singers, notably B.B. King and Howlin' Wolf, encouraged Phillips to form his own label, Sun, and two of the singers he recorded for his own label, Little Junior Parker and Rufus Thomas, had hit records in the black market.

The Memphis blues singers used small bands that featured piano, guitar, and saxophone. No particular dominant style linked them all, but common to many of their records was a kind of intimate atmosphere created by the simple and cheap, but unorthodox, "tape delay echo" recording technique of Phillips. The singers invariably made their personal presence felt on the records, menacingly in Howlin' Wolf's case, impatiently in Junior Parker's. These recordings, and other more traditional blues, and rhythm and blues records issued by Sun, were known to a substantial number of white youths throughout the South, and presented a source of song material and stylistic inspiration that was in many ways more satisfactory than the orthodox country and western culture.

Jimmie Rodgers sang the "white blues" in the 1920s but Elvis Presley was the first to make it work as pop music. According to the legend of his recording debut, his discovery by Sam Phillips was casual and lucky. Presley is said to have attracted the attention of Phillips when he used Sun's studios to cut a record for his mother's birthday present; Phillips encouraged him to make a record with proper accompaniment, and the two men were rewarded with a local hit from one of the sides, "That's All Right."

The story of Presley's discovery has the elements of romance, coincidence, and fate that legends need, and in fact seems to be true, but it is likely that if Phillips and Presley had not met, two other such people would soon have done what they did—merge rhythm and blues with country and western styles and material, and come up with a new style. In the panhandle of west Texas, in Arkansas, in north Louisiana, and in Memphis there were other singers whose cultural and musical experience were comparable to Presley's; indeed, some of them followed him into the Sun studios, while others tried studios in Nashville and Clovis, New Mexico.

3. *Haley News*, 1966.

It is difficult to assess how great a part Sam Phillips played in influencing his singers—among other things, by introducing them to blues records—and how much they already knew. Presley told one interviewer:

> I'd play [guitar] along with the radio or phonograph, and taught myself the chord positions. We were a religious family, going round together to sing at camp meetings and revivals, and I'd take my guitar with us when I could. I also dug the real low-down Mississippi singers, mostly Big Bill Broonzy and Big Boy Crudup, although they would scold me at home for listening to them.
>
> "Sinful music," the townsfolk in Memphis said it was. Which never bothered me, I guess.

In the same interview, Presley stressed the importance of Phillips:

> Mr. Phillips said he'd coach me if I'd come over to the studio as often as I could. It must have been a year and a half before he gave me an actual session. At last he let me try a western song—and it sounded terrible. But the second idea he had was the one that jelled. "You want to make some blues?" he suggested over the phone, knowing I'd always been a sucker for that kind of jive. He mentioned Big Boy Crudup's name and maybe others, too. I don't remember.
>
> All I know is, I hung up and ran fifteen blocks to Mr. Phillips' office before he'd gotten off the line—or so he tells me. We talked about the Crudup records I knew—"Cool Disposition," "Rock Me, Mama," "Hey Mama," "Everything's All Right," and others, but settled for "That's All Right," one of my top favorites . . .[4]

What Presley achieved was certainly not "the same thing" as the men he copied. On "That's All Right" and "Mystery Train" (written and first recorded by Junior Parker for Sun), he evolved a personal version of this style, singing high and clear, breathless and impatient, varying his rhythmic emphasis with a confidence and inventiveness that were exceptional for a white singer. The sound suggested a young white man celebrating freedom, ready to do anything, go anywhere, pausing long enough for apologies and even regrets and recriminations, but then hustling on towards the new. He was best on fast songs, when his impatient singing matched the urgent rhythm from bass (Bill Black) and guitar (Scotty Moore). Each of his five Sun singles backed a blues song with a country and western song, most of them already familiar to the respective audiences; each sold better than its predecessor, and increasing numbers of people discovered Presley either through radio broadcasts or through his stage appearances.

But Presley did not reach the mass popular music audience with his Sun records, which sold mainly to audiences in the South and to the minority country and western audience elsewhere. Only after Presley's contract was bought by RCA-Victor did his records make the national top ten, and the songs on these records were not in a country rock style. At Victor, under the supervision of Chet Atkins, Presley's records featured vocal groups, heavily electrified guitars, and drums, all of which were considered alien by both country and western audiences and by the audience for country rock music. Responding to these unfamiliar intrusions in his accompaniment, Presley's voice became much more theatrical and self-conscious as he sought to contrive excitement and emotion, which he had seemed to achieve on his Sun records without any evident forethought.

Presley's success for Sun, and later for RCA-Victor, encouraged Phillips to try other singers with comparable styles and material, and attracted to his studios young Southerners with similar interests. Carl Perkins and Warren Smith from the Memphis area, Roy Orbison from west Texas, Johnny Cash, Conway Twitty, Charlie Rich from Arkansas, and Jerry Lee Lewis from northern Louisiana brought songs, demonstration tapes, and their ambitions to Phillips, who switched almost completely from black singers to white singers once the latter became commercially successful.

Not all of the singers were as obviously influenced by blues styles as Presley was. Carl Perkins and Johnny Cash, for example, both sang in a much more predominantly country and western style. But, as with Bill Haley, the music and particularly the rhythms of all of them had the emphatic dance beat of rhythm and blues. "Rockabilly" effectively describes this style, which differed from the band ensemble rock 'n' roll of the Comets. Rockabilly has much looser rhythms, no saxophones, nor any chorus singing. Like the New Orleans dance blues singers, the rockabilly singers were much more personal—confiding, confessing—than Haley could ever be, and their performances seemed less calculated and less prepared. But unlike the lyrical, warm instrumentalists in the dance blues, the instrumentalists in rockabilly responded more violently to unpredictable inflections in the singer's voice, shifting into double-time for a few bars to blend with a sudden acceleration in the singer's tempo. Presley's "You're A Heartbreaker" (his third single for Sun) typifies the style, as does Carl Perkins's "Blue Suede Shoes." The latter was the first million-selling record in the rockabilly style, and brought a new dimension to popular music in its defiant pride for the individual's cultural choice.

Later, in 1956, Johnny Cash made *Billboard*'s top twenty with another Sun record, "I Walk The Line," much closer to conventional country and western music in both style and material, and in 1957 the Louisiana pianist-singer Jerry Lee Lewis, heavily influenced by Little Richard, had the first of several big hits with his boogie-based "Whole Lotta Shakin' Goin' On" (also for Sun). Rockabilly became a major part of American popular music, as much in its continuing inspiration for singers from outside the South as in the occasional commercial successes enjoyed by the rockabilly singers other than Presley.

IV.

The nearest equivalent to rockabilly among black styles was the "rocking Chicago blues" style of Chuck Berry, perhaps the major figure of rock 'n' roll, and Bo Diddley. Many of the black singers who had recorded around Memphis before Presley (among them Howlin' Wolf, Elmore James, and James Cotton) moved to Chicago during the early 1950s, where they helped Muddy Waters and others develop the Chicago bar blues style—loud, heavily amplified, shouted to a socking beat.

Chicago became the hotbed for any black musician trying to make a living from the blues, many of whom hoped to work for Muddy Waters or Howlin' Wolf and to record for Chess or its subsidiary Checker. Muddy's harmonica player Little Walter gave Checker two of its biggest rhythm and blues hits in the early 1950s with "My Babe" (1952) and "Juke" (1955), and the Chess label's big rhythm and blues hits of the period were by the soft-voiced club pianist Willie Mabon: "I Don't Know" (1953) and "I'm Mad" (1954). In 1955 the company became one of the first rhythm and blues indies to break into the pop market with Chuck Berry and Bo Diddley, two guitar-playing singers who recorded with blues musicians but aimed their lyrics and dance rhythms at a younger audience.

"Maybellene" was a "formula" song, carefully constructed to meet the apparent taste of the recently emerged mass audience for rock 'n' roll. The song lived out the fast-car fantasy:

> As I was motorvatin' over the hill,
> I saw Maybellene in a Coupe deVille
> Cadillac rollin' on the open road,
> Tryin' to outrun my V8 Ford.[5]

Berry later admitted that an early draft of "Maybellene" was closely modeled on the Bob Wills hit, "Ida Red." But disc jockey Alan Freed was "motivated" to play the record regularly—by being credited as part-author—and the result was instant rock 'n' roll. The beat was much cruder than any Berry ever used again, echoing Bill Haley more than anyone else, and the shouted-back chorus lines were also derived from the Comets' style. Berry's clear enunciation probably enabled his record to "pass for white" on the radio stations that generally kept such stuff off the air.

In contrast to "Maybellene," "Bo Diddley" was not played by many pop stations. The apparent innocence of its nursery rhyme lyric was betrayed by the barely controlled intensity of the churning rhythm from Bo's heavily reverbed guitar. Top three on radio, juke box, and sales charts in the black market, the record's unabashed earthiness discouraged any cover challenges from would-be copycats at the time.

Both singers had immeasurable influence on other rock 'n' roll singers and styles, Berry particularly as a songwriter and guitarist, Diddley as the interpreter of one of the most distinctive rhythms of rock 'n' roll.[6]

V.

"Vocal group rock 'n' roll" was the loosest of the five types of rock 'n' roll, bracketing the groups who sang mainly fast novelty songs together with those who specialized in slow ballads. Where the other four styles developed in reaction to the evolution of electrically amplified guitars and to the emphatic backbeat from drummers, the vocal group style was almost a throwback to earlier eras; almost, but not quite.[7]

Most of the black vocal groups who emerged in this period were young, inexperienced, and amateur singers whose rehearsals were in improvised settings without the benefit of musicians to help with the arrangements. To compensate, each of the backup singers had to evolve a part that was more concerned with rhythmic and percussive impact than with harmonic sophistication, and it was often the ingenious

---

4. *Hit Parade* (Britain), January 1957. 5. Copyright 1955 Arc Music Corp. All Rights Reserved. 6. The distinctive "shave-and-a-haircut, two-bit" syncopation of "Bo Diddley" had been on the pop charts in 1952 in several versions of "Hambone"; it resurfaced on "Willie and the Hand Jive" (1958) by Johnny Otis and again on "Hey Little Girl" (1959) by Dee Clark (with Bo Diddley rumored to be on guitar, playing his trademark riff).

chants that attracted attention to their records.

But although the rehearsals may have been "accappella" (without instruments), most of the records were made with hastily convened backup bands, often the bare minimum of guitar, bass, and drums, with sometimes a saxophone player in the solo break. The paradox for the supervising A&R man was that the less he interfered with a group's own arrangement, the better, although a few companies did find sympathetic arrangers who learned to tidy up the groups' ideas without making them merely conventional. In New York, Atlantic benefited from Jesse Stone's coaching efforts with the Chords, whose "Sh-Boom" made the pop charts in 1954, while Al Silver of Herald Records sent both the Turbans ("When You Dance") and the Nutmegs ("Story Untold") to Leroy Kirkland for help with their arrangements. The most productive team in this period was George Goldner and Richard Barrett, who were respectively the supervisor and arranger at the session that produced "Why Do Fools Fall In Love" by the Teenagers featuring Frankie Lymon, issued on Goldner's Gee label at the end of 1955.

"Why Do Fools Fall In Love" was in many ways the definitive fast novelty vocal group record of the period, combining an unforgettable web of backup noises with a classic teenage-lament lyric. Bass singer Sherman Garnes kicked the song off: "Ay, dum-da di-dum dah dum . . ." and in came Frankie, wailing high in his little boy's cry: "Ooh-wah, oo-ooh wah-ah." And then, with the rest of the group weaving in and out, and saxman Jimmy Wright honking along with them, came the song itself, as simple as a nursery rhyme, and as effective, but sung with such heartfelt conviction that it sounded—like the group's name—teenage, not kindergarten.

The record made the top ten in the States, and then took off around the world, topping the charts in Britain where none of the previous black vocal group records had made any impact. But although the Teenagers had a couple more hits (which was better than most novelty-oriented vocal groups managed), they soon faded into the swamps of obscurity and Frankie Lymon's life wasted away to an inevitable death from a drug overdose in 1968.

Of the other novelty groups who made their mark early, the Crows had no more success after their first hit "Gee" made the pop charts on George Goldner's Rama label in 1954; that record was hardly more than a repetition of the title, chanted over a simple dance beat, and mainly served to prove that the teenage audience was starved of records with an emphatic offbeat. The Chords were next up, with "Sh-Boom," and down they went too, followed by the Charms from Cincinnati, who lasted long enough to chalk up two hits, "Hearts Of Stone" and "Ling Ting Tong," and then one more in 1956, "Ivory Tower," billed as Otis Williams and His Charms, all for DeLuxe Records. In 1955 the El Dorados ("At My Front Door," Vee Jay), the Cadillacs ("Speedoo," Josie), and the Turbans took their turn on the wheel of fortune, and in 1956 another of George Goldner's groups, the Cleftones, made it with "Little Girl Of Mine." Each record implanted itself in the minds of listeners, and several attracted cover versions at the time and revival versions since; but for most of the singers involved, it was a back to day jobs at best, or hustling on the streets at worst. The term "novelty group" seemed to be a euphemism for one-hit wonder, and the one notable exception was the Coasters, who made their mark in 1957 with the Leiber-Stoller productions of "Young Blood" and "Searchin' " and sustained a career of hits until 1964.

For slow groups career prospects were potentially much better because they could hope to move into the supper-club and cabaret world where Las Vegas was the ultimate target. The paradox was, could a group meet the needs of that world and yet satisfy the criteria for play on the teen-oriented rock 'n' roll radio shows? Buck Ram, manager of the Platters and writer of several of their hits, proved that it could be done.

Although there were slow groups making the rhythm and blues charts from all areas of the States, the three that made the biggest impact on the pop charts in rock 'n' roll's breakthrough period were all based in Los Angeles: the Penguins, the Teen Queens, and the Platters. Both the Penguins and the Teen Queens turned out to be one-hit wonders but their records were typical of an ongoing West Coast style, which had previously surfaced on the rhythm and blues charts via "Dream Girl" by Jesse and Marvin (Specialty, 1953) and "Cherry Pie" by Marvin and Johnny (Modern, 1954). In both cases, the singers slurred and dragged their phrases to ludicrous extents in order to declare their heartfelt devotion, and this was the sound that the Penguins brought to the nation in "Earth Angel."

For the professionals in the industry, "Earth Angel" was seen as undeniable proof that the youth of the day had lost their marbles. Was the singer male or female? (Male: Cleveland Duncan.) Where was the song? "Earth angel (*thud,* from the drummer), earth angel (*thud*) (pause) will you be mine? (*thud*)." To compound the felony, the record featured the bane of all professional musicians: triplets, where the pianist just held a chord and hammered it three times on every beat; so simple, no self-respecting musician could bear to do it. But it made for hypnotic dancing, and was what worked. Dootone Records had its one and only hit, and encountered some of the attendant problems when Buck Ram moved in as manager of the group and took them off to Mercury Records along with his other protégés, the Platters.

The Platters had been just one of the countless black vocal groups in Los Angeles, recording for Federal in all the current styles without ever establishing a distinct identity but, after their move to Mercury, all the focus was put on to the voice of lead tenor Tony Williams. The first recording for the new label was "Only You," a song written by Ram, which the group had already recorded for Federal, who had refused to release it. This time around the record went unnoticed again for three months before it began to get play, yet it came to represent a milestone in the era's music.

The backup singers in the Platters never sounded as interesting as most of the other groups of the day, and in many ways the group's records could have been billed as by Tony Williams. He had a genuinely good voice, obviously influenced by gospel, and he threw in a kind of hiccup on the high notes, which became his trademark. Swooping up to stratospheric heights, he declared the now familiar undying devotion in "Only You," and followed through with a better song (again written by Buck Ram), "The Great Pretender." Tailor-made to showcase the highflying voice of Williams, this topped the American pop charts, and set the group up for a long career, achieving Ram's declared ambition to launch "the new Ink Spots."

Later records veered away from the triplet, teen-ballad idiom of the first two hits, but that idiom became part of the basic rock 'n' roll heritage, for better or (quite often) for worse.

These five styles of rock 'n' roll covered most of the records that broke through to the pop charts from 1954 through 1956, and basically set up the "ingredients" which were mixed together in slightly varying combinations for the next thirty years by musicians, producers, and singers aiming at the "youth market." Bill Haley's brand of band ensemble rock 'n' roll was probably the least influential, being the end, rather than a beginning, of a tradition; sometimes derided for his old-fashioned image, Haley was in fact an astute bandleader who outlasted most of his contemporaries by accommodating the backbeat rhythm that was required of the new dance music.

The piano-and-saxophone orientation of New Orleans rock 'n' roll gradually lost favor during the 1960s, when the majority of groups featured guitars as both lead and rhythm instruments, inspired equally by Memphis-style rockabilly and Chicago-style rhythm and blues. The gospel attack of Little Richard had incalculable influence, both directly and through the other gospel-styled singers who found more favor after he had crashed into public view. And many of the performers who synthesized these influences worked as groups, incorporating vocal harmonies that took off from the Teenagers and the other vocal groups. Between them, these styles provided the basis for all the major artists and producers of the 1960s—obviously the Four Seasons, the Beach Boys, and the Motown groups in the States, and the Beatles and Rolling Stones in Britain, and less obviously but just as certainly, Bob Dylan and Sly Stone. In most cases, the second generation was able to make more from its records than the innovators had, in terms of money, fame, and prestige, as they reclaimed the music from the businessmen who tried to reproduce the effects of rock 'n' roll without risking the personal elements that had been fundamental in the first place.

FIRST PUBLISHED IN CHARLIE GILLETT, *THE SOUND OF THE CITY: THE RISE OF ROCK AND ROLL*. NEW YORK: OUTERBRIDGE & DIENSTFREY, DISTRIBUTED BY E.P. DUTTON, 1970.

---

7. In the early 1970s, this style was retrospectively dubbed doo-wop, a brilliant evocation of the sounds made by the accompanying vocal group singers, and literally sung by the Turbans in "When You Dance."

"THROUGH 1955 AND ON INTO 1956, BILL HALEY HELD COMPLETE CONTROL... AND HE WAS EVERYTHING —PROPHET, FACE, SINGER, EXPLORER— AND NO ONE ELSE COUNTED."

NIK COHN, WRITER, 1996

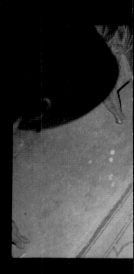

Bill Haley and His Comets and LaVern Baker, concert, Sports Arena, Hershey, Pennsylvania, April 23, 1956, by Ed Feingersh.

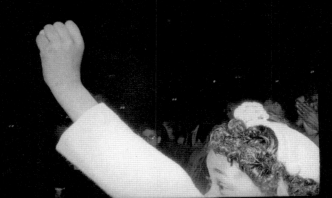

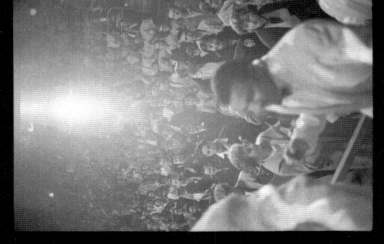
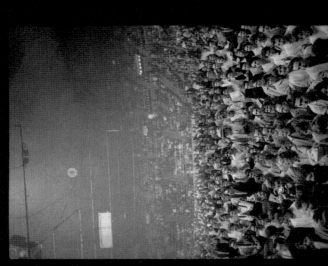

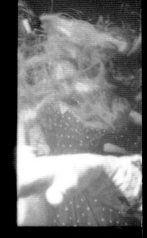

Bill Haley and His Comets and LaVern Baker, concert, Sports Arena, Hershey, Pennsylvania, April 23, 1956, by Ed Feingersh.

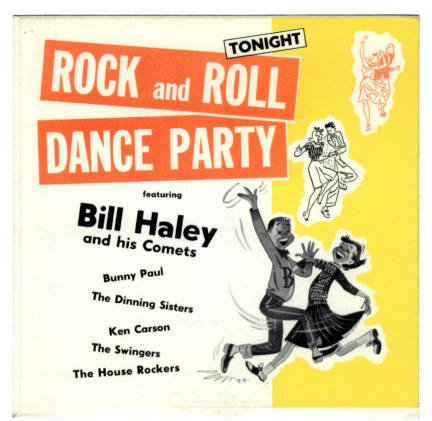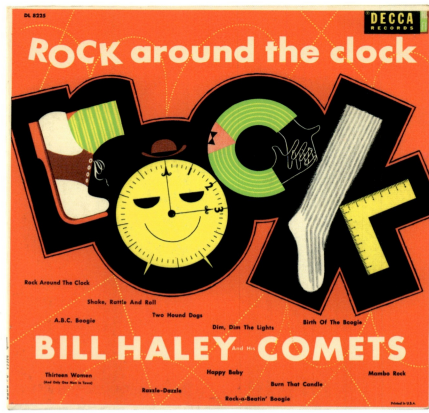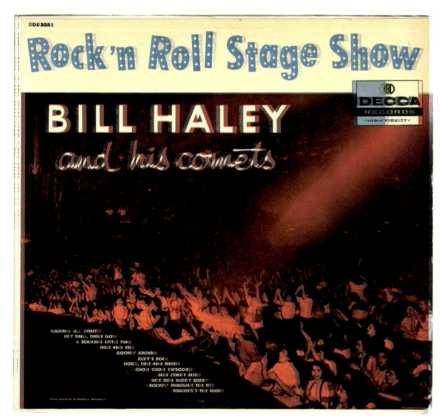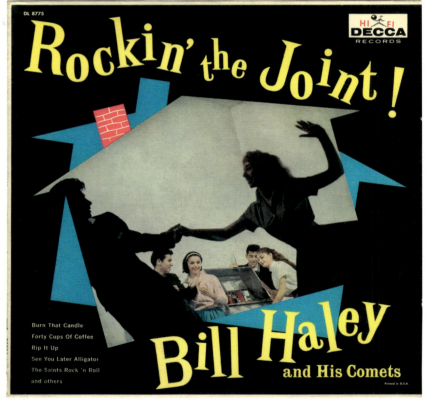

Bill Haley and His Comets, *Tonight Rock And Roll Dance Party*, Somerset, LP, mid-1950s. **Bill Haley and His Comets,** *Rock Around The Clock*, Decca, LP, 1956.
Bill Haley and His Comets, *Rockin' The Joint!*, Decca, LP, 1958. **Bill Haley and His Comets,** *Rock 'n' Roll Stage Show*, Decca, LP, 1956.

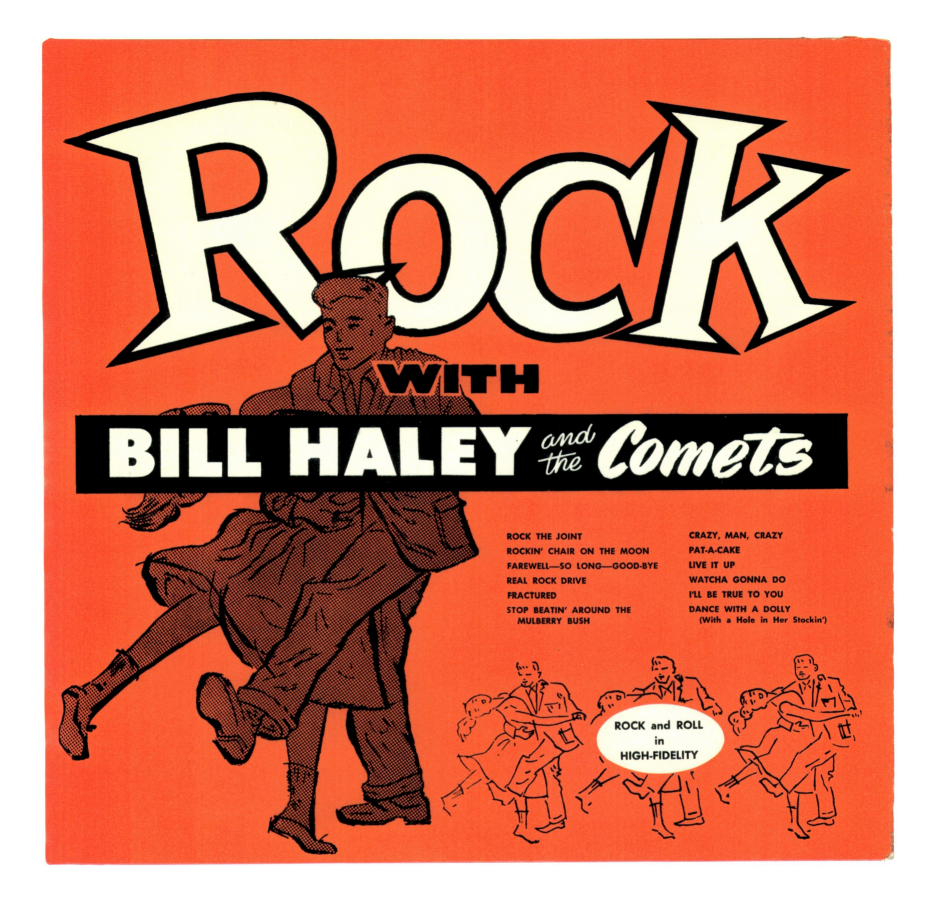

Bill Haley, *Rock With Bill Haley and The Comets*, Essex, LP, 1956 (recordings from the early 1950s).

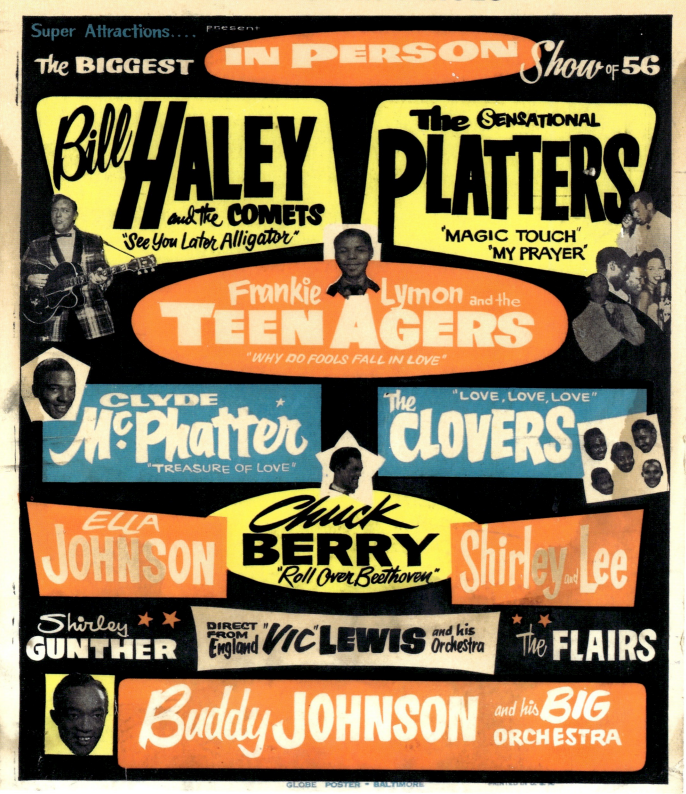

"The Biggest Show of 1956" concert poster, October 11, 1956, Providence, Rhode Island.

Advertisement for Essex Records, *The Cash Box*, magazine, January 17, 1953.

BO DIDDLEY:
"MY MUSIC HAS A LITTLE BIT OF A SPIRITUAL TASTE, BUT IT'S ALSO PRIMITIVE. I PLAY THE GUITAR AS IF I WAS PLAYING THE DRUMS."

Bo Diddley, c.1958.

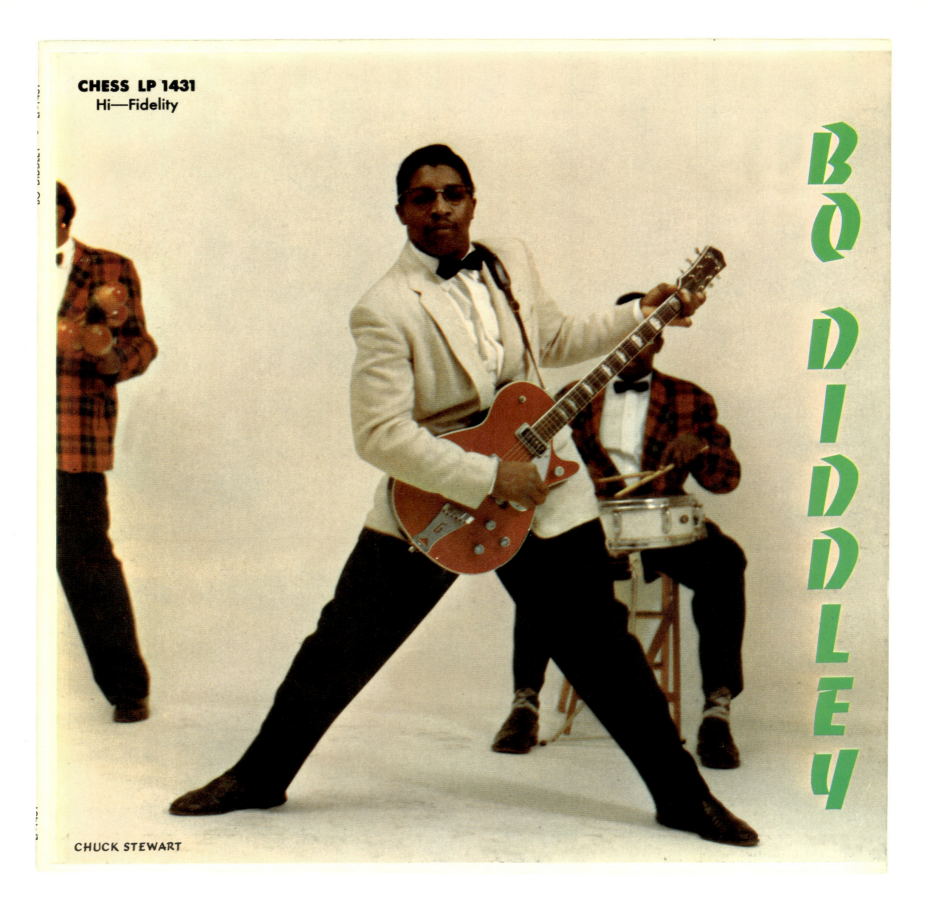

Bo Diddley, *Bo Diddley*, Chess, LP, 1958.

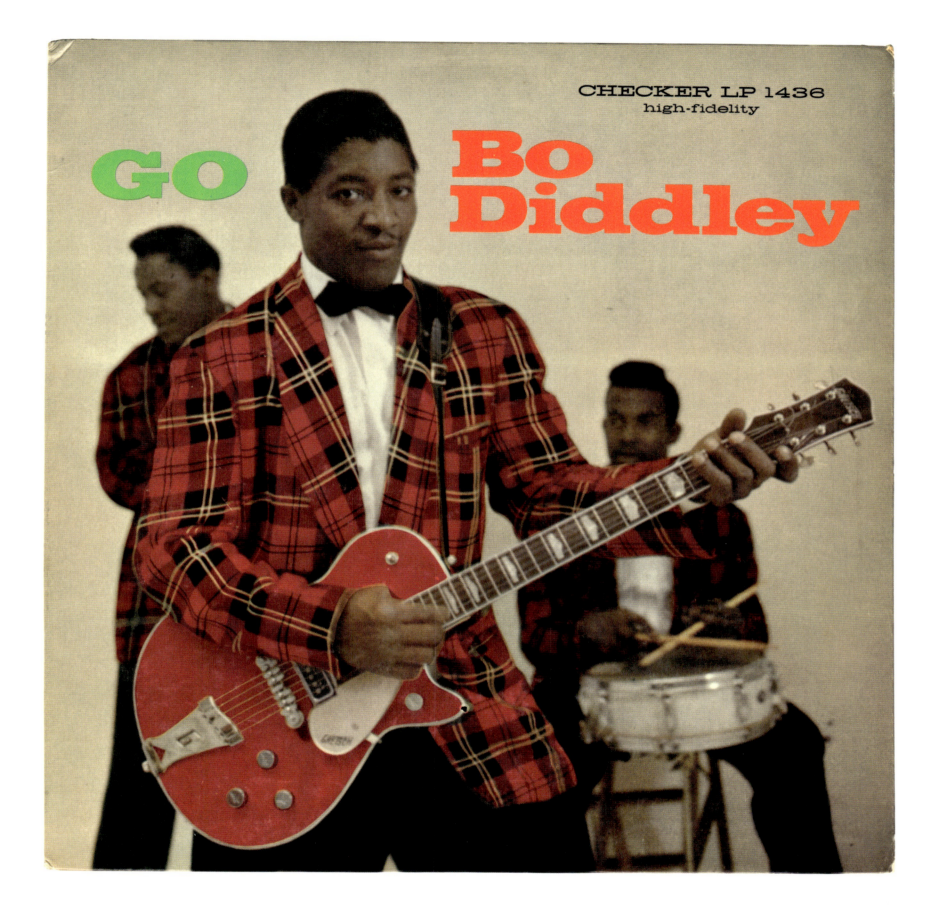

Bo Diddley, *Go Bo Diddley*, Checker, LP, 1959.

"Top 10 Rhythm And Blues Review" concert poster, September 27, 1955, Chattanooga, Tennessee.

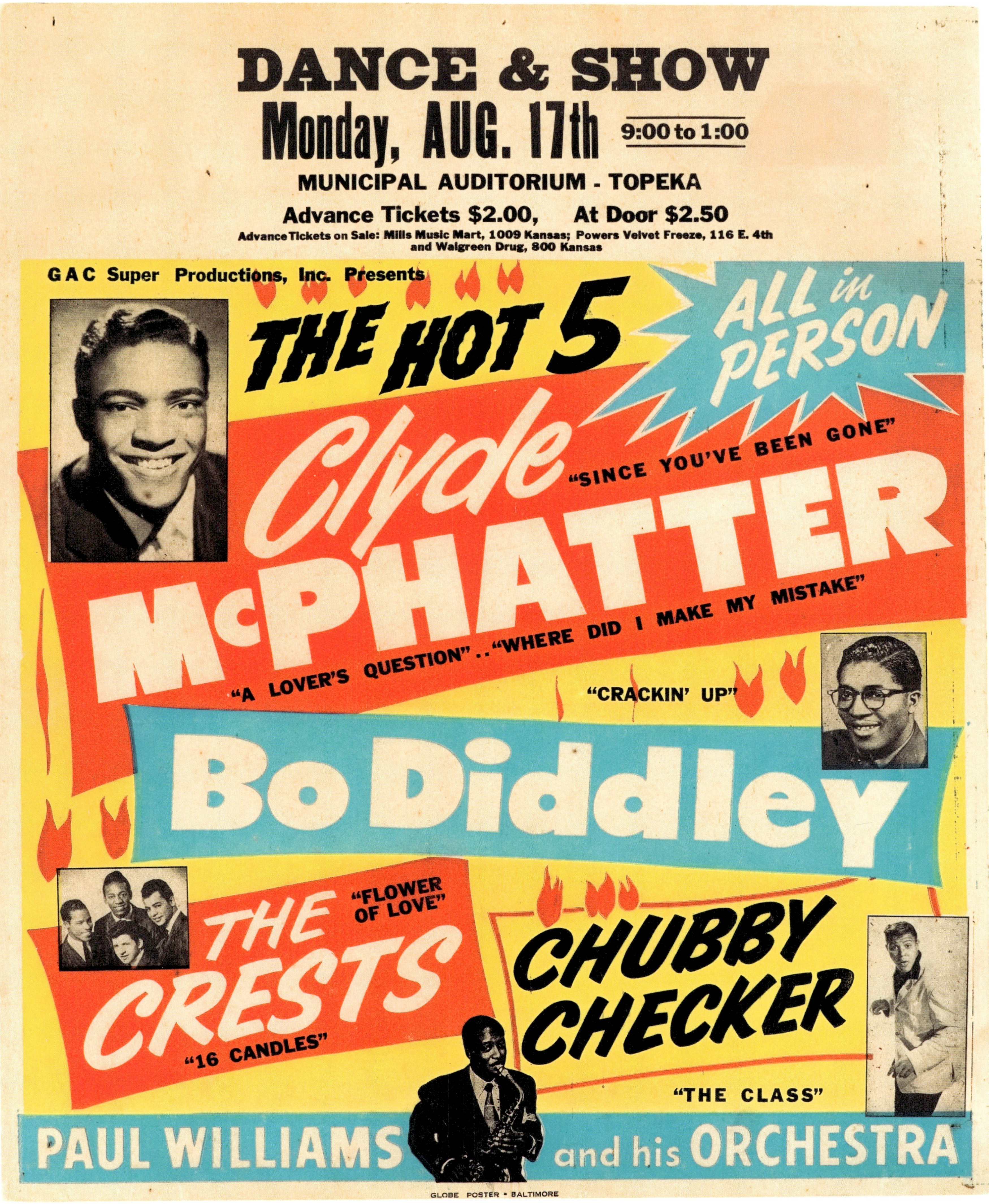

"The Hot 5" concert poster, August 17, 1959, Topeka, Kansas.

"IF YOU TRIED TO GIVE ROCK 'N' ROLL ANOTHER NAME, YOU MIGHT CALL IT CHUCK BERRY."

—JOHN LENNON

Chuck Berry, Chicago, Illinois, c.1957.

Chuck Berry, *One Dozen Berrys*, Chess, LP, 1958.

Chuck Berry, "Maybellene," Chess, single, 1955.
Chuck Berry, "Thirty Days," Chess, single, 1955.
Chuck Berry, "Roll Over Beethoven," Chess, single, 1956.

Chuck Berry, "Johnny B. Goode," Chess, single, 1957.
Chuck Berry, "Rock & Roll Music," Chess, single, 1957.
Chuck Berry, "Sweet Little Sixteen," Chess, single, 1957.

Chuck Berry, Sheet Music for "Johnny B. Goode," 1957.

Chuck Berry, Sheet Music for "Carol," 1958.

Chuck Berry concert poster, August 31, 1957, Seattle, Washington.

"Big Rock And Roll Show" concert poster, October 14, 1955, Chattanooga, Tennessee.

"<u>FATS</u> WAS SUPERHOT. FATS COULD BURN A PIANO, AND FATS HAD A VOCAL SOUND THAT EVERYBODY LOVED."

—ART NEVILLE, MUSICIAN

Fats Domino, Brooklyn Paramount, New York, November 21, 1957, by Charlotte Brooks.

Fats Domino, Brooklyn Paramount, New York, November 21, 1957, by Charlotte Brooks.

Fats Domino, Brooklyn Paramount, New York, November 21, 1957. Charlotte Brooks.

Fats Domino in his hotel room the night of his concert at the Brooklyn Paramount, New York, November 21, 1957, by Charlotte Brooks.

Fats Domino backstage, Brooklyn Paramount, New York, November 21, 1957, by Charlotte Brooks.

Fats Domino's musicians during their tour, 1956.

Fats Domino and Dave Bartholomew, Cosimo Matassa's studio (J & M Studio), New Orleans, Louisiana, July, 1957.

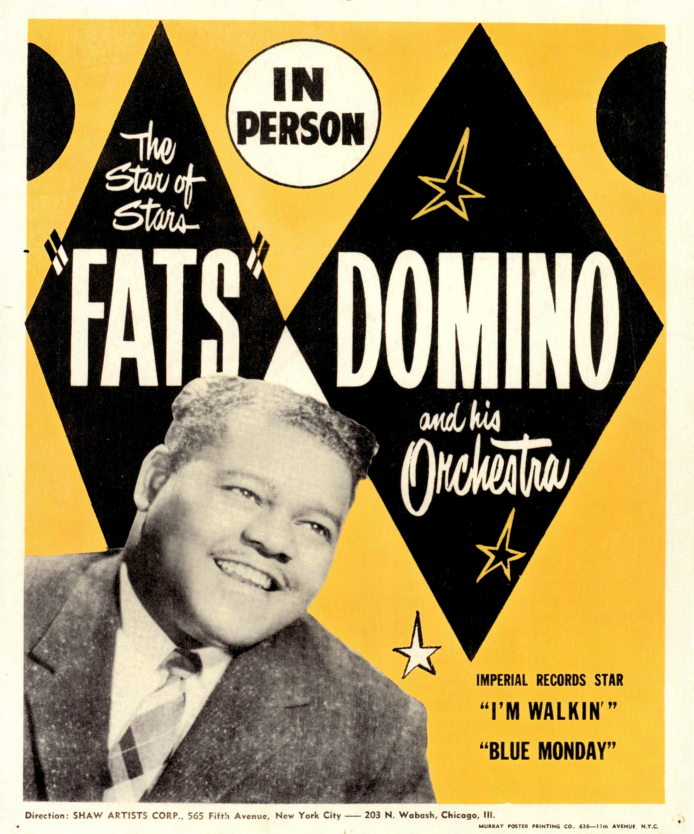

Fats Domino concert poster, February 22, 1958, Rock Island, Illinois.

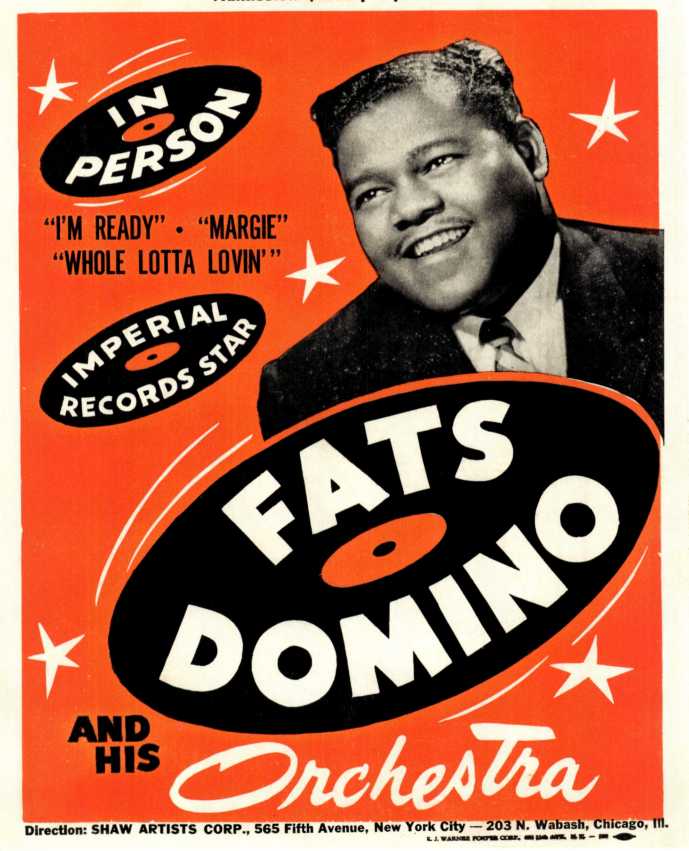

Fats Domino concert poster, July 22, 1959, Topeka, Kansas.

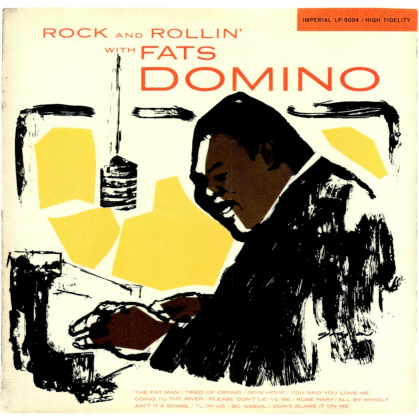

Fats Domino, *This Is Fats Domino!*, Imperial, LP, 1956. Fats Domino, *Rock And Rollin' With Fats Domino*, Imperial, LP, 1956.
Fats Domino, *Here Stands Fats Domino*, Imperial, LP, 1957. Fats Domino, *This Is Fats!*, Imperial, LP, 1957.

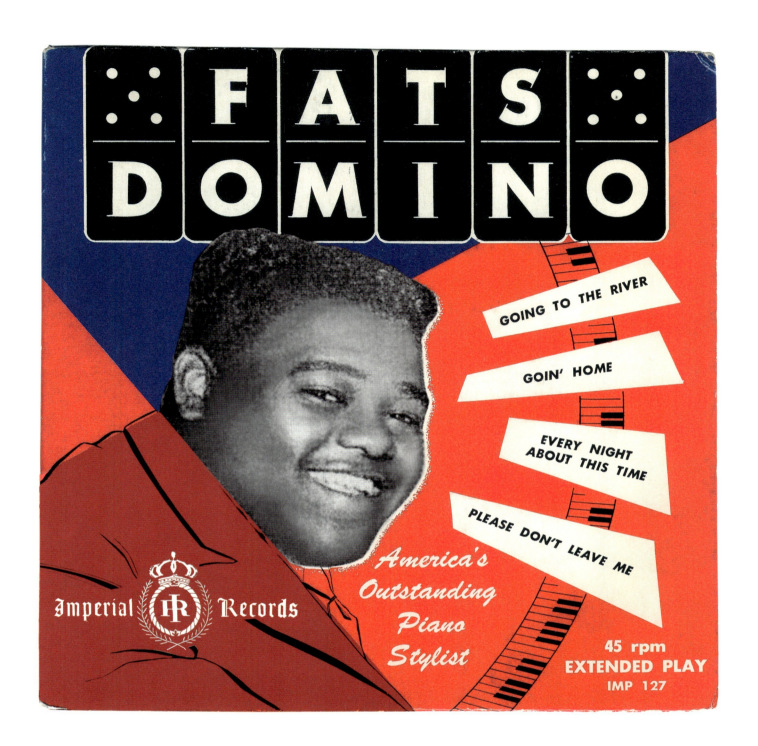

Fats Domino, *Fats Domino*, Imperial, 45 EP, c.1956.

LITTLE RICHARD:

"WHEN THE WHITE KIDS WOULD BUY MY RECORDS, THEY'D HAVE TO HIDE 'EM FROM THEIR PARENTS."

Little Richard, Los Angeles, California, mid-1950s.

Little Richard, c.1956.

Little Richard concert poster, October 30, 1953, location unknown.

Little Richard concert poster, August 6, 1957, Louisville, Kentucky.

Little Richard, "Long Tall Sally," Specialty, 78 rpm, 1956.

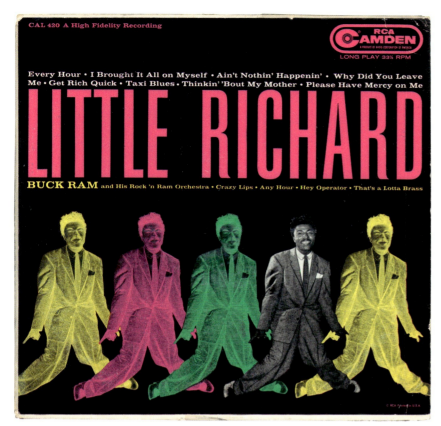
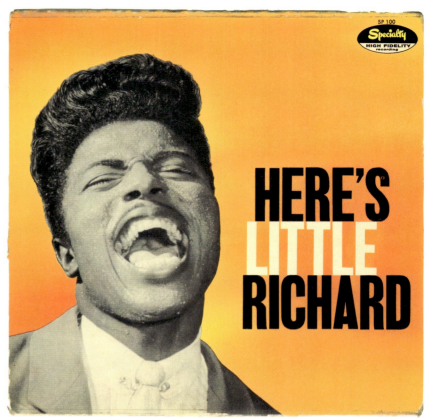
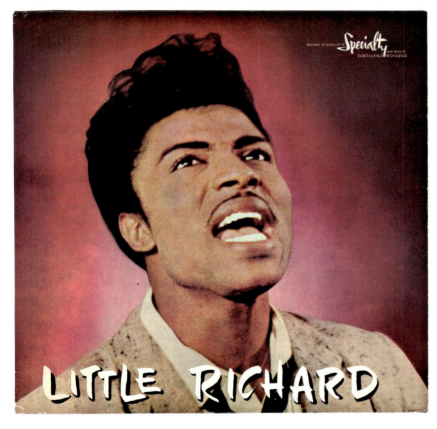

Little Richard, *Little Richard*, RCA Camden, LP, 1956. Little Richard, *Here's Little Richard*, Specialty, LP, 1957.
Little Richard, *Little Richard*, Specialty, LP, 1958. Little Richard, *The Fabulous Little Richard*, Specialty, LP, 1959.

Little Richard, "Tutti Frutti," Specialty, single, 1955.
Little Richard, "The Girl Can't Help It," Specialty, single, 1956.
Little Richard, "She's Got It," Specialty, single, 1956.

Little Richard, "Keep A Knockin'," Specialty, single, 1957.
Little Richard, "Lucille," Specialty, single, 1957.
Little Richard, "Good Golly, Miss Molly," Specialty, single, 1958.

The Cash Box

VOLUME XIX — NUMBER 32

APRIL 26, 1958

Jerry Lee Lewis, young Rock and Roll sensation of the Sun label, signs the contract to head the Alan Freed R & R package now touring the United States. The Freed show, "The Big Beat", is about midway through its 44 day trek, and has been playing to standing room only in all cities since it left New York. Freed, lower left, hands the pen to Lewis. Jack Hooke, associate of Freed, who buys all the talent for Freed's shows, stands between Freed and Lewis. Milt Shaw, Shaw Agency, who books the show, places the contract for Lewis to sign.

JERRY LEE LEWIS:
"OTHER PEOPLE—THEY PRACTICE AND THEY PRACTICE AND THEY PRACTICE... THESE FINGERS OF MINE, THEY GOT BRAINS IN 'EM. YOU DON'T TELL THEM WHAT TO DO—THEY DO IT. GOD GIVEN TALENT."

The Cash Box, magazine, April 26, 1958.

Jerry Lee Lewis, Cafe de Paris, New York, June 10, 1958.

Jerry Lee Lewis, "High School Confidential," Sun, single, 1958.

Jerry Lee Lewis, *Jerry Lee Lewis*, Sun, LP, 1958.

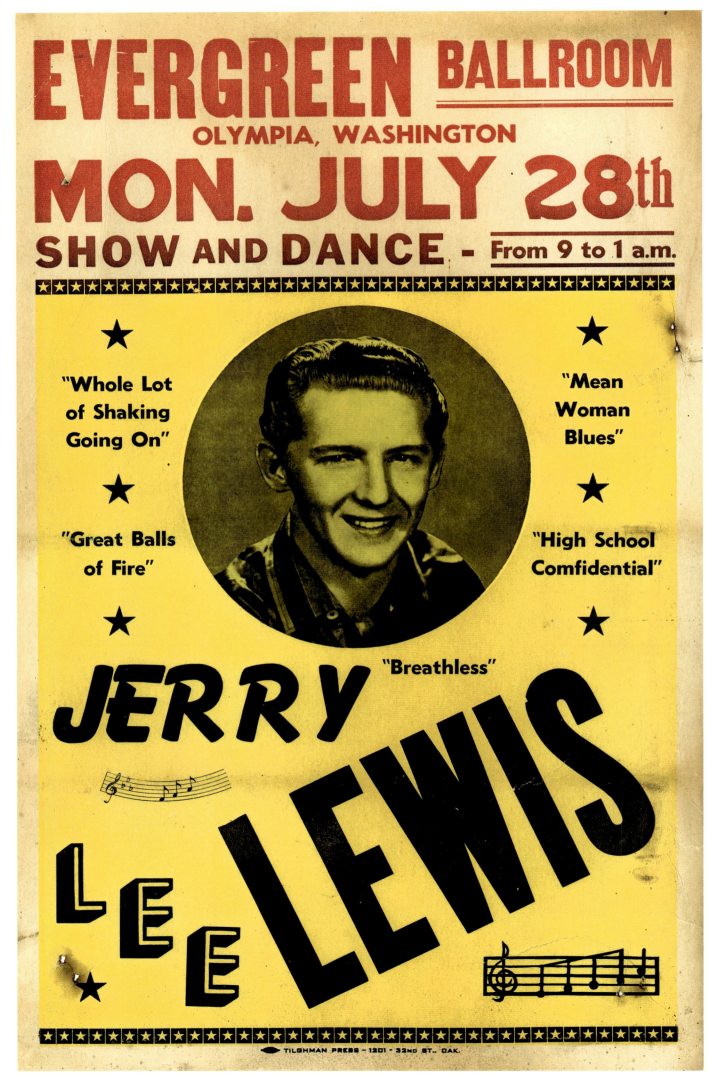

Jerry Lee Lewis concert poster, July 28, 1958, Olympia, Washington.

Lobby card for the film *High School Confidential!* by Jack Arnold featuring Jerry Lee Lewis as himself.

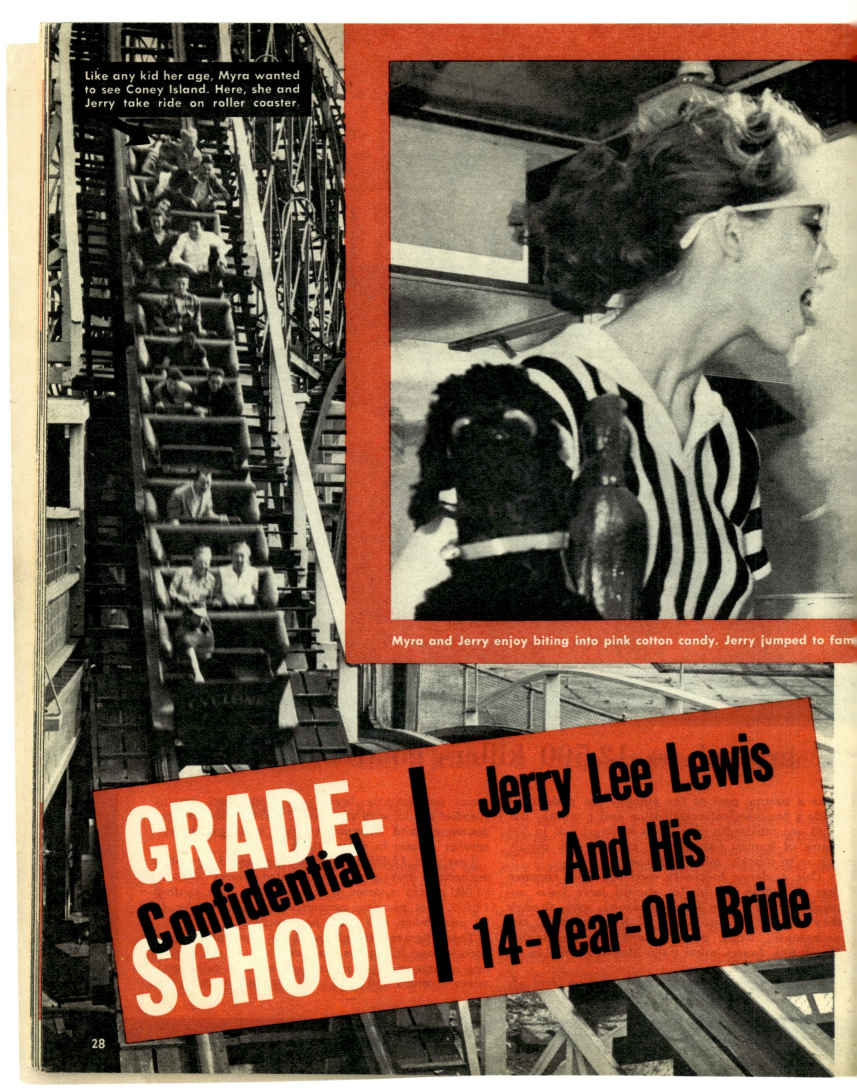

Like any kid her age, Myra wanted to see Coney Island. Here, she and Jerry take ride on roller coaster.

Myra and Jerry enjoy biting into pink cotton candy. Jerry jumped to fam

GRADE-SCHOOL Confidential | Jerry Lee Lewis And His 14-Year-Old Bride

in one movie and has since replaced Elvis Presley.

The first intimate, inside story of what it feels like to be the child married to America's No. 1 Rock and Roller— singer, Jerry Lee Lewis.

By RENEE FRANCINE

MYRA GALE IS SUCH a little child. Just turned 14, she is a bright child, who, like other children, might be spending the summer at a girl scout camp, or at a day camp away from the city.

She has her favorite dolls and toys and likes licorice and two-for-a-penny taffies and gum and chocolate drops. By rights she should be in bed at 8:30 p.m. after watching TV or catching up on her reading of "Black Beauty."

But not Myra. Myra is a housewife. She's Myra Gale Lewis, wife of Elvis Presley's home-front replacement, git-tarrin' Jerry Lee Lewis. Myra basks in her 22-year-old husband's success with the recent No. 1 rock-and-roll tune, "High School Confidential," from his movie of the same name.

Right now she's out in Hollywood watching Lewis make a movie and matching her childish innocence against glittering urbanity.

What will the child say at the Brown Derby when they refuse to serve her a drink?

What will she say at Mike Lyman's when they ask her if she can stay up late enough to see the floor show?

She's going to be hurt in Hollywood, if CONFIDENTIAL's afternoon spent with the incredible couple is any indication.

First there was Coney Island, where Myra blended with all the other gay children. She liked the rides, but food was her major spree. A hot dog, then corn on the cob, finally cotton candy. Just a bite of each, then throw it away and on to something else.

"Get me some watermellon, Jerry," the child pleaded. "I promise I'll eat it all."

Then she wanted to go back to Manhattan, to their hotel suite.

There, Lewis stretched his lanky, lean body on a bed as the Child hovered over him.

"I just lovin' my baby," *(Continued on next page)*

Here, reporter Renee Francine, gets Confidential story straight from young Mrs. Lewis at a New York City hotel.

"BUDDY HOLLY WAS THE GENTLEMAN OF ROCKA- BILLY, THE FIRST SOFT ROCKER."

NICK TOSCHES, WRITER

Buddy Holly, New York, c.1958.

Buddy Holly, *The "Chirping" Crickets*, Brunswick, LP, 1957.

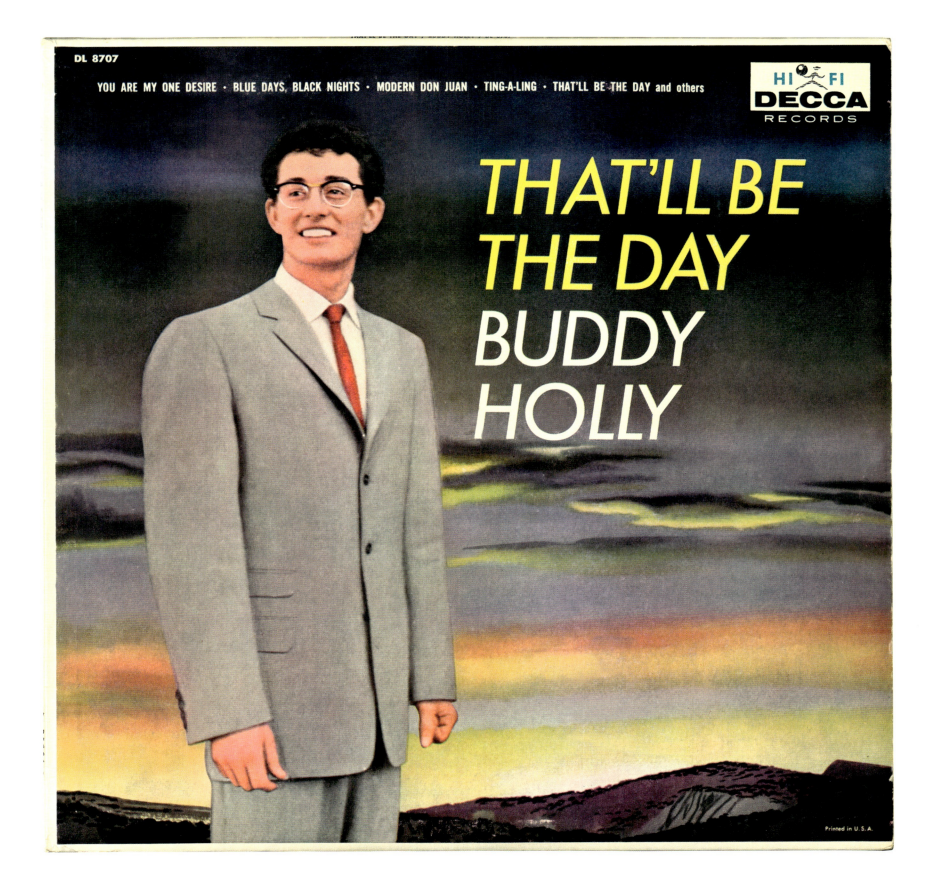

Buddy Holly, *That'll Be The Day*, Decca, LP, 1958.

Buddy Holly and his friends backstage during the *America's Teenage Recording Stars Tour*, Community War Memorial Theater, Rochester, New York, October 15, 1958, by Lew Allen.

348

"Winter Dance Party" concert poster, January 25, 1959, Mankato, Minnesota.
Buddy Holly, The Big Bopper, and Ritchie Valens will disappear one week later in an airplane accident.

In 2004, William Eggleston photographed what was once Norman Petty's studio in Clovis, New Mexico. It has remained largely unchanged since Buddy Holly and his band, The Crickets, recorded their demo of the hit "That'll Be the Day" within its walls. These large format photographs present the historical three-room recording complex, where the band's biggest hits, including "Peggy Sue," "Oh, Boy!," and "Maybe Baby," were cut for Brunswick and Coral Records over an eighteen-month period, from 1957 to 1958.

Untitled (Buddy Holly LP Record Cover, Blue Satin Jacket On Chair), 2004.

BUDDY HOLLY BY WILLIAM EGGLESTON

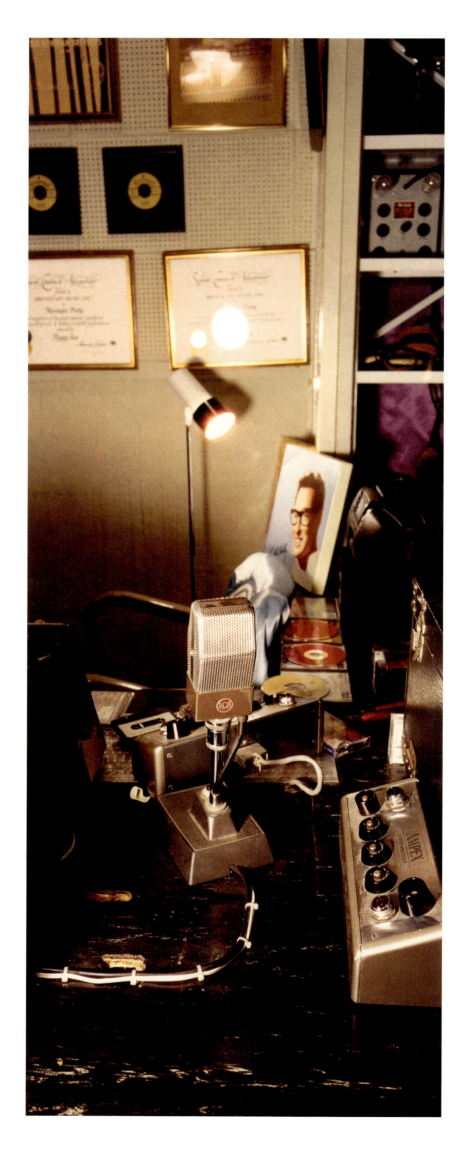

Untitled (Desktop With Microphone And Controls, Lamp), 2004.

Untitled (Orange Peggy Sue Sheet Music Framed On Wall, Buddy Holly, Certificate Above), 2004.

Untitled (B&W Portrait Of Couple Norman & Vi Petty, Sugartime, Maybe Baby, Gold 45), 2004.

Untitled (Ceramic Leopard Head Bowl, Bowls On Shelf, Curtains, Pillows, Retro), 2004.

Untitled (Lamp On Speaker, Eye Glasses, Clock, Records On Wall), 2004.

Untitled (Upright Recording Console, B&W Portrait Of Couple), 2004.

Untitled (Retro Clock On Wall, Framed Gold Records & CDs On Wall), 2004.

Untitled (Front View Of Recording Mixer On Desk), 2004.

"THE KIDS GET TOGETHER IN ONE ANOTHER'S HOME, TURN ON <u>ALAN FREED'S</u> WINS PROGRAM, AND LET THE PLACE START JUMPING."

RAY PARRIS, MUSICIAN, 1955

Alan Freed concert programs, 1955 to 1958.

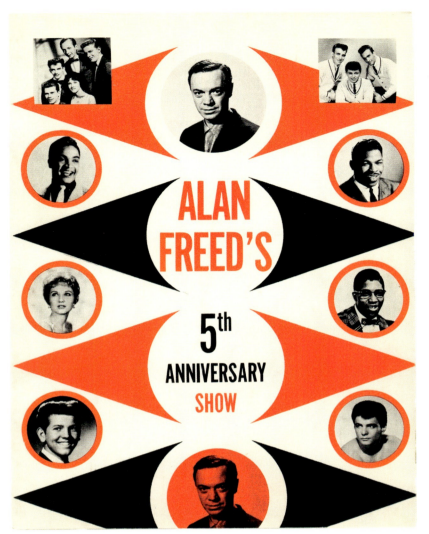
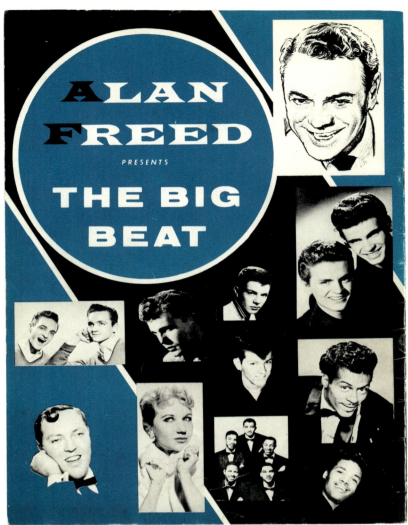
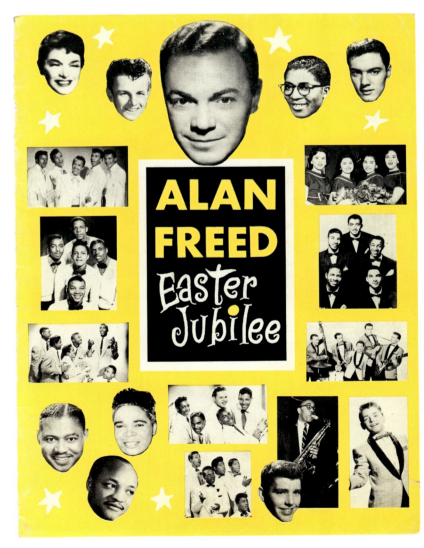
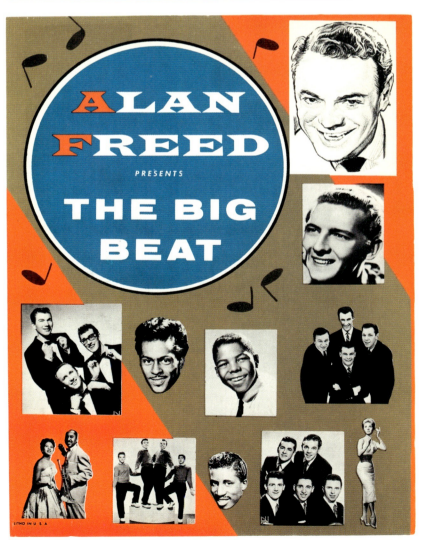

Alan Freed, *Alan Freed's Rock 'n Roll Dance Party*, volume 2, Coral, LP, 1956.

Alan Freed, *The Alan Freed Rock 'n Roll Show*, Brunswick, LP, 1959.

Rufus Thomas and Elvis Presley, *WDIA Goodwill Revue*, Ellis Auditorium, Memphis, Tennessee, December 7, 1957, by Ernest C. Withers.

RUFUS THOMAS
BY PETER GURALNICK

Rufus Thomas possessed a wide range of talents. He was a singer, a dancer, a comedian, and a radio DJ, and he was highly accomplished in each of these roles. None of his talents, however, defined his *mark*, the impact he made on both the world at large and the world around him. You might be tempted to describe Rufus Thomas as a larger-than-life personality, but that would be doing him an injustice. For Rufus Thomas was a life force, as anyone who ever encountered him on stage, screen, or simply on the street would attest. His music—blues and Louis Jordan-influenced jump to start off with, then nothing but pure cosmic (and comic) funk—brought a great deal of joy to the world, but his personality brought even more, conveying a message of grit, determination, indomitability, above all a bottomless appreciation for the human comedy that left little room for the drab or the dreary in his presence.

He was born in 1917 in Cayce, Mississippi, and grew up in Memphis, where he attended Booker T. Washington High School. There he met the fabled Professor Nat D. Williams, history teacher and entertainer extraordinaire, who schooled him in both comedy routines and academics and, after graduation, brought Rufus in as his sidekick hosting Amateur Night at the Palace Theater on Beale Street. When Nat quit, Rufus became the MC, later following Nat to WDIA, "the Mother Station of the Negroes," where Nat had become the first black DJ on the first all-black station in the nation, in 1949.

Rufus had already completed his show business education by then, traveling all over the South with the Rabbit Foot Minstrels tent show ("I was a tap dancer, and I used to do some scat singing. If it came under the heading of show business, I did it.") in the years immediately following high school graduation. He gave up the tent shows to get married, took a job in a local textile plant, and had three musical children, Marvell, Carla, and Vaneese, all of whom would pursue successful professional careers of their own. But he always kept his mind on show business, and when Sam Phillips opened up his Memphis Recording Service in 1950, Rufus was one of the first to show up at its door.

His early recordings, released on the Chess label, were not commercially successful, but when Phillips started his own Sun label, it was Rufus Thomas who had the fledging company's first hit in 1953. "Bear Cat (The Answer To Hound Dog)" was, as the subtitle suggests, an undisguised, flavorful, and witty response to the Big Mama Thornton original, going to #3 on the rhythm and blues charts and putting Sun Records on the map. This in turn led directly to an eighteen-year-old named Elvis Presley finding his way to the Memphis Recording Service to make a record "for his mother." Phillips recorded Elvis commercially the following year, trying him out early on Rufus' version of "Tiger Man," which would years later become a staple of his Vegas act. Elvis' arrival in any case marked the end of Rufus' first brief fling with stardom. Sun Records was essentially a one-man operation, and Sam Phillips would from this point on devote his energies to what became known as rock 'n' roll. "Me and Sam Phillips," remarked Rufus ruefully, "we were tighter than the nuts on the Brooklyn Bridge, but when Elvis and Carl Perkins and Johnny Cash come along, no more blacks did he pick up at all."

The experience left him embittered—but not for long. He always played Elvis' records on the air, even if the station looked askance, and when Elvis showed up at the WDIA Goodwill Review in 1956, one of the only whites in a sea of black faces, it was Rufus who introduced him *con brio*. "I took him onstage by the hand, and when he did that little wiggle that they wouldn't let him do on television, the crowd just went crazy!" Although he was shut out of the recording studio for the most part during these years, Rufus stayed busy with all his other tasks, not least of which was to play his customary role of Beale Street ambassador and wisecracking man about town to soulful perfection.

Then in 1960 a little label that had been operating fitfully for the last couple of years moved to south Memphis, and Rufus sensed an opportunity. Satellite (soon to be renamed Stax) had originally been modeled on Sun and had up till then focused primarily on rockabilly and country. With its move to his neighborhood, though, Rufus felt it might be time for a change. He persuaded Stax owner Jim Stewart to cut a duet on him and his eighteen-year-old daughter, Carla, and it was a hit. Just as with Sun, said Rufus, "I was the beginning of Stax. I made the first record that made money for them, me, and Carla."

He went on, of course, to have hits into the 1960s and 1970s ("Walking The Dog" and "Do The Funky Chicken," among others, not to mention such action follow-ups as "Do The Funky Robot," "Do The Funky Penguin," and "Do The Push And Pull," each accompanied by its own striking new steps and costumes). He never strayed far from the blues, though, and he continued to do his radio show and entertain into his eighties, showing off both his dances and his legs in hot-pink outfits and high lace-up boots and proudly (and more and more accurately) proclaiming himself to be "The World's Oldest Teenager."

But you can't quantify the achievements of someone like Rufus Thomas any more than it's possible to pinpoint the siren call of Beale Street. Spending any amount of time with Rufus, you were inevitably caught up in his energy field—it was no longer a matter of studying history, you were *living* history. In Italy, in the 1990s, he became not just the hit but the heart and soul of the Porretta Sweet Soul Music Festival in Emilia-Romagna. By the time I arrived in 1995, they had named the park in which the festival was held after him, requiring a special legislative act to override a national prohibition against naming public institutions for living people. Everywhere he went in Porretta and its environs, he was hailed with cries of "Rufalone!" as he sashayed down the street in lordly fashion.

He took it all as his due. He stood in awe of no man (or woman), though he sometimes stood in envy. Elvis Presley, B.B. King, Frank Sinatra, and Michael Jackson were all simply regarded by him as his peers, and while he had the capacity to feel sorry for himself, he had the even greater capacity to triumph over adversity, real or imagined. "All my life," he liked to say, "I wanted to be an entertainer. My models were Fats Waller and Louis Armstrong, and a fellow named Gatemouth Moore who came out of Memphis by way of Topeka. They were all good entertainers, very very versatile, always able to do more than one thing, and they helped, they made a way if they could, for somebody else to make it, too. Well, I believe that was my whole work, helping people. And still is. It's enough room for everybody to be on top. Ain't nothing *but* room up there. It's a big enough space up there for everybody, so why can't you share it with somebody? *You* got the chance, now go ahead and share it with somebody else."

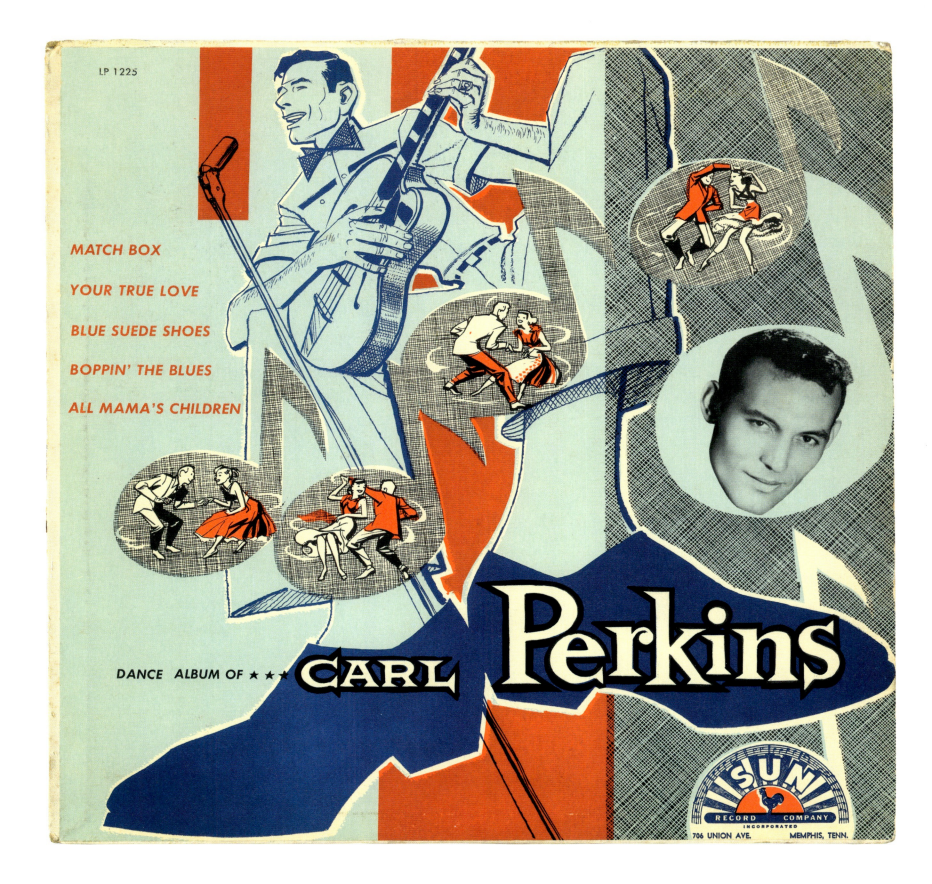

Carl Perkins, *Dance Album Of Carl Perkins*, Sun, LP, 1957.

Gene Vincent and His Blue Caps, *Bluejean Bop!*, Capitol, LP, 1957.
Gene Vincent, Los Angeles, c.1958 (opposite).

Eddie Cochran, c.1958.

"Top Record Stars of '56" concert poster, July 31, 1956, Oklahoma City, Oklahoma.

"ROCK 'N' ROLL'S COMING IN THE MID-FIFTIES WAS NOT SO MUCH A SINGLE EVENT OR A SERIES OF EVENTS AS AN OPENING OF AMERICA'S SONIC FLOODGATES." ROBERT PALMER, MUSIC HISTORIAN, 1995

"America's Greatest Teen-Age Recording Stars" concert poster, January 19, 1958, Rochester, New York.
The Everly Brothers, 1958, by Don Cravens (opposite).

Johnny Cash concert poster, December 9, 1956, Ventura, California.

Johnny Cash, *Johnny Cash With His Hot And Blue Guitar!*, Sun, LP, 1956.

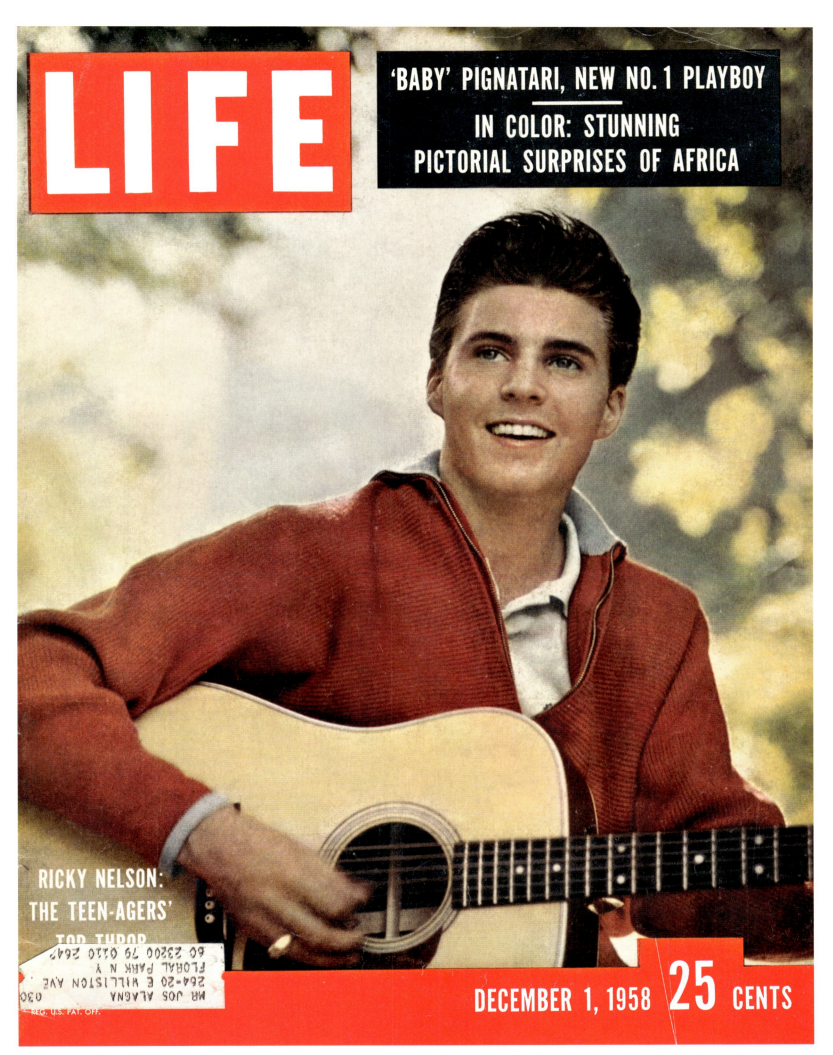

Life, magazine, December 1, 1958.
Ricky Nelson headshot for the film *Rio Bravo*, 1959 (opposite).

The Platters, 1956.

The Platters, *The Platters*, volume 2, Mercury, LP, 1957.

The Teenagers, c.1956.
LaVern Baker, New York, c.1955 (opposite).

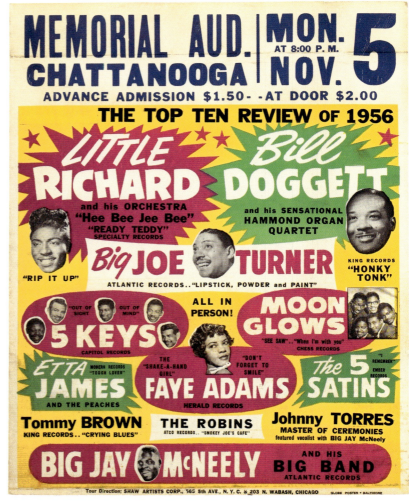

The "5" Royales concert poster, February 7, 1954, Wichita, Kansas. "The Top Ten Review of 1956" concert poster, November 5, 1956, Memorial Auditorium, Chattanooga, Tennessee. Alan Freed, The Big Beat concert poster, April 19, Kansas City, Missouri. James Brown with the Famous Flames concert poster, July 28, 1956, Columbus, Ohio.

The Midnighters concert poster, November 15, 1957, location unknown. Ray Charles concert poster, February 12-13, 1957, location unknown. "The Biggest Show of Stars for '57" concert poster, February 24, 1957, Topeka, Kansas. "The Biggest Show of Stars for '57" concert poster, November 5, 1957.

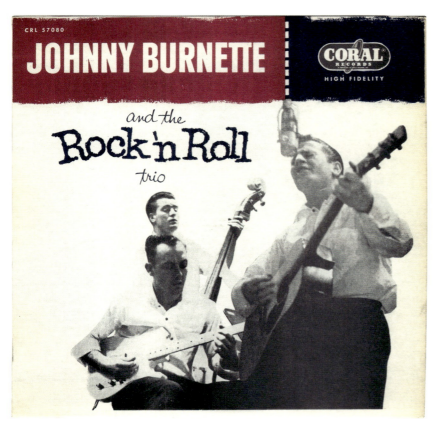

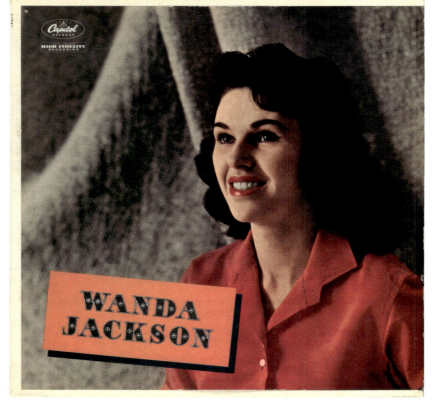

Johnny Burnette, *Johnny Burnette And The Rock'n Roll Trio*, Coral, LP, 1956. Del Vikings, *They Sing... They Swing*, Mercury, LP, 1957. The Champs, *Go Champs Go!*, Challenge, LP, 1958. Wanda Jackson, *Wanda Jackson*, Capitol, LP, 1958.

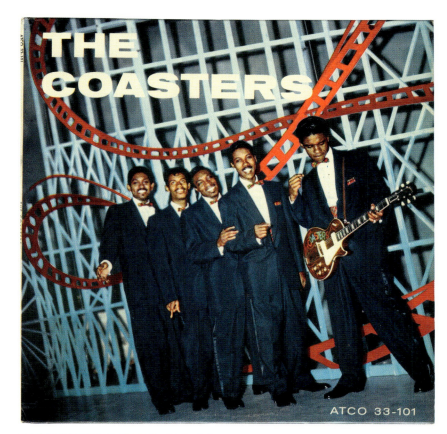

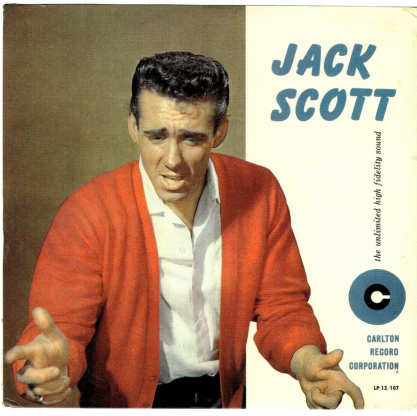
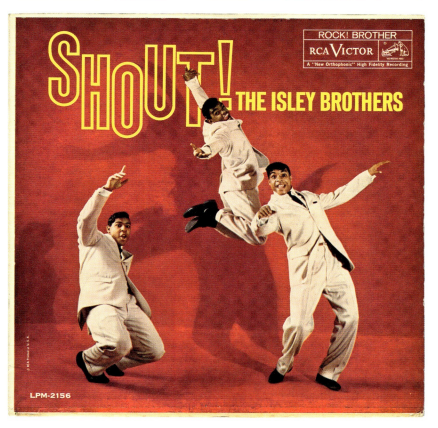

The Coasters, *The Coasters*, Atco, LP, 1958. The Big Bopper, *Chantilly Lance featuring The Big Bopper. Hellooo Baby!*, Mercury, LP, 1959. Jack Scott, *Jack Scott*, Carlton, LP, 1959. The Isley Brothers, *Shout!*, RCA Victor, LP, 1959.

OTIS AND DOC

BY PETER GURALNICK

Doc Pomus and Otis Blackwell, Maine, 1990.

Doc Pomus and Otis Blackwell met in 1949 at one of the little blues joints that dotted Brooklyn in the late 1940s and early 1950s. Otis, a diminutive black teenager in a ubiquitous derby hat, was working as a clothes presser while singing and writing songs on the side. "Otis had that gospel quiver in his voice," Doc wrote in a 1983 recollection. "He walked the floor when he sang, pointing his finger at the audience like a storefront reverend."

Doc, on the other hand, was a heavy-set young white guy with a pencil-thin mustache who stood stock-still when he sang, leaning on the crutches and steel leg braces he had been forced to rely on since contracting polio in 1931 at the age of six. Born Jerome Solon Felder, he had taken the stage name when he started working the blues circuit and writing songs. It made him feel, he said, like "some kind of hip midnight character," and besides it helped disguise his new calling from his conventional middle-class Jewish family.

They were instantly drawn to each other, both out of a common passion for the music and the seemingly unattainable dreams that they shared. Otis grew up in the predominantly black Bedford-Stuyvesant section of Brooklyn (Doc grew up, practically next door, in Williamsburg), but was first inspired by the country music he heard every Saturday afternoon at his neighborhood movie theater. "[Western star] Tex Ritter was my man. But where I lived I couldn't find musicians to play that type of music. So I started singing the blues."

Doc himself came under the spell of the blues when he heard Big Joe Turner's "Piney Brown Blues" at the age of fifteen. "It was," he said, "the transformation of my life." One night two or three years later he was hanging out at George's Tavern in Greenwich Village, listening to Frankie Newton's jazz combo. Just as the proprietor was about to throw him out for nursing a single beer the whole evening, Doc came up with the perfect alibi. "I'm a blues singer," he said. "I'm here to do a song." The song he sang, without any further preparation or ado, was, naturally, "Piney Brown Blues."

Doc was the first to break through. He was living in one of the transient midtown hotels that had become his home when Atlantic Records opened its doors on the ground floor of the Jefferson Hotel in 1947. He was, according to Atlantic founder Ahmet Ertegun, the first real songwriter to show up at the Atlantic office. One of the biggest thrills of his life came when his idol, Big Joe Turner, recorded his classically elegant "Still In Love" for Atlantic in 1952, a thrill that was only matched when Ray Charles cut a chilling version of his "Lonely Avenue" four years later.

By then Otis had achieved at least equal stature, first with Little Willie John's sinuous treatment of "Fever," then, on July 3, 1956, with Elvis Presley's recording of "Don't Be Cruel." Otis' subsequent success with Elvis ("All Shook Up" was only the first of many follow-ups), not to mention his delivery of such incendiary material as "Great Balls Of Fire" and "Breathless" to Jerry Lee Lewis the following year, gave him the opportunity to introduce Doc to Elvis' song publishers Hill and Range. Doc by this time had a young songwriting partner, Mort Shuman, and with Shuman he now wrote his first rock 'n' roll hits, top ten numbers for teen idols Fabian and Jimmy Clanton, "A Teenager In Love" for Dion and the Belmonts, and, in 1960, the song that would define the lyrical realism of his best work, the Drifters' "Save The Last Dance For Me."

In 1960, too, he started to write for Elvis, in whom he had sensed a kindred spirit from the first (when he initially heard "Mystery Train," he said with a fellow blues singer's perspective, it sounded like "someone coming out of the swamp"). He and Otis had huge hits with Elvis in 1961 and 1962—Doc with "Little Sister" and "His Latest Flame," Otis with "Return To Sender"—and each continued to write rhythm and blues-inflected numbers for him for release on both singles and movie soundtracks.

They remained friends to the end. Neither ever went back to a singing career but both remained fixed on their original creative vision. Doc defined songwriting success as putting technique at the service of feeling; his entire aesthetic was centered on writing from within, like the great blues singers whom he admired. What he valued most in Otis' writing was its simplicity, the utter uniqueness of his approach. "He is a complete original," Doc wrote appreciatively. "You hear a few bars, and you know it's him."

When I met Otis in 1990, he was living in Nashville, seemingly using up every penny he had gotten on his copyright renewals to make an album that he felt the world would not be able to ignore. Some of the musicians working the sessions tried to persuade him there was no need for him to spend his money so lavishly (or with such unstinting generosity), but Otis never seemed to consider cutting back and one weekend even flew in singer Dee Clark, who had recently suffered a stroke, because he thought sitting in on the session, if only as an observer, would cheer him up.

Otis himself had a debilitating stroke the following year, and the album was never finished. Doc died that same year, in 1991. He kept writing almost up to his last breath—working with his last (and most *simpatico*) songwriting partner, Dr. John, in his hospital room at Sloan-Kettering.

The songs that he wrote in the last ten years of his life were clearly among his greatest and most personal, matching, and in some cases surpassing, the quality of his biggest hits. With them he achieved the directness of expression that he had been striving for all his life. He knew it, and was proud of it—but he was just as proud of the faith he had kept with the music and the musicians that had inspired him.

There's a wonderful picture of Doc and Otis in their later years, at an arts fair in Maine that was honoring the work of both. Doc is sitting in his wheelchair, wearing a straw hat and a custom-made African shirt, as Otis, in a gesture of spontaneous affection, rests his head, almost cuddles up against one massive shoulder. Both men seem utterly relaxed, there is a contented smile on the face of each, and it is, of course, in many ways an altogether transparent picture of enduring friendship. In other ways its meaning remains opaque. Who could ever have imagined that two such very different personalities, growing up within a few miles of each other but separated by elements of class, education, and race, could have been brought together by a love they shared for something neither would have presumed to define? There they are, having arrived at the same destination neither by inheritance nor by choice but by something that chose them. You could write a song about it.

7 RECORDS
BY GREIL MARCUS

"STAGGER LEE THREW SEVEN... BILLY SWORE THAT HE THREW EIGHT."
Lloyd Price, "Stagger Lee" (1959)

I'm not going to cheat. I was asked to create a portrait of rock 'n' roll as it took shape between 1939 and 1959 through portraits of a handful of records, and I will. I won't use one record to talk about fifteen others. I won't go back to the forty-song LP collection of early Los Angeles group harmony singles I found in a bin outside of a Mexican restaurant for fifty cents. Nevertheless—

Early rock 'n' roll was so rich—so different from the world as everyone understood it, so different from every other sort of music, so different, one moment to the next, from *itself*—so crazy, so ridiculous, so stupid, so profound—that the problem is not simply that of limiting its story to seven or ten or even a thousand records. One could answer this charge solely with doo-wop records. You could do it with records from the Sun label ("It was like Paris in the 1920s," singer, bandleader, and producer Jim Dickinson once said of the black and white bohemian milieu that came and went through the doors of Sam Phillips' studio. "We saw a change in Memphis that affected the whole world"). You could do it with Clyde McPhatter records or Elvis Presley, records written and produced by Jerry Leiber and Mike Stoller, or for that matter records a teenage Phil Spector wished he'd produced but didn't (his first credited production worth remembering, Johnny Nash's shimmering "Some Of Your Loving," did not appear until 1961). Records solely from the Atlantic label. From New Orleans, or Chicago, Detroit, Los Angeles, Texas, or New York. You could choose your number from any year between 1953 through 1956 and call it quits—but not from any year before that.

It is not hard to go back to the 1940s or the very early 1950s and find prototypes, precursors, sketches, and models of what in 1951 in Cleveland, Ohio, on the radio, Alan Freed would call "rock 'n' roll." With only the barest exceptions—the Orioles' 1948 "It's Too Soon To Know" more than any other—you will not find the real thing. It doesn't matter that records with some variation of "rock" or "rocking" or even "rock and roll" were common in the 1940s—Roy Brown's 1947 "Good Rockin' Tonight," Wild Bill Moore's 1948 "We're Gonna Rock, We're Gonna Roll"—or that the likes of Freddie Slack's 1946 "The House Of Blue Lights" or Jackie Brenston's "Rocket '88' " are commonly wheeled onstage not only as early rock 'n' roll records but as the *first* rock 'n' roll record.

These records and many like them have rock 'n' roll themes. They may have rock 'n' roll shape. But they are not rock 'n' roll. The rhythms are slack, satisfied, finished. The singing is plummy, accepting, eager to please. No musician stands out, no one makes a fool of himself without signaling that he's only kidding. No one goes too far—which means that the music most of all affirms that the world is precisely as it seems, that there is no too far to reach.

Whole intellectual industries are devoted to proving that there is nothing new under the sun, that everything comes from something else—and to such a degree that one can never tell when one thing turned into something else. But it is the moment when something appears as if out of nowhere, when a work of art carries within itself a thrill of invention so strong that the work is itself its own manifesto—a moment that, in historical time, may be repeated again and again, until, as culture, that moment of appearance can seem to define art itself—that counts.

"We didn't know it," the Los Angeles rhythm and blues bandleader Johnny Otis once said of Fats Domino's "The Fat Man," "but there was a whole new art form brewing." That is the story. That's where history is made; that's where history is started over, as if for the first time, the slate wiped clean, one or a multitude rushing forward promising that anything is possible, and then proving it.

That's how I see it—and from that perspective, there is no reason to be responsible to tradition, to account for all the innovators, to follow the progression of the form (there is no such thing—the most shocking aspect of early rock 'n' roll records, as they sounded when they were first heard and as they sound now, is how many were *perfect*, simultaneously the first and last word the form needed to say). Because early rock 'n' roll was so rich, one can dive with a blindfold and earplugs into a vault filled with singles as Uncle Scrooge's was filled with money and come out clutching a few prizes that both raise the question of rock 'n' roll and answer it.

Fats Domino, "The Fat Man," Imperial, LP, 1950.

Fats Domino
THE FAT MAN
Imperial, 1950

In 2005, in the days after Hurricane Katrina destroyed New Orleans, word spread that Fats Domino could not be found. The Ninth Ward, where he was born in 1928, was gone, a graveyard underwater. People searched the fetid refugee camp of the Superdome, and the diasporas that were springing up in Baton Rouge and Houston, but Domino was already counted among the dead when he showed his face.

In the culture of celebrity that has overwhelmed the United States over the last twenty-five years, it seemed impossible that a famous person could suffer like an ordinary one—weren't celebrities protected, even made, by God? If a famous person could be swept away in a storm, faceless, uncounted, like anybody else, didn't that mean that there was no difference between a famous person and an ordinary one—and if that were so, how would the citizens of the republic understand their place on earth?

He was just two months short of twenty-one when he sat down at the piano in the J & M Studio on the corner of Rampart and Dumaine streets in New Orleans. It was December 10, 1949. The notes were no longer painted on the keys, as they had been when Domino was a small boy, but they might have been. There was an eight-man band behind him, but as the record opened, the piano was all you heard.

It came out like a river bursting over a dam, cymbal noise that sounded like the hiss of shellac, a strange, cantering high-step of a beat—the river surging, but then somehow developing a mind of its own, looking around at the trees and cars and people it was sweeping up and carrying with it, paying attention to its own movement, realizing it could change, that it could laugh, that it could make the screaming men and women fighting for breath turn their faces toward each other and dance with their eyes.

There was no beginning to the rolls of pleasure that came off of the piano—the first note felt as if it had been caught in the middle of some other song—and no end, because the sound was so sweet you couldn't bear the thought that it could end. Everything else was lagniappe: the five-foot-five-inches, 224-pound man squeaking a high "They call, they call me the fat man, 'cause I weight two hundred pounds" over the sliding bass rumbles under his fingers, the weird wah-wah passage he sings for an instrumental break, the saxophones now creeping up behind him, letting you see the band not playing with him but swaying, as if they were not his musicians but his audience, unable to stay still in their seats.

It was his first record—how many times in the history of rock 'n' roll, in a freedom promised by the form, has a performer done his or her best work the first time he or she stepped forward to be heard? It sold a million copies. In the next ten years, Fats Domino might have sold a hundred million more, but never again was he as loose in the water as he was that first time.

Best heard on *The Fats Domino Jukebox* (Crescent City Soul, 2002)

The Jewels, "Hearts of Stone," R and B, single, 1954.

The Jewels
HEARTS OF STONE
R and B, 1954

Rock 'n' roll was unlikely. The idea was that you turned on the radio expecting to hear something you could never have expected to hear—and you did.

The Jewels were a Los Angeles doo-wop group, but without the teenage romanticism of the Penguins or Ritchie Valens; one of them looked at least forty. "Haaaaaaaaaaaaarts made of stone," was the sound the leader opened his mouth to make, the first word a flag unfurling, the next three the line pulling the first word up the pole, where it stopped cold. The words were recognizable English; they were shaped like speech, as if the idea was to make a point, communicate a meaning. But then instantly the language changed. The leader was upended by a chorus that could have been made by a troupe of Hollywood gorillas pounding their chests. "Doody wah-dah do," they chanted, and if this wasn't a true, authentic, unmediated cultural transmission from an Africa of four hundred years before, then it was a cheap degraded parody of cannibals dancing around an iron pot, and it sounded better than the real thing ever could. The leader kept on, "Hearts made of stone, will never break," but now he sounded square. Listening now, you want him out of the way, so you can see who those fools behind him really are.

This was big rock, a big beat, but far more than that it was at once crazy and bottomless. Here were people who were somehow unafraid to appear in public, or at least the imaginary public of the airwaves, acting as if "wadda-wadda-wadda" held more truths than Shakespeare—and you believed it.

It is one of the great lost records. Except in Los Angeles, it was not a hit. Immediate cover versions by Otis Williams and the Charms, a black country and western singer passing as the leader of a rhythm and blues group (#1 on the rhythm and blues charts), by Red Foley, a white country singer (#4, country), and by the Fontaine Sisters, a white vocal group (#1 on the pop charts)—in every case a cold, straight treatment, taking the Jewels' record, a thing in itself, and extracting a mere composition, something that could have been written by anyone and in their hands felt as if it had been written by no one—literally shut the Jewels' mouths. "Once, at a show in Cleveland," the rhythm and blues historian Marv Goldberg writes, "the Jewels found themselves on the same bill as the Charms—and it was the latter group which got to sing 'Hearts Of Stone.'"

In essence, it was a murmur—loud, pounding, but insisting amid the noise it made that, as the punk group the Germs would put it in the same town more than a quarter of a century later, that what we do is secret. Was it that murmur—or the way, after the unstoppable "But they'll say no no (NO) no no (NO) no no (NO) no no (NO) no no (NO) no no (NO) no no (NO)" breakdown in the middle of the piece, the whole ensemble slid over the edge of the rhythm into a release that only people grasping for a melody can provide? We speak in unknown tongues, the Jewels said, and you can, too.

Best heard on *The Jewels!—B-Bomb Baby* (Gold Dust, 1996)

Little Richard, "Ready Teddy," Specialty, single, 1958.

Little Richard
READY TEDDY
Specialty, 1956

When Jerry Lee Lewis first appeared on national television, on *The Steve Allen Show* in 1957, Allen had tables and chairs thrown across the stage as Lewis hammered out "Whole Lotta Shakin' Goin' On." What would he have done with Little Richard? Set him on fire?

What made rock 'n' roll different from the music that came before it was contingency and doubt, which when brought together exploded into freedom. You hear it in the rhythms, in the lift and reach of the vocals, in the way you can actually feel a singer or a band surprised at what they're hearing, at what they themselves are doing. It's Scotty Moore exclaiming "Damn, nigger!" in wonderment and awe in the midst of Elvis' first session in Memphis in 1954; it's the runaway train of the third take of "Ready Teddy," again in the J & M Studio in New Orleans, but this day the seven musicians realizing that a runaway train means they can get away. From everything. From their lives as they were raised to live them. From the expectations of everyone around them, themselves most of all. From white America, and into an escape into the America that was always promised and has never been. Into sex, drink, drugs, an endless night with the hint of a dawn as the smile the night offers those who can hold off sleep.

Ping! goes the guitar, out of place, the guitarist unable to stop *his* smile, because this is take three, he knows what's coming, but he knows what's coming is going to go farther than it has before. This time it's Lee Allen's sax break that breaches the levee each man carries with himself. With the band crashing behind him like buildings blown up in sequence, Allen sounds like three of himself, negating every screaming shock Richard has already delivered. Earl Palmer, the most elegant of drummers, is smashing up a bar. Richard himself holds back at first, as if intimidated by the force he has himself let loose, but then bearing down harder on his piano, until you can almost feel it resisting him: *Leave something for the poor!* You shake your head in disbelief that anything like this could ever have happened, that it could have been recorded, that it is present before you now as if it is happening for the first time, not a representation of anything but the event itself.

It is probably the eighth take when they get the version that will be sent out into the world to convulse those who can hear it and confuse everyone else. Convulse—until the very moment when silence takes over, when the train goes into the air, into a kind of suspension, where if you look down you'll fall, but you don't look down, and suddenly everything is quiet. In an instant, then, noise is gone and the world is defined only by what is severe, cool, geometric, Malevich's erasure of chaos, his few planes signifying the opening of all doors, but not yet, because in this moment you stand still, gazing into the future. This is what happens when the band disappears and Richard goes into a trance. "I shuffle to the left," he says; "I shuffle to the right." Yes, you think, in a trance yourself, that must be it.

Best heard on Little Richard, *The Specialty Sessions* (1989–1990)

Buchanan and Goodman, "The Flying Saucer," Luniverse, single, 1956.

Buchanan and Goodman
THE FLYING SAUCER PARTS 1 & 2
Luniverse, 1956

The notion that rock 'n' roll was so strange it had to come from outer space was not arcane. It was part of the deep self-consciousness of the music, and the self-consciousness of its audience. There was the sense that something truly new was taking shape, that people were caught up in a great game without rules or expectations. There was a sense that all of this was a joke. And there was the sense that to commit oneself to novelty, adventure, and excitement as completely as the new music and its fans seemed to have done was to risk that your whole sense of who you were, what life was for, and what the future promised, might vanish in an instant.

The thrill of rock 'n' roll was frightening. The message that unscrolled at the beginning of the 1983 film *Strange Invaders*—a parody of 1950s flying saucer movies—seemed like a smug look back at the grown-ups who didn't get it: "It was a simple time, of Eisenhower, twin beds, and Elvis from the waist up—a safe, quiet moment in history. As a matter of fact, except for the communists and rock 'n' roll, there was not much to fear. Not much at all . . . until that night." But even its truest fans were, in moments, afraid of Rock 'n' Roll. It made promises you might not be able to live up to. It affirmed a utopia of fun, speed, and pathos everyday life might never match. And, in a belief that united the people who hated the music and the people who loved it, almost everyone was certain that it would end.

This was not the tone of Billy Lee Riley's 1956 "Flying Saucers Rock 'n' Roll," a crash-through-the-swamp in which Riley, who could sing like a chainsaw when it was called for, insisted that not only had spacemen "brought rock 'n' roll all the way from Mars," but that "the little green men taught me how to do the bop." And it was not the tone of "The Flying Saucer," in which two comedy writers produced an idiot's version of Orson Welles' 1938 radio play *The War Of The Worlds*. The device was simple and irresistible: a flying saucer is about to land on earth, and everybody—humans and aliens—speaks in rock 'n' roll. "Are you there?" says a reporter, knocking on the spaceship door: a sample from the Smiley Lewis hit has the spaceman answering, "I *hear* you knocking, but you can't come in." The "outer-space disc jockey" plays "Earth Angel." "And now I believe we're about to hear the words of the first spaceman ever to land on earth," says the reporter. What do you think he says? Why, he sounds just like Little Richard: "A WOP BOP A LOO BOP A LOP BAM BOOM!"

Rock 'n' roll was weird; it was also ordinary language. All those stupid little catchphrases and throwaways and nonsense syllables could say anything. Think of the greatest of all alien-invader movies, Tim Burton's 1996 *Mars Attacks!* (where the only defense against the Martians is Slim Whitman's "Indian Love Call," an anti-rock record that melts their brains), with Jack Nicholson's president of the United States pleading "Can't we all just . . . get along?" before the smiling little Martian smokes him—and then give the story back to Buchanan and Goodman's president, and imagine how right the moment they conjured up was, a world-historical crisis changed into a stomp not even Martians could resist: "Here is a news item from Washington," a broadcaster says, in a nervous tone that matches that of the first reports of the assassination of President John F. Kennedy all too closely. "The president has just issued a statement to the spacemen, and we quote—" And then, in a perfect cut-in, Carl Perkins is the president of the United States. There's a lift as the chief steps out, his guitar bouncing in his hands, his legs jumping, a welcome so warm you just know everything is going to work out fine: "You can do anything, but lay off of my blue suede shoes." No White House speechwriter could have come up with that.

Best heard on Dickie Goodman, *All Time Novelty Hits* (Goodman Brothers, 2006) and the anthology *Weird, Wild & Wacky* (Time-Life, 1991)

Dion and the Belmonts, "I Wonder Why," Laurie, single, 1958.

Dion and the Belmonts
I WONDER WHY
Laurie, 1958

Contingency and doubt were never more at the heart of the rock 'n' roll style than in doo-wop. All doo-wop began a cappella—or, as it was spelled in New York and New Jersey, where a whole cult grew up around unaccompanied vocal groups, "acappella"—which meant that as groups formed on street corners or at the bottom of high-school stairwells, there was nothing to fall back on. The voices of yourself and the guys around you had to make every change, find every transition hidden in the melody, create a unique drama out of the same old ballads—"The Glory Of Love," "A Sunday Kind Of Love," "Gloria"—everybody else sang. Some of the most unearthly of all early rock 'n' roll recordings are early 1960s a cappella rehearsals by the Detroit harmony group Nolan Strong and the Diablos, "Since I Fell For You" and "(So Long) Gee, I Hate To See You Go," sung with an affection, a comradeship almost from beyond the grave—each singer forced not only to speak to every other singer, but obligated, somehow, to speak for every other singer even as he heard them speaking to him—that neither Sam Cooke, Jesse Belvin, Jerry Butler, or anyone else ever quite touched.

The first record Dion and the Belmonts made had musical instruments on it, but you barely noticed, if you noticed at all. In fact, there are no instruments until Carlo Mastrangelo and then the rest of the group make it through the first thirteen seconds—which might as well be the whole of the song. When they repeat the same figures at the end of the recording—with drums, bass, and piano now behind them—it has lost its flair, the trembling joy that comes when you're working without a net.

Dion is the formal leader—singing words in English, "When you're with me, I'm sure you're always true," etc.—but Mastrangelo, mouthing "Din din din din din din din" until he finally reaches the long "Dah" that allows the other singers into the music—never surrenders the song. His low tenor is everywhere, constant, his doo-wop language pulling back against the chiming high notes that Dion and the other Belmonts hit again and again, ringing bells as Mastrangelo races through every back alley in the Bronx, bringing the news.

They are faster than sound. They achieve what true speed in rock 'n' roll always has—tenths, hundredths of seconds where a match is struck in the midst of the storm. You revel in the rush, but it's those moments of suspension that call you back—for me, the slight shift one minute thirty-nine seconds in, just after the outrageous "Wop/ Wop/ Wop wop wop" from four Italian boys (because it's the doo-wop syllable with the percussive force they need, and because they are mouthing a forbidden word) when two notes from the bass guitar turn the song over, physically, like Astaire leading Rogers. But you don't imagine the Belmonts dancing—their matching suits, their matching gestures, elbows to one side, knees to the other—you imagine them doing back flips. It's a figure-skating final in the Olympics, and everyone else has come out with some Celine Dion number or "I Will Always Love You" or even some flaccid techno track—and then the judges throw down their cards and run for their lives.

Best heard on *The Very Best of Dion and the Belmonts* (EMI, 2005). See also Nolan Strong and the Diablos, *Daddy Rock* (Fortune, 1984)

The "5" Royales, "The Slummer The Slum," King, single, 1958.

The "5" Royales
THE SLUMMER THE SLUM
King, 1958

Rock 'n' roll was not afraid of its own stupidity. "The Purple People Eater," a hit in the summer of 1958, was so fascinatingly moronic people simply could not turn away from it; in San Francisco, a new top forty station announced itself by playing the record for twenty-four hours straight. The "5" Royales were a vocal group from Winston-Salem, North Carolina, led by the guitarist Lowman Pauling, who ran rings around Eric Clapton and Jimi Hendrix before they ever stepped on a stage. They made many great records, including the original versions of "Think" (taken by James Brown) and "Dedicated To The One I Love" (the Shirelles), but in a career played out mostly in the shadows, "The Slummer The Slum" was their strangest.

"Slummer the slum," the group hammered down, sounding for all the world as if they were promoting a new dance, the Slumety Stomp, when hidden in their sound was a three-word protest song. The leader announced himself as if he were the Lone Ranger—but the Lone Ranger with a scary, stop-time rhythm he used instead of silver bullets. The words Paulman wrote were among the most Gothic, and at the same time the most shameless, in all of American music.

"Don't try
To figure out
Where I come from
Now, don't try
To figure out
Where I come from"

He could have stopped right there—

"I could be a smart guy from Wall Street
I could be the Purple People Eater's son"

But you couldn't tell—maybe it *was* a new dance. The leader sang as hard metal notes flew out of his fingers:

"Well, now, that's only one difference
That's only one difference
Between me and you
You've got money in your pocket
And I've got a hole in my shoe
All from doing the slummer the slum . . ."

The song ends, and you can't believe what you've just heard—the guitar playing that is absolutely modern, a style still waiting for someone to catch up with it. And then you hear the words, and you can't believe they mean what they say. Figure out where he came from? Not a chance in the world.

Best heard on *Monkey Hips and Rice: The "5" Royales Anthology* (Rhino, 1994)

The Fleetwoods, "Come Softly To Me," Dolphin, single, 1959.

The Fleetwoods
COME SOFTLY TO ME
Dolphin, 1959

The sounds traveled across the country, around the world. One spot they lighted down was Olympia, Washington. There at Olympia High School, seniors Gretchen Christopher and Barbara Ellis were auditioning for a third girl to sing the Five Satins' "In The Still Of The Night" with them. The audition didn't work out; disappointed, they sat down at the piano and worked out a song called "Come Softly." Then they began looking for a trumpet player for a new arrangement of "Stormy Weather." Gary Troxel of the Blue Comets showed up. Nothing worked—except a new sound. Rearranged around the Del Vikings' "Come Go With Me," and renamed "Come Softly To Me," to take some of the sex out of the title, the song was a #1 hit. The feeling was soft and gentle, but behind Troxel's lead—"Dum dum, dum do dum, doobey do"—Christopher and Ellis, almost whispering "Come softly, darling," were implacable, hard, demanding. The record was a dream the radio dreamed for you—even if the truest version of the dream was never on the radio at all. That is an a cappella rehearsal, where the singers surrender themselves completely, exposed to the melody, allowing it to strip them naked, leaving them unashamed. "Oh!" says Christopher or Ellis. "I was busy kissing Gary." She giggles. "Tee hee," Troxel says, as if he's too nice for these sluts, but hell, he's a guy, and when a girl throws herself at you, what are you going to do? And then the song takes them all into its tunnel. As the era ends, they disappear into it; they don't even wave goodbye.

Best heard on *Come Softly To Me: The Very Best Of The Fleetwoods* (EMI, 1993)

CHUCK BERRY

Charles Edward Anderson Berry was born on October 18, 1926 in St. Louis, Missouri and lives in Wentzville, Missouri. He was introduced to Leonard Chess, head of Chess Records in Chicago, by blues great Muddy Waters. "Maybellene," his first single for Chess, was released in 1955 and inspired by the old-time fiddle tune "Ida Red," popularized by the country acts Roy Acuff and His Smoky Mountain Boys, and Bob Wills and His Texas Playboys. His songs such as "School Days," "Sweet Little Sixteen," and "Almost Grown" chronicle teenage life in the United States during the 1950s. Other classic hits written and recorded by Chuck Berry include "Roll Over Beethoven," "Rock & Roll Music," "Johnny B. Goode," "Carol," and "Back In The U.S.A." By marrying country and western guitar lines to a rhythm and blues beat behind incisive and witty lyrics, he created a style that is widely influential to the present day. His songs have been recorded by the Beatles, the Rolling Stones, the Beach Boys, Elvis Presley, Jerry Lee Lewis, Buddy Holly, Carl Perkins, Ricky Nelson, Johnny Rivers, Buck Owens, George Jones, the Yardbirds, the Animals, Rod Stewart, Bob Seger, Linda Ronstadt, Emmylou Harris, Electric Light Orchestra, the Grateful Dead, and Jimi Hendrix. He appeared in the films *Rock, Rock, Rock*, *Mister Rock And Roll*, *Go, Johnny Go!*, and *Jazz On A Summer's Day*.

EDDIE COCHRAN

Born Edward Ray Cochrane on October 3, 1938 in Albert Lea, Minnesota, Eddie Cochran died in an automobile accident in which Gene Vincent was seriously injured on April 17, 1960 in Chippenham, Wiltshire, England. He was the singer, guitarist, and frequently the writer of such rock anthems as "Summertime Blues," "C'mon Everybody," "Somethin' Else," "Nervous Breakdown," "Cut Across Shorty," and "Twenty Flight Rock."

BO DIDDLEY

Bo Diddley was born Otha Ellas Bates on December 30, 1928 in McComb, Mississippi. Also known as Ellas McDaniel, his stage name was derived from the diddley bow, a primitive one-stringed musical instrument. He currently lives in Archer, Florida. At seven years of age, he moved to Chicago, Illinois, where he took up the violin, replacing it with the guitar at the age of ten. After seeing bluesman John Lee Hooker, he decided to become a musician. In 1955 he joined the Chess Records' Checker label. "Bo Diddley" and its b-side "I'm A Man" was his first single, and each side became a #1 rhythm and blues hit. His lyrics were frequently adapted from children's songs and other folk material, and he popularized what came to be known as the Bo Diddley Beat in his music. A propulsive, rumba-based rhythm played by guitar and maracas, it is closely related to hambone, a street style in which rhythm is produced by slapping and patting the arms, legs, chest, and cheeks in order to accompany recited rhymes. Among the many artists whose recordings employ variations of the Bo Diddley Beat are Buddy Holly ("Not Fade Away"), Johnny Otis ("Willie And The Hand Jive"), Dee Clark ("Hey Little Girl"), Elvis Presley ("His Latest Flame"), the Who ("Magic Bus"), the Strangeloves ("I Want Candy"), Smokey Robinson and the Miracles ("Mickey's Monkey"), and Bruce Springsteen ("She's The One"). With its emphasis on an insistent, primitive rhythm and frequently spoken-sung lyrics, his music may be considered a precursor of both hip hop and rap.

FATS DOMINO

Antoine Domino was born on February 26, 1928 in New Orleans, Louisiana, and adopted the name Fats as a tribute to his hero Fats Waller. He continues to live in his hometown. Inspired by Albert Ammons, he joined trumpeter Dave Bartholomew's band on piano in the mid-1940s. Signed as a solo artist to Imperial Records of Los Angeles, his first recording was a variation of Champion Jack Dupree's "Junker's Blues" that he called "The Fat Man," which rose to #2 on the national rhythm and blues charts in 1949. After a string of top ten rhythm and blues hits in the early 1950s, his "Ain't It A Shame" crossed over and cracked the pop top ten in 1955, despite a cover by Pat Boone that attained the #1 position. "Ain't It A Shame" is the first of eleven top ten singles that he was to score over the next five years. With thirty-five top forty singles overall, he was the best-selling African American recording artist of the 1950s, appealing equally to white and black audiences. Other big hits, all recorded in New Orleans, include "I'm In Love Again," "Blueberry Hill," "Blue Monday," "I'm Walkin'," "Whole Lotta Loving," and "Walking To New Orleans." Many of his hits were cowritten with his producer and bandleader Dave Bartholomew. His was a key influence on Allen Toussaint and the New Orleans rhythm and blues artists of the 1960s whom he produced, Paul McCartney of the Beatles, and Billy Joel. He appeared in the films *The Girl Can't Help It*, *Jamboree*, *The Big Beat*, and *Shake, Rattle And Rock!*

BILL HALEY

Born William John Clifton Haley Jr. on July 6, 1925 in Highland Park, Michigan, Bill Haley died on February 9, 1981 in Harlingen, Texas. Bill Haley began his career in the post war 1940s as the singer in a number of country bands, among them the Down Homers, the Four Aces of Western Swing, and the Saddlemen, in the Northeastern United States. Looking to vary his repertoire, he released the proto-rock anthem "Rock The Joint" as by Bill Haley and the Saddlemen on the Philadelphia-based Essex label in 1952. The recording featured an eight-bar guitar solo by Danny Cedrone, which he duplicated note for note two years later on "Rock Around The Clock." Billed as Bill Haley with Haley's Comets, his "Crazy Man, Crazy" made the pop charts for Essex in 1953. Signing with Decca Records in 1954, the band, now known as Bill Haley and His Comets, entered a New York studio with Milt Gabler, producer of Louis Jordan in the 1940s, and recorded "(We're Gonna) Rock Around The Clock" which, released as the b-side of "Thirteen Women (And Only One Man In Town)," failed to make an impression. However, when "Rock Around The Clock" was heard playing over the opening credits of the film *Blackboard Jungle*, it became a #1 hit in the U.S. and an international phenomenon in 1955. In the meantime, a cover of "Big" Joe Turner's #1 rhythm and blues hit "Shake, Rattle And Roll" had climbed to #7 on the pop charts for Bill Haley and His Comets in 1954, whose other hits would include "See You Later, Alligator," "R-O-C-K," "Razzle Dazzle" and "Burn That Candle." These songs were also featured in the band's performances in the films *Rock Around The Clock* and *Don't Knock The Rock*. Bill Haley and His Comets was the first band to introduce and popularize rock 'n' roll music on an international scale.

BUDDY HOLLY

Born Charles Hardin Holley on September 7, 1936 in Lubbock, Texas, Buddy Holly died on February 3, 1959 near Clear Lake, Iowa. After a false start to his career with Decca Records in Nashville, during which a version of "That'll Be The Day" was recorded but unreleased, Buddy Holly re-recorded the song with his band, the Crickets, at Norman Petty's studio in Clovis, New Mexico in 1957. This new version secured them a contract with the Decca subsidiaries Brunswick and Coral Records in which the Crickets' recordings were released by Brunswick while those by Buddy Holly as a solo artist appeared on the Coral label. "That'll Be The Day" rose to #1 on the pop charts and #2 rhythm and blues, and was followed in short order by the hits "Peggy Sue," "Oh, Boy!" and "Maybe Baby." The Crickets' original lineup of Buddy Holly, lead guitar, Niki Sullivan, rhythm guitar, Joe B. Mauldin, bass, and Jerry Allison, drums, establishes the look and sound of the classic, two guitars, bass, and drums rock band. In late 1958 Buddy Holly split from the Crickets and producer Norman Petty, married, and moved to Greenwich Village in New York City. He was killed in the crash of a small plane along with Ritchie Valens and J.P. "The Big Bopper" Richardson in early 1959, an event immortalized in the 1972 song "American Pie" by Don McLean as "the day the music died." The Beatles, who named themselves in honor of the Crickets, recorded Buddy Holly's "Words Of Love" and the Rolling Stones recorded his "Not Fade Away" during the early phase of the British invasion. Other acts that have covered his songs include Bobby Vee, the Everly Brothers, Carl Perkins, Bobby Fuller, Waylon Jennings, Mickey Gilley, Linda Ronstadt, Blind Faith, Santana, Commander Cody and the Lost Planet Airmen, the Grateful Dead, Peter and Gordon, the Beach Boys, and the Hollies, whose name is an homage to Buddy.

JERRY LEE LEWIS

Born on September 29, 1935 in Ferriday, Louisiana, Jerry Lee Lewis currently lives in Nesbit, Mississippi. His earliest inspiration was Jimmie Rodgers, whose meld of country and blues styled vocals he combined with gospel fervor and boogie-woogie piano to create a musical persona all his own. At the age of twenty-one, he moved to Memphis, where he played piano on Carl Perkins and Billy Lee Riley sessions at Sun Records. His own Sun recordings were billed as by Jerry Lee Lewis and His Pumping Piano. His biggest hits, "Whole Lotta Shakin' Goin' On," "Great Balls Of Fire," and "Breathless," were equally successful in the pop and rhythm and blues fields. Jerry Lee Lewis' career suffered a precipitous ten-year decline after it was revealed he had taken his thirteen-year-old cousin as his third wife (prior to divorcing the second). He reemerged with "Another Place, Another Time" in 1968, the first in a long line of country hits he enjoyed throughout the 1970s while never straying far from his rock 'n' roll roots. The spontaneity and dynamism of his style had a pervasive influence on the entirety of rock 'n' roll; his piano playing has influenced the work of Leon Russell, Billy Joel, and Elton John. He appeared in the films *Jamboree* and *High School Confidential!*, in which he performed the title song.

CARL PERKINS

Carl Lee Perkins was born on April 9, 1932 near Tiptonville, Tennessee, and died on January 19, 1998 in Jackson, Tennessee. His single "Blue Suede Shoes" and its b-side "Honey Don't," recorded at the end of 1955 at the Sun Studio in Memphis, was the first rockabilly record to top the pop, rhythm and blues, and country charts. His guitar skills have had a strong influence on George Harrison of the Beatles, who recorded several of his songs, including "Honey Don't," "Matchbox," and "Everybody's Trying To Be My Baby."

ELVIS PRESLEY

Elvis Aron Presley was born on January 8, 1935 in Tupelo, Mississippi and died of a heart attack on August 16, 1977 in Memphis, Tennesse.
He recorded bluesman Arthur "Big Boy" Crudup's "That's All Right" for Sun Records in 1954, when he was nineteen years old. A version of bluegrass pioneer Bill Monroe's "Blue Moon Of Kentucky" was on its b-side. Accompanied by Scotty Moore on guitar and Bill Black on bass, their subsequent four Sun singles continued the pattern of coupling a blues song with a country song. He signed with RCA Victor in late 1955, under the guidance of Colonel Tom Parker, the impresario who would manage him throughout the length of his career. His first recording for the label, "Heartbreak Hotel," hit #1 on the pop and country charts and was #3 in the rhythm and blues field. With sensational television performances throughout 1956 on Tommy and Jimmy Dorsey's Stage Show and the Milton Berle, Steve Allen, and Ed Sullivan shows, he was acclaimed by his teenage public as "The King Of Rock And Roll." Though puritan America was offended by his suggestive on-stage behavior, nothing could slow his momentum. Both sides of his single, "Hound Dog" and "Don't Be Cruel," would top all three charts, pop, country, and rhythm and blues, making it the most successful record of the 1950s. He served in the U.S. Army from March 24, 1958 through March 5, 1960, and resumed his career upon his discharge, focusing on recording and films. He had starred in *Love Me Tender*, *Loving You*, *Jailhouse Rock*, and *King Creole* prior to his Army service, and made 27 more feature films over the course of his career. Elvis Presley returned to television in 1968 in what came to be known as his "Comeback" special. It was a resounding success, after which he spent the remainder of his life as a highly popular concert attraction. Drawing inspiration from all the music that had preceded him, he, in turn, influenced many of those who came after, from the rockabillies who followed in his wake, to international stars such as Cliff Richard and Johnny Hallyday, from the British invasion of the Beatles and the Rolling Stones to punk rockers like the Sex Pistols and the Clash.

LITTLE RICHARD

Richard Wayne Penniman was born on December 5, 1932 in Macon, Georgia and resides today in Los Angeles, California. In the early 1950s, he recorded for RCA Victor and, with the Tempo Toppers, for Peacock Records in a traditional rhythm and blues mode. However, he found his voice upon signing with Specialty Records of Los Angeles in 1955. Inspired by the blues shouting of Billy Wright and the gospel stylings of Marion Williams, his uninhibited, exhilarating vocals on "Tutti Frutti" proved to be a breakout performance in spite of a cover record by Pat Boone. Similar smash hits, recorded in New Orleans with producer Bumps Blackwell, followed in rapid succession, including "Long Tall Sally," "Rip It Up," "Ready Teddy," "The Girl Can't Help It," "Lucille," "Jenny, Jenny," "Keep A-Knockin'," and "Good Golly, Miss Molly." He quit the music business at his peak in 1958 to go to college, where he earned a degree in theology. Ordained as a minister, he returned to record gospel music and, ultimately, pop music, too. He has had a major impact on the music world: Paul McCartney of the Beatles cited him as a primary influence, and James Brown, Otis Redding, Jimi Hendrix, and Prince, each in his own way, followed in his footsteps. Elvis Presley recorded four Little Richard songs during his first year at RCA Victor. Little Richard appeared in the films *The Girl Can't Help It*, *Don't Knock The Rock*, and *Mister Rock And Roll*.

GENE VINCENT

Born Vincent Eugene Craddock on February 11, 1935 in Norfolk, Virginia, Gene Vincent died on October 12, 1971 in Newhall, California. Recorded for Capitol with his band the Blue Caps, his first hit single, "Be-Bop-A-Lula" (1956) and its b-side "Woman Love," was banned by some radio stations due to suggestive content. He eventually moved to Great Britain where he became a major influence on the early English rock scene.

39-59 CHRONOLOGY

BY GREGG GELLER

1938

DECEMBER 23
From Spirituals To Swing, a concert featuring, among others, Count Basie and His Orchestra, Jimmy Rushing, Helen Humes, Big Bill Broonzy, Sister Rosetta Tharpe, Big Joe Turner, and the boogie-woogie pianists Albert Ammons, Meade Lux Lewis, and Pete Johnson is held at Carnegie Hall in New York City. Boogie-woogie, which dates back to the 1920s, will become a defining musical trend of the ensuing decade.

1939

APRIL 20
Her label, Columbia Records, having rejected the idea, Billie Holiday records the anti-lynching anthem "Strange Fruit" for producer Milt Gabler's Commodore Records in New York City.

JULY 5
Roy Acuff and His Smoky Mountain Boys record the old-time fiddle tune "Ida Red" for Vocalion Records in Memphis. The same label's Bob Wills and His Texas Playboys had recorded a western swing version of the song in Dallas eight months earlier. It will be the inspiration for Chuck Berry's "Maybellene" sixteen years later.

SEPTEMBER 3
When Germany invades Poland, Great Britain and France declare war on Germany. World War II begins.

OCTOBER 14
Broadcast Music Inc., or BMI, is founded by radio executives seeking an alternative to the long-established ASCAP. The new, nonprofit, performing rights organization is the first to represent songwriters in the fields of jazz, blues, gospel, country, and folk music, thus providing them entrée to exposure they had never previously been afforded.

DECEMBER 7
The Cats and the Fiddle vocal group record the prototypical doo-wop ballad "I Miss You So" for Bluebird Records in Chicago.

DECEMBER 24
A second *From Spirituals To Swing* concert is held at Carnegie Hall.

1940

MAY 12
Germany invades and occupies France.

SEPTEMBER 7
"Blueberry Hill" by Glenn Miller and His Orchestra on Bluebird peaks at #2 on the pop charts for the first of four weeks in which it is kept from the top slot by "I'll Never Smile Again" by Victor's Tommy Dorsey and His Orchestra with the Pied Pipers, featuring Frank Sinatra on his first #1 record. "Blueberry Hill" will stall yet again at #2 in a version by Fats Domino sixteen years later.

1941

APRIL 23
Accompanied by Big Bill Broonzy on guitar, Lil Green records "Why Don't You Do Right?" for Bluebird in Chicago. It is derived from the Harlem Hamfats' 1936 Decca recording of "The Weed Smoker's Dream."

DECEMBER 7
Japan attacks the American fleet at Pearl Harbor in Hawaii, drawing the United States into World War II.

1942

MAY 26
Lionel Hampton and His Orchestra record "Flying Home" for Decca Records in New York. It features a tenor sax solo by Illinois Jacquet, which becomes the model for the myriad of honking saxophone solos that will follow over the next twenty years.

JULY 27
Peggy Lee, fronting Benny Goodman and His Orchestra, records an uptempo version of Lil Green's "Why Don't You Do Right?" for Columbia Records in New York. It remains her signature song until she records the Little Willie John hit "Fever" sixteen years later.

DECEMBER 30
Having left Tommy Dorsey and His Orchestra three months earlier, Frank Sinatra appears on the bill at New York's Paramount Theater for the New Year's show as an extra added attraction to Benny Goodman and His Orchestra featuring Peggy Lee. His solo turn is greeted by hysterical, swooning teenage fans known as "bobby-soxers" and his two-week engagement is extended to eight weeks.

1943

OCTOBER 23
"Boogie Woogie," Tommy Dorsey and His Orchestra's 1938 Victor Records hit revival of "Pine Top's Boogie Woogie" from 1928, re-enters the pop charts for a thirty-week run, then charts again in each of the two succeeding years.

1944

APRIL 15
Featuring Nat Cole on piano and vocals, "Straighten Up And Fly Right" by the King Cole Trio, on Capitol Records, enters the Harlem Hit Parade where it will ultimately achieve a #1 ranking. Two weeks later, it enters the pop charts where it will peak at #9 and, a month after that, the folk charts, peaking at #1.

JUNE 6
D-Day. The Allies, under the command of General Dwight D. Eisenhower, land in Normandy and begin the push to reclaim Europe from the Axis Powers.

JULY 2
At producer Norman Granz's first *Jazz At The Philharmonic* concert in Los Angeles, Illinois Jacquet, in a performance of "Blues, Part 2" with Jack McVea, Nat Cole, Les Paul, and others, elaborates and expands upon his "Flying Home" solo. The sensational event is recorded "live," one of the first such recordings to be made available commercially.

OCTOBER 21
"I Wonder" by Pvt. Cecil Gant, billed as "The G.I. Sing-Sation" by his label Gilt-Edge Records, enters the Harlem Hit Parade. Taking the country by storm, it peaks at #1. Though Gilt-Edge fades from the scene, it is a harbinger of hundreds of independent labels that will emerge in the years following World War II, notably Specialty, King, Chess, Atlantic, Savoy, Apollo, Modern, Aladdin, Imperial, Sun, Duke, and Peacock.

1945

APRIL 12
Franklin Delano Roosevelt, president of the United States, dies at sixty-three. Harry S. Truman succeeds him.

APRIL 30
Nazi Führer Adolf Hitler, fifty-six, commits suicide in his bunker in Berlin as the Allies bear down on Germany.

MAY 7
Germany agrees to an unconditional surrender in Reims, France.

MAY 8
Victory in Europe Day. Cease-fire in Europe takes effect at one minute past midnight.

JUNE 9
The Decca recording of "Who Threw The Whiskey In The Well" by Lucky Millinder and His Orchestra, featuring vocalist Wynonie Harris, enters the race records charts, where it will spend twenty weeks, eight of them at #1, and cross over to the pop charts, peaking at #7.

AUGUST
Helen Humes and the Bill Doggett Octet record "Be-Baba-Leba" for Philo Records in Los Angeles, which peaks at #3 on the race records charts and paves the way for a plethora of nonsense lyrics.

AUGUST 6
The United States drops the atomic bomb on Hiroshima and, three days later, on Nagasaki.

AUGUST 11
"The Honeydripper (Parts 1 & 2)" by Joe Liggins on Exclusive Records enters the race records charts where it will spend twenty-seven weeks, eighteen of them at #1, and cross over to the pop charts, peaking at #13.

AUGUST 15
Victory in Japan Day. The Allies announce that Japan has agreed to end all military operations in the Pacific. World War II is over.

SEPTEMBER 2
Japan signs a formal surrender agreement on board the battleship USS *Missouri*.

1946

MAY 18
Boogie-woogie pianist Freddie Slack's recording of "The House Of Blue Lights" for Capitol Records, featuring Ella Mae Morse on vocals, enters the pop charts where it will reach #8. It is the biggest of several hits in the style, including "Cow Cow Boogie," "Down The Road Apiece" and "Beat Me, Daddy (Eight To The Bar)" in which he is involved.

SEPTEMBER 6
Bluesman Arthur "Big Boy" Crudup records "That's All Right" for RCA Victor in Chicago.

SEPTEMBER 16
Bill Monroe and His Blue Grass Boys record "Blue Moon Of Kentucky" for Columbia Records in Chicago.

SEPTEMBER 30
T-Bone Walker, pioneer of the electric guitar, records "Bobby Sox Blues" with Jack McVea's All-Stars for Black & White Records in Hollywood. The song, addressed to a teenager with "a head full of nothing but stage, screen, and radio" presages Chuck Berry's "Sweet Little Sixteen," still eleven years in the future.

1947

FEBRUARY 8
"Open The Door, Richard" by Jack McVea enters the race records charts. Based on a vaudeville routine performed by comedian Dusty Fletcher since the 1930s, his Black & White Records release is soon joined by versions by Count Basie on RCA Victor, Louis Jordan on Decca, the Three Flames on Columbia, and Fletcher himself on National, all of which go top ten on the pop charts as well, where they are joined by versions by the Charioteers on Columbia and the Pied Pipers on Capitol.

APRIL 15
Jackie Robinson of the Brooklyn Dodgers breaks the color line, becoming the first black player in Major League Baseball.

JULY
Roy Brown records "Good Rockin' Tonight" for Deluxe Records in New Orleans but it doesn't hit the charts until after a version by Wynonie Harris has done so the following year, when it peaks at #11.

JULY 5
U.S. Secretary of State George Marshall, in a commencement address at Harvard University, proposes the European Recovery Program in which the United States will, during the next four years, fund the economic reconstruction of Western Europe after the devastation of World War II. The Marshall Plan proves to be a resounding success.

AUGUST 9
"Move It On Over" is the first of thirty-six singles by Hank Williams on the MGM label to hit the folk or country and western charts during the next six years; thirty-three of them reach the top ten, with eleven going all the way to #1.

OCTOBER 14
U.S. Air Force pilot Chuck Yeager becomes the first man to break the sound barrier.

DECEMBER 28
Wynonie "Mr. Blues" Harris records Roy Brown's "Good Rockin' Tonight" for King Records in Cincinnati. In twenty-five weeks on the race records charts, it peaks at #1.

1948

JANUARY 30
Avatar of nonviolent civil disobedience, Mohandas Gandhi is assassinated by a Hindu fanatic in New Delhi.

MAY 14
The State of Israel is established.

JULY
The Orioles, with Sonny Til singing lead, record "It's Too Soon To Know" for It's a Natural Records in New York. A #1 single on the race records charts, it also dents the pop charts, peaking at #13.

JULY 26
By executive order President Harry S. Truman ends racial segregation in the U.S. military.

NOVEMBER
John Lee Hooker records "Boogie Chillen" in Detroit, which will top the race records charts for Modern Records.

NOVEMBER 6
Vernon and Gladys Presley and their thirteen-year-old son Elvis move to Memphis from Tupelo, Mississippi.

1949

MARCH 31
RCA Victor introduces the 7-inch, 45 rpm single, and a record changer on which to play it, to compete with Columbia's 33 1/3 rpm long-player, which bowed the previous June.

APRIL 2
"Drinkin' Wine Spo-Dee-O-Dee" by "Stick" McGhee and His Buddies is the first single from the new Atlantic label to hit the race records charts, peaking at #2 for four weeks.

JUNE 25
At the urging of its staff writer Jerry Wexler, the trade magazine *Billboard* changes the name of the race records charts to rhythm and blues.

OCTOBER 8
"Saturday Night Fish Fry (Parts I & II)" by Louis Jordan and His Tympany Five enters the newly-named rhythm and blues charts where it will become his seventeenth #1 hit and fiftieth chart record of the decade on Decca Records under the guidance of producer Milt Gabler. Among the others are classics such as "Caldonia," "Let The Good Times Roll," and "Choo Choo Ch'Boogie."

DECEMBER 1
Johnny Otis records "Double Crossing Blues," featuring the vocals of the Robins and thirteen-year-old Little Esther Phillips for Savoy Records in Los Angeles. It goes on to spend nine weeks at #1 on the rhythm and blues charts.

DECEMBER 10
Fats Domino enters Cosimo Matassa's J&M Studios in New Orleans with bandleader Dave Bartholomew for the first time. They record "The Fat Man," the first of his long string of hit singles for Imperial Records over the thirteen years that follow.

1950

JANUARY
Sam Phillips opens the Memphis Recording Service at 706 Union Avenue, where his motto is "We Record Anything—Anywhere—Anytime." He is soon recording local area bluesmen B.B. King and Howlin' Wolf and placing their masters with the independent labels RPM in Los Angeles and Chess in Chicago, respectively.

JUNE 25
Communist forces from the North invade South Korea. The Korean War begins.

SEPTEMBER
Ruth Brown records "Teardrops From My Eyes" with producers Ahmet Ertegun and Herb Abrahmson for Atlantic Records in New York. The song earns her the moniker "Miss Rhythm" and becomes the first of her twenty-four rhythm and blues hits during the next decade, twenty-one of which hit the top ten, with five peaking at #1, a level of consistency that led Atlantic to become known as "The House That Ruth Built."

DECEMBER
Nineteen-year-old Sam Cooke is asked to replace R.H. Harris as lead singer of the Soul Stirrers, a top gospel quartet of the day, where he will become the biggest matinee idol in that genre over the course of the next five years.

DECEMBER 16
"The Shot Gun Boogie" by Tennessee Ernie Ford on Capitol Records enters the country charts where it will spend fourteen weeks at #1 during its twenty-five week stay and cross over to the pop charts for thirteen weeks, peaking at #14.

DECEMBER 30
The Dominoes, a vocal group led by pianist Billy Ward and featuring lead singer Clyde McPhatter, record "Sixty Minute Man," a song with double entendre lyrics, for Federal Records in New York. Highlighted by the work of bass man Bill Brown, the single spends fourteen weeks atop the rhythm and blues charts during a total chart run of thirty weeks, even crossing over to the pop charts for nine weeks.

1951

MARCH 5
Bandleader and talent scout Ike Turner and his Kings of Rhythm record "Rocket '88'" at Sam Phillips' Memphis Recording Service. Billed as a single by its vocalist Jackie Brenston, and his Delta Cats, it is picked up by Chess Records of Chicago and becomes a #1 rhythm and blues hit, considered by many to be the first rock 'n' roll record.

JUNE 11
Twenty-nine-year-old, white disc jockey Alan Freed debuts a nightly rhythm and blues radio show on WJW, Cleveland. Soon dubbed *The Moondog Rock 'n' Roll House Party*, it attracts both black and white teenage listeners.

OCTOBER 16
Johnnie Ray and the Four Lads record the emotional ballad "Cry" under the direction of Mitch Miller for Columbia Records in New York. Released on the company's rhythm and blues subsidiary label, OKeh Records, it is a sensation, hitting #1 on both the pop and rhythm and blues charts.

Little Richard Penniman records his first four sides, in a conventional urban blues style, for RCA Victor in Atlanta, Georgia. They fail to make a mark.

1952

MARCH 13
Lloyd Price records "Lawdy Miss Clawdy" with Dave Bartholomew's band, including Fats Domino on piano, for Specialty Records in New Orleans. It hits #1 on the rhythm and blues charts for seven weeks.

MARCH 21
The Moondog Coronation Ball, a dance promoted by Alan Freed and starring the Dominoes, Varetta Dillard, and Paul Williams and His Orchestra at the Cleveland Arena, draws capacity, mostly black crowds, and has to be shut down when the overflow throngs grow unruly.

APRIL
Essex Records of Philadelphia releases "Rock The Joint" by local country-western combo Bill Haley and the Saddlemen, a remake of a 1949 rhythm and blues hit by Jimmy Preston and His Prestonians that features prominent slap-back bass and a memorable guitar solo by Danny Cedrone of the Esquire Boys.

AUGUST 13
Willie Mae "Big Mama" Thornton records Jerry Leiber and Mike Stoller's "Hound Dog" with Johnny Otis and His Orchestra for Peacock Records in Los Angeles. It hits #1 on the rhythm and blues charts for seven weeks.

DECEMBER 31
With his new single "I'll Never Get Out Of This World Alive" climbing the charts, country superstar Hank Williams sets out by car from Knoxville, Tennessee for Canton, Ohio where he is booked to perform at a concert on New Year's Day. He dies at the age of twenty-nine, probably of acute alcohol poisoning, in the backseat of his Cadillac somewhere en route.

1953

JANUARY 20
Dwight D. Eisenhower is inaugurated as president of the United States.

MARCH 5
Josef Stalin, leader of the Soviet Union and General Secretary of its Communist Party, dies at seventy-four.

APRIL
Clyde McPhatter departs the Dominoes to form his own group, the Drifters. He is replaced as lead singer in the Dominoes by Jackie Wilson.

MAY 23
"Crazy Man, Crazy" by Bill Haley with Haley's Comets on Essex Records, enters the pop charts, where it will spend ten weeks, peaking at #12.

JULY
Elvis Presley, a recent graduate of Humes High School, visits the Memphis Recording Service, where he makes an acetate recording of two songs, "My Happiness" and "That's When Your Heartaches Begin," ostensibly as a present for his mother.

JULY 27
A cease-fire in the Korean War is decreed at Panmunjeom.

AUGUST 9
Clyde McPhatter and the Drifters record Jesse Stone's "Money Honey" with producers Ahmet Ertegun and Jerry Wexler at the group's second session for Atlantic Records in New York City.

1954

JANUARY 2
As the year begins "Money Honey," Clyde McPhatter and the Drifters' first single for Atlantic Records tops the rhythm and blues charts.

"Oh! My Pa-Pa" by Eddie Fisher is #1 on the pop charts for the first of eight weeks. Fisher, from Philadelphia, was the top teen singing idol of the pre rock 'n' roll early 1950s.

JANUARY 4
For the second time in six months, eighteen-year-old Elvis Presley records two songs at the Memphis Recording Service for his personal use. On this occasion they are: "I'll Never Stand In Your Way" and "It Wouldn't Be The Same Without You."

JANUARY 7
Muddy Waters records Willie Dixon's "Hoochie Coochie Man" with producer Leonard Chess for Chess Records in Chicago. It reaches #3 on the rhythm and blues charts.

JANUARY 11
The Will Mastin Trio starring Sammy Davis Jr. desegregates the Las Vegas Strip when they not only open at the Last Frontier but also, for the first time, live at the resort while appearing in its showroom.

JANUARY 14
The Midnighters record "Work With Me Annie" for Federal Records in Cincinnati. It reaches #1 on the rhythm and blues charts but fails to cross over to the pop charts. An answer record, "The Wallflower," written and produced by Johnny Otis and recorded by Etta James, also reaches #1 rhythm and blues; this song, as covered by Georgia Gibbs and now known as "Dance With Me Henry," reaches #1 on the pop charts a year later. Meanwhile, the Midnighters continue to mine the "Annie" craze they had started with their subsequent Federal hits "Annie Had A Baby" and "Annie's Aunt Fanny."

JANUARY 21
The United States launches *Nautilus*, the first atomic-powered submarine.

FEBRUARY 4
Clyde McPhatter and the Drifters record "Honey Love," "White Christmas," "The Bells Of St. Mary's," and "What'cha Gonna Do" with producers Ahmet Ertegun and Jerry Wexler for Atlantic Records at Fulton Recording Studios in New York.

FEBRUARY 15
Big Joe Turner records "Shake, Rattle And Roll" with producers Ahmet Ertegun and Jerry Wexler for Atlantic Records in New York City.

FEBRUARY 26
Marilyn Monroe entertains the troops in Korea.

MARCH 1
The United States tests a hydrogen bomb, one thousand times more powerful than the atomic bomb that destroyed Hiroshima, above Bikini Atoll in the Marshall Islands of the Pacific.

MARCH 6
The Crows' recording of "Gee" on George Goldner's Rama Records label is the first doo-wop record to enter the *Billboard* pop charts, reaching as high as #14. A month later, in a case of "reverse crossover," it enters the rhythm and blues charts where it will peak at #2.

MARCH 15
The Chords record "Sh-Boom" with producers Ahmet Ertegun and Jerry Wexler for Atlantic Records' Cat label in New York City.

APRIL 8
Decca Records signs Bill Haley and His Comets.

APRIL 12
Atlantic Records releases "Shake, Rattle And Roll" by Big Joe Turner.

Bill Haley and His Comets record "Rock Around The Clock" with producer Milt Gabler for Decca Records in New York City.

APRIL 22
The Army-McCarthy hearings begin. This probe of Communist infiltration of the U.S. Army, government, and society in general is televised over the course of the next two months, leading to the downfall of demagogic Senator Joseph McCarthy.

MAY 1
The Moondog Coronation Ball, a dance promoted by Cleveland, Ohio disc jockey Alan Freed at the Sussex Avenue Armory in Newark, New Jersey, draws huge crowds. Attractions include the Harptones, the Clovers, Muddy Waters, Charles Brown, and the Buddy Johnson Orchestra featuring Ella Johnson.

MAY 7
France is defeated by Communist forces at Dien Bien Phu in Vietnam.

MAY 8
Big Joe Turner's "Shake, Rattle And Roll" enters the *Billboard* rhythm and blues charts, where it remains for thirty-weeks, three of them at #1. It does not cross over to the pop charts.

MAY 10
"Rock Around The Clock" is released as the b-side of the single "Thirteen Women (And Only One Man In Town)" by Bill Haley and His Comets.

MAY 17
In the *Brown* v. *Board of Education* decision, the U.S. Supreme Court rules that separate but equal facilities are inherently unconstitutional, banning segregation in public schools.

JUNE
"Riot In Cell Block No. 9" by the Robins, with Richard Berry guesting on lead vocals, is the third single released by Spark Records, a new label helmed by the record's writer-producers Jerry Leiber and Mike Stoller in Los Angeles. Berry, a stalwart on the local rhythm and blues scene, would go on to write and record "Louie Louie" which, as later covered by the Kingsmen, became one of the most notorious hits of the 1960s.

JULY 3
"Sh-Boom" by the Chords enters the *Billboard* pop charts where it will spend sixteen weeks, reaching a peak of #5.

WJW, Cleveland disc jockey Alan Freed announces he will move his *Moondog Rock And Roll Party* to WINS, New York.

JULY 5
Elvis Presley, accompanied by Scotty Moore on guitar and Bill Black on bass, records what will become his first single release, bluesman Arthur "Big Boy" Crudup's "That's All Right" with producer Sam Phillips at Sun Records, 706 Union Avenue, Memphis, Tennessee.

JULY 7
With their single "Thirteen Women (And Only One Man In Town)" languishing, Bill Haley and His Comets cover Big Joe Turner's "Shake, Rattle And Roll" with producer Milt Gabler for Decca Records in New York City.

JULY 8
WHBQ, Memphis disc jockey Dewey Phillips introduces "That's All Right" by Elvis Presley on his *Red, Hot And Blue* show at approximately 9:30 p.m. The response is immediate and overwhelming.

JULY 10
A cover record of "Sh-Boom" by the Crew-Cuts, a white Canadian act on Mercury Records, enters the *Billboard* charts where it will spend twenty weeks, nine of them at #1.

JULY 19
Sam Phillips releases Elvis Presley's "That's All Right" on his Sun Records label. A version of bluegrass pioneer Bill Monroe's "Blue Moon Of Kentucky" is on the flip side.

AUGUST
"Shake, Rattle And Roll" by Bill Haley and His Comets is released by Decca Records.

AUGUST 21
Bill Haley and His Comets' "Shake, Rattle And Roll" enters the *Billboard* pop charts, where it will peak at #7 during its twenty-seven-week run.

SEPTEMBER
The Penguins record "Earth Angel," cowritten by Jesse Belvin, for Doo Tone Records in Los Angeles. It rises to #1 on the rhythm and blues charts and to #8 on the pop charts.

SEPTEMBER 7
Disc jockey Alan Freed makes his WINS, New York debut.

OCTOBER
Clyde McPhatter of the Drifters is drafted into the U.S. Army.

OCTOBER 2
Elvis Presley, making his debut at the Grand Ole Opry in Nashville, sings "Blue Moon Of Kentucky." He is not invited to return.

OCTOBER 16
Elvis Presley makes his first appearance on the Louisiana Hayride out of Shreveport, Louisiana, performing "That's All Right" and "Blue Moon Of Kentucky."

OCTOBER 18
The first commercially available transistor radio, the Regency TR-1, is introduced.

OCTOBER 20
LaVern Baker records "Tweedle Dee" with producers Ahmet Ertegun and Jerry Wexler for Atlantic Records in New York. It scores a #4 position on the rhythm and blues charts and peaks at #14 on the pop charts despite Georgia Gibbs's #2 cover disc.

OCTOBER 24
Clyde McPhatter records his final session as the lead singer of the Drifters.

NOVEMBER
The Algerian War of Independence from France begins.

NOVEMBER 18
Ray Charles records "I Got A Woman" with producers Ahmet Ertegun and Jerry Wexler for Atlantic Records at the WGST radio station in Atlanta, Georgia. The song, based on the traditional gospel hymn "Jesus Is All The World To Me" will top the rhythm and blues charts but fail to cross over to pop.

DECEMBER 25
Johnny Ace, twenty-five, dies playing Russian Roulette backstage at the Civic Auditorium in Houston, Texas. His Johnny Otis-produced "Pledging My Love" debuts on the charts three weeks later, ultimately spending ten weeks at #1 on the rhythm and blues charts and reaching #17 on pop.

1955

JANUARY 14
Alan Freed's *Rock 'n' Roll Jubilee Ball*, his first New York City show, is held at St. Nicholas Arena. Attractions include Fats Domino, Clyde McPhatter and the Drifters, Ruth Brown, Big Joe Turner, the Harptones, the Clovers, the Moonglows, Charles Brown, Varetta Dillard, Dakota Staton, and the Buddy Johnson Orchestra featuring Ella Johnson.

MARCH 2
Bo Diddley records "Bo Diddley" and "I'm A Man" with producer Leonard Chess for Chess Records' Checker label in Chicago.

MARCH 15
Fats Domino records "Ain't It A Shame" with producer Dave Bartholomew for Imperial Records in Hollywood.

MARCH 19
The film *Blackboard Jungle*, starring Glenn Ford and Sidney Poitier, opens; Bill Haley and His Comets' "Rock Around The Clock" plays over its opening credits.

APRIL 6
Winston Churchill resigns; he is replaced as British Prime Minister by Anthony Eden.

APRIL 12
Dr. Jonas Salk announces that his polio vaccine has cured the dreaded disease.

MAY
Johnny Cash records his first single "Cry! Cry! Cry!" backed with "Hey Porter" with producer Sam Phillips for Sun Records in Memphis. It hits #14 on the country charts.

MAY 7
"Bo Diddley" backed with "I'm A Man" by Bo Diddley enters the *Billboard* rhythm and blues charts where it ultimately rises to the #1 position. The single fails, however, to cross over to the pop charts.

MAY 14
The Warsaw Pact, an Eastern European mutual defense agreement, is signed.

"Rock Around The Clock" by Bill Haley and His Comets enters the *Billboard* charts.

MAY 21
Chuck Berry records "Maybellene" with producer Leonard Chess for Chess Records in Chicago.

JUNE 3
Buddy Holly opens for Elvis Presley at the Cotton Club in his hometown of Lubbock, Texas.

JULY 9
"Rock Around The Clock" by Bill Haley and His Comets tops the *Billboard* pop charts, the first single by a rock 'n' roll act to do so. It will remain on the charts for twenty-four weeks, eight of them at #1, and rise as high as #3 on the rhythm and blues charts.

JULY 16
"Ain't It A Shame" by Fats Domino enters the *Billboard* pop charts. It will ultimately peak at #10 on the pop charts while spending eleven weeks at #1 on the rhythm and blues charts.

JULY 30
"Only You (And You Alone)" by the Platters on Mercury Records, a remake of their 1953 recording for Federal Records, enters the rhythm and blues charts where it will peak at #1 and cross over to reach #5 on the pop charts.

AUGUST 7
Bill Haley and His Comets appear on Ed Sullivan's *Toast Of The Town*, performing "Rock Around The Clock."

AUGUST 15
Elvis Presley signs a contract naming Col. Tom Parker his "special advisor." The Colonel, a carnival veteran and more recently the manager of RCA Victor recording artist Eddy Arnold, is in partnership with another RCA country star, Hank Snow, in a management company and booking agency, Hank Snow Enterprises and Jamboree Attractions.

AUGUST 20
"Maybellene" by Chuck Berry enters the *Billboard* pop charts. It will ultimately peak at #5 on the pop charts while spending eleven weeks at #1 on the rhythm and blues charts.

AUGUST 28
Emmett Till, a fourteen-year-old African American boy visiting from Chicago, is brutally murdered in Money, Mississippi for allegedly whistling at a white woman.

SEPTEMBER
The Robins' "Smokey Joe's Cafe," written and produced by Jerry Leiber and Mike Stoller for their own Spark Records label, is acquired by Atlantic Records' Atco subsidiary. Leiber and Stoller agree to join Atlantic on a non-exclusive basis as independent producers.

SEPTEMBER 14
Little Richard records "Tutti Frutti" for Specialty Records at Cosimo Matassa's J&M Studios in New Orleans, Louisiana.

SEPTEMBER 17
Pat Boone's cover record of Fats Domino's "Ain't It A Shame," now known as "Ain't That A Shame," reaches #1 on the *Billboard* pop charts, where it remains for two weeks, and even achieves a #14 ranking on the rhythm and blues charts.

SEPTEMBER 19
The Drifters, with Johnny Moore singing lead, record Jerry Leiber and Mike Stoller's "Ruby Baby" with producer Nesuhi Ertegun for Atlantic Records in Los Angeles. It reaches #10 on the rhythm and blues charts.

SEPTEMBER 30
Actor James Dean crashes his silver Porsche 550 Spyder and dies at age twenty-four.

OCTOBER
Atco releases "Smokey Joe's Cafe" by the Robins; only two members of the group, Carl Gardner and Bobby Nunn, agree to move with writer-producers Jerry Leiber and Mike Stoller to the new label. Joined by Billy Guy and Leon Hughes, they become a new group named the Coasters.

OCTOBER 13
Allen Ginsberg introduces his poem "Howl" at the Six Gallery in San Francisco.

OCTOBER 20
Bill Haley and His Comets and Elvis Presley play Cleveland, where they are filmed for a documentary about the disc jockey Bill Randle entitled *The Pied Piper Of Cleveland*. It has yet to be seen.

OCTOBER 29
The film *Rebel Without A Cause*, starring James Dean, Natalie Wood, and Sal Mineo, premieres at the Astor Theater in New York City.

NOVEMBER 20
Bo Diddley appears on *The Ed Sullivan Show*; asked to perform Tennessee Ernie Ford's then-current hit "Sixteen Tons," he instead plays his own "Bo Diddley" and is banned from the program for life.

NOVEMBER 21
In an agreement engineered by Col. Tom Parker, Elvis Presley's Sun Records contract and master recordings are assigned to RCA Victor Records of New York in return for a payment of $35,000 to Sun.

DECEMBER 1
An African American woman named Rosa Parks refuses to relinquish her seat on a Montgomery, Alabama bus. A boycott of the Montgomery public transportation system, led by Rev. Martin Luther King, Jr., begins.

DECEMBER 5
The Teenagers, featuring thirteen-year-old Frankie Lymon, record "Why Do Fools Fall In Love" for George Goldner's Gee Records label in New York. It will top the rhythm and blues charts while peaking at #6 pop.

DECEMBER 12
Backstage at a show in Amory, Mississippi, Johnny Cash suggests to fellow Sun artist Carl Perkins that he write a song about blue suede shoes. One week later, Perkins records "Blue Suede Shoes" with producer Sam Phillips at Sun Studios in Memphis, Tennessee.

DECEMBER 21
LaVern Baker records Lincoln Chase's "Jim Dandy" with producers Ahmet Ertegun and Jerry Wexler for Atlantic Records in New York. A #1 rhythm and blues hit, it peaks at #17 on the pop charts as well.

1956

JANUARY
Howlin' Wolf records "Smokestack Lightnin'" with producers Leonard Chess and Willie Dixon for Chess Records in Chicago.

JANUARY 10
Elvis Presley records "Heartbreak Hotel" at RCA Studios in Nashville, Tennessee.

JANUARY 11
The first Coasters session for Atco Records is held in Los Angeles, produced by Jerry Leiber and Mike Stoller. "Down In Mexico" backed with "Turtle Dovin' " is their first single; it reaches #8 on the rhythm and blues charts, but fails to chart pop.

JANUARY 14
"Tutti Frutti" by Little Richard enters the *Billboard* pop charts. It will peak at #2 on the rhythm and blues charts and #17 on the pop charts.

JANUARY 27
Elvis Presley's first RCA Victor single "Heartbreak Hotel" backed with "I Was The One" is released.

JANUARY 28
Elvis Presley makes the first of six national television appearances over the next two months on the Dorsey Brothers' *Stage Show* in New York City, during the course of which he will perform "Shake, Rattle And Roll/Flip, Flop And Fly," "I Got A Woman," "Baby, Let's Play House," "I Was The One," "Money Honey," "Tutti Frutti," and "Blue Suede Shoes" (two times each), and "Heartbreak Hotel" (three times).

FEBRUARY 4
Nikita S. Khrushchev, First Secretary of the Communist Party of the U.S.S.R., denounces the rule of Joseph Stalin.

James Brown records "Please, Please, Please" with producer Ralph Bass for Federal Records at King Studios, in Cincinnati, Ohio.

FEBRUARY 18
"The Great Pretender" by the Platters on Mercury Records begins the first of two weeks at #1 on the pop charts. It will also spend eleven weeks at #1 on the rhythm and blues charts.

MARCH 4
Clyde McPhatter records "Treasure Of Love" with producers Ahmet Ertegun and Jerry Wexler at his second solo session for Atlantic Records at Capitol Studios in New York; the disc reaches #1 on the rhythm and blues charts and peaks at #16 pop.

MARCH 10
"Blue Suede Shoes" by Carl Perkins is the first record to appear on the *Billboard* pop, rhythm and blues, and country and western charts simultaneously.

MARCH 14
The film *Rock Around The Clock* premieres in Washington, D.C. It features Alan Freed, Bill Haley and His Comets, the Platters, and Freddie Bell and the Bellboys.

MARCH 21
A serious automobile accident causes Carl Perkins to miss his national television debut, scheduled two days later on *The Perry Como Show*.

MARCH 31
"Heartbreak Hotel" becomes the second record to appear on the *Billboard* pop, rhythm and blues, and country and western charts simultaneously.

APRIL 2
Johnny Cash records "I Walk The Line" with producer Sam Phillips for Sun Records in Memphis, which goes on to top the country charts and peak at #17 pop.

APRIL 3
Elvis Presley makes his first appearance on *The Milton Berle Show*, performing "Heartbreak Hotel" and "Blue Suede Shoes" from the deck of the U.S.S. Hancock at the San Diego Naval Station. Two months later his bump-and-grind rendition of "Hound Dog" on the same show generates outrage and protest.

APRIL 7
Alan Freed's *Rock 'n' Roll Dance Party* bows over the CBS Radio Network. It is the first regularly scheduled, nationally broadcast program devoted to rock 'n' roll.

APRIL 10
Nat King Cole is physically attacked by white supremacists while performing onstage in Birmingham, Alabama.

APRIL 19
Cpl. Clyde McPhatter is discharged from the U.S. Army.

APRIL 23
Elvis Presley, billed as "the Atomic-Powered Singer," begins a two-week engagement at the Venus Room of the New Frontier Hotel in Las Vegas, Nevada, during the course of which he catches a performance of Jerry Leiber and Mike Stoller's "Hound Dog" by Freddie Bell and the Bell Boys.

MAY 4
Gene Vincent records "Be-Bop-A-Lula" and "Woman Love" in Nashville for Capitol Records. The single will reach #8 on the rhythm and blues charts and #7 pop.

MAY 5
"Heartbreak Hotel" by Elvis Presley reaches #1 on the *Billboard* top one-hundred charts.

JULY 1
Elvis Presley makes his first and only appearance on *The Steve Allen Show*, performing "I Want You, I Need You, I Love You" and "Hound Dog" at the Hudson Theater in New York City.

JULY 2
Elvis Presley records Leiber-Stoller's "Hound Dog" and Otis Blackwell's "Don't Be Cruel" at RCA Studios in New York City.

Johnny Burnette and the Rock 'n' Roll Trio records Tiny Bradshaw's "The Train Kept A-Rollin' " for Coral Records in Nashville. While it fails to make an immediate impact, their version provides the model for recordings of the song by the Yardbirds in the 1960s and Aerosmith in the 1970s.

JULY 26
Egypt seizes the Suez Canal.

AUGUST 11
The painter Jackson Pollock dies at forty-four.

AUGUST 18
Elvis Presley's double-sided hit "Hound Dog" backed with "Don't Be Cruel" hits #1 on the pop charts for the first week of an eleven-week run. Each song will also rank #1 on both the rhythm and blues and country and western charts.

SEPTEMBER
The novel *Peyton Place* by Grace Metalious is published. Its explicit sexual references cause a sensation.

SEPTEMBER 9
Elvis Presley makes his first appearance on *The Ed Sullivan Show*. It is estimated that more than 50,000,000 viewers tune in to see him perform "Don't Be Cruel," "Love Me Tender," "Ready Teddy," and "Hound Dog" from Hollywood, California.

SEPTEMBER 17
Decca Records releases its first single, "Jambalaya" backed with "Bigelow 6-200," by eleven-year-old Brenda Lee.

OCTOBER
A revolt against Communist rule forces the withdrawal of Soviet troops from Budapest, Hungary.

Jesse Belvin records "Goodnight My Love" for Modern Records in Los Angeles. Alan Freed will adopt the song as his radio show's closing theme.

OCTOBER 28
Elvis Presley makes his second appearance on *The Ed Sullivan Show*, performing "Don't Be Cruel," "Love Me Tender," "Love Me," and "Hound Dog" in New York City.

OCTOBER 29
Israel attacks Sinai Peninsula in Egypt and drives toward Suez Canal.

NOVEMBER
Jerry Lee Lewis records his first single, "End Of The Road" backed with "Crazy Arms," with producer Sam Phillips for Sun Records in Memphis.

NOVEMBER 1
Hungary withdraws from the Warsaw Pact.

NOVEMBER 3
"Love Me Tender" by Elvis Presley, the title song of his forthcoming first feature film, is #1.

NOVEMBER 4
Soviet troops return with tanks and reassert control in Budapest, Hungary.

NOVEMBER 5
Great Britain and France attack Port Said on the Suez Canal.

The Nat King Cole Show, the first television variety program hosted by an African American, is broadcast on the NBC network.

NOVEMBER 6
A cease-fire is declared in the Suez affair.

President Dwight D. Eisenhower and Vice-President Richard M. Nixon are reelected in the United States.

NOVEMBER 8
The Drifters, with Johnny Moore on lead vocals, record Jerry Leiber and Mike Stoller's "Fools Fall In Love" with producers Ahmet Ertegun and Jerry Wexler for Atlantic Records in New York. It reaches #10 on the rhythm and blues charts, but only #69 pop.

NOVEMBER 16
Elvis Presley's first film, *Love Me Tender*, premieres in New York City.

DECEMBER
Fee Bee Records of Pittsburgh releases "Come Go With Me" by the Del Vikings, a local interracial vocal group. The master is soon picked up by Dot Records, where it becomes the first rock 'n' roll record by an integrated act to achieve national chart success, peaking at #4 on the pop charts and #2 rhythm and blues.

The film *Don't Knock The Rock* opens, featuring Bill Haley and His Comets, Little Richard, and the Treniers, as does *Rock Rock Rock*, featuring Alan Freed, Chuck Berry, the Moonglows, the Flamingos, Bo Diddley, Frankie Lymon and the Teenagers, LaVern Baker, and the Johnny Burnette Trio.

DECEMBER 1
The film *The Girl Can't Help It* opens, starring Jayne Mansfield and Tom Ewell and featuring Fats Domino, Gene Vincent, Eddie Cochran, the Platters, the Treniers, and Little Richard, who sings the title song; the film *Shake, Rattle And Rock* opens too, featuring Fats Domino and Big Joe Turner.

DECEMBER 4
Elvis Presley and Johnny Cash drop by a Carl Perkins recording session at Sun Studios in Memphis where Jerry Lee Lewis is playing piano. The ensuing jam session is recorded for posterity, its four principals forever to be known as the Million Dollar Quartet.

DECEMBER 12
Sam Cooke, lead singer of the Soul Stirrers gospel quartet, records a pop single, "Lovable" backed with "Forever," for Specialty Records in New Orleans. In an attempt to avoid alienating the Soul Stirrers' religious following, the disc is released under the name Dale Cook but fails to fool anyone or achieve much renown.

DECEMBER 21
The Montgomery, Alabama bus boycott ends successfully; all public transportation in the city is desegregated.

1957

JANUARY
The Southern Christian Leadership Conference is formed; Rev. Martin Luther King, Jr. is elected as the first president of the new civil rights organization.

JANUARY 6
Elvis Presley makes his third and final appearance on *The Ed Sullivan Show*, this time shown only from the waist up and performing "Hound Dog," "Love Me Tender," "Heartbreak Hotel," "Don't Be Cruel," "Too Much," "When My Blue Moon Turns To Gold Again," and "Peace In The Valley" in New York City.

FEBRUARY
Jerry Lee Lewis records his second single "Whole Lotta Shakin' Goin' On" backed with "It'll Be Me" with producer Sam Phillips for Sun Records in Memphis. It tops the rhythm and blues charts and peaks at #3 on the pop charts. "Whole Lotta Shakin' Goin' On" had originally been recorded by Big Maybelle with producer Quincy Jones for OKeh Records in 1955.

FEBRUARY 7
Bill Haley and His Comets commence a tour of Great Britain, their first overseas performances by a major U.S. rock 'n' roll act.

FEBRUARY 15
The Coasters record the two-sided hit "Searchin' " backed with "Young Blood," written and produced by Jerry Leiber and Mike Stoller (Doc Pomus is the cowriter of "Young Blood") for Atco Records in Los Angeles. Both sides top the rhythm and blues charts; "Searchin' " peaks at #3 on the pop charts, while "Young Blood" reaches #8.

FEBRUARY 25
Buddy Holly and the Crickets record "That'll Be The Day" for Brunswick Records at producer Norman Petty's studio in Clovis, New Mexico. It reaches #2 on the rhythm and blues charts while topping the pop charts.

MARCH
The Everly Brothers record "Bye Bye Love" for Cadence Records in Nashville. It reaches #2 on the pop charts and #5 rhythm and blues.

MARCH 19
Elvis Presley purchases a Memphis mansion named Graceland.

APRIL 10
Ricky Nelson sings Fats Domino's "I'm Walkin' " on his family's television series, *The Adventures Of Ozzie And Harriet*, the first of his many such musical performances on the program.

APRIL 13
"All Shook Up" by Elvis Presley, written by Otis Blackwell, is #1 on the pop charts for the first of nine weeks, while also topping the rhythm and blues and country and western surveys.

MAY
Sam Cooke departs the Soul Stirrers gospel group, for which he had been lead singer.

JUNE
Dissent magazine publishes Norman Mailler's essay "The White Negro."

JUNE 1
Sam Cooke records "You Send Me" with producer Bumps Blackwell for Specialty Records in Los Angeles. Rejected by label head Art Rupe, it is ultimately released on the new Keen Records label where it tops both the rhythm and blues and pop charts.

JUNE 30
The Everly Brothers make the first of many appearances on *The Ed Sullivan Show*, performing "Bye Bye Love."

JULY 6
Paul McCartney is introduced to John Lennon after witnessing his skiffle group, the Quarrymen, perform a song variously identified as "Be-Bop-A-Lula," "Baby, Let's Play House," and "Come Go With Me" at St. Peter's Church in Woolton, England. John soon asks Paul to join the group.

JULY 9
Elvis Presley's second film, *Loving You*, opens. The title song is written by Jerry Leiber and Mike Stoller.

JULY 12
Jackie Wilson records "Reet Petite (The Finest Girl You Ever Want To Meet)" for Brunswick Records in New York. It is the first of five hits cowritten by Berry Gordy for the artist to make the pop charts over the next two years.

111

JULY 19
Frankie Lymon is seen dancing with a white girl on Alan Freed's WABC-TV, New York dance show *Big Beat*. Two weeks later WABC cancels the show.

JULY 28
Jerry Lee Lewis appears on *The Steve Allen Show*, performing "Whole Lotta Shakin' Goin' On."

AUGUST
The novel *On The Road* by Jack Kerouac is published.

AUGUST 5
Dick Clark takes his daily Philadelphia-based dance program, now named *American Bandstand*, national via the ABC television network.

AUGUST 31
While on tour in California, Johnny Cash and Carl Perkins meet Columbia Records Nashville A&R head Don Law.

SEPTEMBER
The film *Mister Rock And Roll* opens, featuring Alan Freed, Chuck Berry, Little Richard, Frankie Lymon and the Teenagers, LaVern Baker, Clyde McPhatter, and the Moonglows.

The Everly Brothers record "Wake Up Little Susie" for Cadence Records in Nashville. It will ultimately top the pop, rhythm and blues, and country and western charts.

SEPTEMBER 9
President Dwight D. Eisenhower signs the Civil Rights Act of 1957, a voting rights bill, into law. It is the first Civil Rights legislation enacted in the United States in eighty-two years.

SEPTEMBER 17
Wanda Jackson cuts a rockabilly rendition of Annisteen Allen's 1954 rhythm and blues record "Fujiyama Mama" for Capitol Records in Hollywood. While never a hit in the U.S. it becomes extremely popular in Japan.

SEPTEMBER 23
The Crickets' "That'll Be The Day" on Brunswick Records is #1 for a week.

SEPTEMBER 24
Nine black students attempt to integrate Central High School in Little Rock, Arkansas. President Dwight D. Eisenhower federalizes troops to control unruly mobs, protect the students, and enforce integration.

SEPTEMBER 26
The Leonard Bernstein–Stephen Sondheim musical *West Side Story*, a depiction of juvenile delinquent New York City street gangs, opens at the Winter Garden on Broadway.

OCTOBER
Jerry Leiber and Mike Stoller transfer their base of operations from Los Angeles to New York.

OCTOBER 1
In the midst of a two-week tour of Australia, Little Richard announces he is forsaking rock 'n' roll for religion.

OCTOBER 4
The U.S.S.R. launches *Sputnik*, the first man-made satellite to orbit Earth.

OCTOBER 6
Jerry Lee Lewis records Otis Blackwell's "Great Balls Of Fire" with producer Sam Phillips for Sun Records in Memphis. It peaks at #3 on the rhythm and blues charts and #2 pop.

OCTOBER 21
Elvis Presley's third film, *Jailhouse Rock*, opens. The title song is written by Jerry Leiber and Mike Stoller; it reaches #1 on the pop charts for a seven-week stay, also becoming #1 in the rhythm and blues and country and western fields.

DECEMBER 1
Sam Cooke makes his second appearance in a month on *The Ed Sullivan Show*, performing "You Send Me" on both occasions; Buddy Holly and the Crickets make their first appearance on the same show, performing "That'll Be The Day" and "Peggy Sue." In a second and final appearance on the show a month later they perform "Oh, Boy!"

DECEMBER 11
Jerry Lee Lewis marries his thirteen-year-old second cousin Myra Gail Brown in Hernando, Mississippi. She is the daughter of his bass player J.W. Brown.

1958

JANUARY 1
The European Economic Community is formed.

Carl Perkins leaves Sun Records and inks a pact with Columbia Records.

JANUARY 28
Little Richard enters the Oakwood Theological Seminary in Huntsville, Alabama.

FEBRUARY 1
George Harrison is introduced to the Quarrymen at a basement club called the Morgue and joins John Lennon and Paul McCartney in the Liverpool, England-based skiffle group.

MARCH
Buddy Holly and the Crickets launch a month-long tour of Great Britain.

MARCH 17
The Coasters record "Yakety Yak," written and produced by Jerry Leiber and Mike Stoller, for Atco Records in New York; it will ultimately reach #1 on both the rhythm and blues and pop charts.

MARCH 24
Elvis Presley is inducted into the U.S. Army.

MARCH 27
Nikita S. Khrushchev becomes premier of the U.S.S.R.

APRIL
The film *Go Johnny Go!* opens, featuring Alan Freed, Chuck Berry, Jimmy Clanton, Eddie Cochran, Jackie Wilson, the Flamingos, Ritchie Valens, the Cadillacs, Harvey Fuqua, and Jo-Ann Campbell.

APRIL 7
Wanda Jackson records "Let's Have A Party" which, known simply as "Party," had already been cut by Elvis Presley and the Collins Kids for Capitol Records in Hollywood. But it does not become her biggest rock 'n' roll hit until 1960.

APRIL 28
Jerry Leiber and Mike Stoller assume production of the Drifters. They record their own "Drip Drop" in what turns out to be the last session of the original, but Clyde McPhatter-less, group. It fails to chart rhythm and blues and reaches only as high as #58 on the pop charts.

"Rumble" by Link Wray on Cadence Records enters the charts. This instrumental by a guitarist who pioneers the use of distortion and feedback, climbs as high as #16 on the pop charts and #11 rhythm and blues despite its controversial sound.

MAY 3
Rioting breaks out at the Boston stop of Alan Freed's *Big Beat Spring 1958* tour. He is charged with anarchy and inciting a riot. Though the charges are later dropped, he resigns from WINS and switches to WABC, New York.

MAY 22
Jerry Lee Lewis embarks on a tour of England, which is consumed by scandal and canceled after three performances when it is learned that his recent bride is also his thirteen-year-old cousin.

MAY 30
The "original" Drifters begin a final, week-long engagement at the Apollo Theater in Harlem, at the end of which their manager George Treadwell, who owns their name, replaces them with the members of a group that had opened the bill, the Crowns.

JUNE 1
Charles de Gaulle becomes premier of France.

JUNE 4
Elvis Presley's fourth film, *King Creole*, opens. The title song is written by Jerry Leiber and Mike Stoller.

JULY
The Teddy Bears record "To Know Him Is To Love Him" for Dore Records in Los Angeles. It is written, arranged, and produced by Phil Spector, a member of the group. His first recording, it becomes his first #1 pop record and reaches #10 on the rhythm and blues charts as well. Spector, the inventor of "The Wall Of Sound," will go on to become one of the most important and successful producers of the 1960s.

JULY 24
Johnny Cash participates in his first recording session for Columbia Records at Owen Bradley Studios in Nashville. He officially signs a contract with the label one week later.

AUGUST 14
Elvis Presley's mother, Gladys, dies at age 46.

AUGUST 15
Buddy Holly marries Maria Elena Santiago in Lubbock, Texas and subsequently moves to Greenwich Village in New York City.

SEPTEMBER 22
Pfc. Elvis Presley embarks aboard the USS *Randall* for active duty in Germany.

SEPTEMBER 28
A new French Constitution is adopted.

OCTOBER 28
Buddy Holly and the Crickets split up.

NOVEMBER 11
Hank Ballard and the Midnighters record "The Twist" for King Records in Cincinnati. Bearing a striking similarity to Clyde McPhatter and the Drifters' "What'cha Gonna Do," it is relegated to the b-side of "Teardrops On Your Letter." But, as the result of a later recording by Chubby Checker for Parkway Records, "The Twist" reemerges as the greatest dance craze of the 1960s.

DECEMBER 1
Ricky Nelson appears on the cover of *Life* magazine.

DECEMBER 21
Charles de Gaulle is elected president of the 5th Republic of France.

DECEMBER 29
"La Bamba," the b-side of Ritchie Valens' #2 pop hit "Donna" on Del-Fi Records, enters the pop charts in its own right, where it will ascend to the #22 position after the seventeen-year-old's death.

1959

JANUARY 1
Fidel Castro assumes power in Cuba.

JANUARY 12
Berry Gordy founds Tamla-Motown on an $800 loan from his family. His first release is "Come To Me" by Marv Johnson. A local hit in Detroit, it is picked up for national distribution by United Artists Records.

FEBRUARY 3
A small plane carrying Buddy Holly, Ritchie Valens, and J.P. "The Big Bopper" Richardson crashes outside of Clear Lake, Iowa. There are no survivors.

FEBRUARY 9
Lloyd Price's "Stagger Lee" on ABC-Paramount Records reaches #1 on the pop and rhythm and blues charts for the first of four weeks. A revival of the 1950 New Orleans rhythm and blues hit "Stack-A'Lee" by Archibald, the song actually traces its roots back to late-nineteenth-century folklore.

FEBRUARY 18
Ray Charles records "What'd I Say" with producers Ahmet Ertegun and Jerry Wexler for Atlantic Records in New York. A #1 rhythm and blues hit, it becomes the first Ray Charles single to reach the top ten of the "Hot Hundred," peaking at #6 for pop.

MARCH 6
The "new" Drifters, with one Benjamin Earl Nelson on lead vocals, record "There Goes My Baby" for Atlantic Records in New York. A Leiber-Stoller production, it is the first big rock 'n' roll hit to prominently feature strings, reaching #1 rhythm and blues and #2 pop.

MARCH 9
His contract with Atlantic Records having expired, Clyde McPhatter signs a new deal with MGM Records calling for a guarantee in excess of $50,000 per year.

JULY 11
An unbilled appearance at the *Newport Folk Festival* by eighteen-year-old Joan Baez causes a sensation.

JULY 24
Nikita S. Khrushchev and Richard M. Nixon debate the relative merits of Communism and Capitalism at a kitchen exhibit in Moscow.

AUGUST
Sam Cooke, with partners J.W. Alexander and S.R. Crain, establishes SAR Records, among the first African-American owned and operated labels. The Soul Stirrers, with new lead singer Johnnie Taylor, are the first act to record for the new company.

Barrett Strong records "Money (That's What I Want)" for Berry Gordy's Tamla label. It reaches #2 on the rhythm and blues charts and #23 pop.

OCTOBER
Johnny Hallyday records what will become his first single for Disques Vogue. "T'aimer Follement," an adaptation of Floyd Robinson's hit "Makin' Love," is backed with "Laisse Les Filles."

NOVEMBER 1
Ray Charles leaves Atlantic Records and signs with ABC-Paramount, which offers him ownership of his master recordings.

NOVEMBER 6
The Legislative Oversight Committee of the U.S. House of Representatives announces its intention to investigate allegations that radio station personnel are accepting bribes in return for airplay.

NOVEMBER 21
Alan Freed is dismissed by the radio station WABC, New York, after refusing to sign a statement that he had never accepted funds or gifts in return for promoting or playing records.

NOVEMBER 28
The final broadcast of Alan Freed's WNEW TV show *Big Beat* is aired.

DECEMBER
Sam Cooke negotiates a new recording contract with RCA Victor Records, which is signed on January 1, 1960.

DECEMBER 17
Benjamin Earl Nelson, now calling himself Ben E. King, cuts his first solo sides for Atlantic Records in New York.

DECEMBER 22
Chuck Berry is arrested and charged with violating the Mann Act. Subsequently convicted, he serves a two-year term in prison.

DECEMBER 28
As the decade draws to a conclusion, the ballad "Why" by Frankie Avalon of Philadelphia is ensconced at #1 on the *Billboard* "Hot Hundred." Fellow Philadelphian Fabian's "Hound Dog Man" is also in the top ten.

Acknowledgements

The Fondation Cartier pour l'art contemporain would like to warmly thank the people who created this exhibition
Gilles Pétard, who gave it direction;
Gregg Geller, whose expertise and enthusiasm were invaluable in the realization of the project.

We would also like to extend our gratitude to Nathalie Crinière and Eve-Marine Basuyaux from Agence NC, who designed and gave form to the exhibition with great talent;
Atelier La Bonne Merveille for the exhibition's graphic design;
Gérard Chiron for the sound design;
Frédéric Lecomte for his writing and creation of sound clips;
Jean-Jacques Burnel for lending his voice;
Klaus Blasquiz for his expertise and the use of his collection for the sound studio.

We also thank
The film directors Patrick Montgomery and Mathieu Zeitindjioglou;
Tatiana Maksimenko and Morphofilms for their audiovisual production;
Le Chaînon manquant (Serge Garcin, Olivier Paoli) for their documentary research;
Chandor Chury for the mixing.

We would like to extend our deepest appreciation to the people and to the institutions who contributed to this project for their trust, advice, commitment, and support, and, in particular, to the collectors without whom this exhibition would not have been possible:
Michel Aphesberro
Mitch Diamond
Léon Dierckx
Daniel Doan
Michel Fraile
Pete Frame
Gregg Geller
Pete Howard
Bexley Jackson
Michel Lenoir
Michael J. Malone
Alain Dominique Perrin
Gilles Pétard
Christian Sutteur
David Swartz
Barry Weinstein

We also extend our sincere thanks to the institutions who loaned us numerous works essential to this exhibition:

The Rock and Roll Hall of Fame and Museum in Cleveland, its President, Terry Stewart and Vice-President, James Henke. We would also like to recognize the entire team and in particular Howard Kramer, Director of the Curatorial Department, whose enthusiasm and dedication were essential to this project's success, as well as Emmanuel (Jun) Francisco, assisted by Kristin Stempfer for their logistical support.
The Experience Music Project in Seattle: Jacob McMurray, Senior Curator, Jason Emmons, Director of Curatorial Affairs, Erynn Summers, Curatorial Assistant, and Angie Battalio-Bunker, Registrar, for their attention and logistical assistance.

We would like to thank the photographers Alfred Wertheimer and William Eggleston for the use of their invaluable works in addition to the photographers who accepted to loan their works:
Lew Allen
Eve Arnold
Charlotte Brooks
Bruce Davidson
Elliott Erwitt
Clemens Kalischer
Wayne Miller
Ernest C. Withers

We would also like to thank the following galleries for their loans and their collaboration on this project:
Howard Greenberg Gallery, New York:
Howard Greenberg, Margit Erb
Keith de Lellis Gallery, New York: Keith de Lellis
Panopticon Gallery, Boston:
Tony Decaneas and Boris Samarov
Staley-Wise Gallery, New York: Takouhy Wise

And those who remained alongside us throughout the planning of this project, we thank:
Robert Gordon, Peter Guralnick, Greil Marcus, Grazia Quaroni

And those who gave their precious advice and time:
John Bakke, Nik Cohn, François Jouffa, Pierre Lescure, Philippe Manœuvre, Eddy Mitchell, Philippe Paringaux, Line Renaud, Nick Tosches

We thank everyone who participated in the creation of this book:
Xavier Barral and the entire Atalante/Paris team, in particular Florent Moglia, Annette Lucas, Pierre Vorméringer, Mathilde Altenhoven, Franck Davisseau, Amélie Doisteau, Anne Jeandet, Marine Jourdy, Colombe de Panafieu, Emilie Rigaud, and Ben Salesse;
Gerhard Steidl and the entire team of Steidl, in particular Julia Braun, Bernard Fischer, and Frank Hertel.

As well as the authors who contributed new texts especially for the book:
Peter Guralnick
Greil Marcus
Florent Mazzoleni

Finally, we would like to express our appreciation to the individuals who contributed in diverse ways to the exhibition and its book:
Bob Abramson, Dix Hills, New York
Patrick Bardou, Marseille
Estate of Ralph Bartholomew Jr., Singer Island, Florida
Patrick Bastat, Saint-Gratien
Steve Bello, New York
Stanley Booth, Brunswick, Georgia
Christine Borgoltz, Paris
Jean Bubley, Brooklyn, New York (and the Estate of Esther Bubley)
Michelle Cahill, Seattle, Washington
Rick Coleman, Los Angeles, California
Jamie Conlan, New York
Éric Didi, Paris
Sébastien Donadieu, Paris
Joël Dufour, Levallois-Perret
Robert Wayne Dye, Memphis, Tennessee
Winston Eggleston, Memphis, Tennessee
Sharyn Felder, New York
Johanna Fiore, New York
Judith Fisher Freed, Santa Monica, California
Lance Freed, Los Angeles, California
Holly George-Warren, Phoenicia, New York
Arminda Gouveia, Paris
Jean-Bernard Hebey, Suresnes
Guillaume Huret, Paris
Kate Izor, New York
Jennifer Krause, Stockbridge, Massachusetts
Andria Lisle, Memphis, Tennessee
Kurt Mohr, Paris
Victor Pearlin, Boston, Massachusetts
Nina Pearlman, New York
Randy Poe, Los Angeles, California
Marc Richard, Paris
Jake Riviera, London
Maxime Schmitt, Paris
Dr. Christiana Sekaer, Dobbs Ferry, New York
Bob Shatten, Boston, Massachusetts
Kevin Eugene Smith, San Gabriel, California
Vivian Thatos, New York
Jean-William Thoury, Paris
Richard Whelan, New York
Ernest Zwonicek, Geneva

Institutions, associations, and companies
Alfajukebox, Saint-Ouen: Alain Cugnod
Andy Warhol Foundation: Thomas Sokolowski, Sally King-Nero
ARC (ARChive of contemporary music), New York: Bob George
Brooks Museum, Memphis, Tennessee: Kaywin Feldman
Cadillac France, Paris: Berry Van Gestel
Center for Southern Folklore, Memphis, Tennessee: Judy Peiser
Chrysler Museum, Norfolk, Virginia: Brooks Johnson
Cité de la Musique, Paris: Emma Lavigne, Curator
Éditions Allia, Paris: Estelle Roche
Elvis my happiness, Paris: Jean-Marie Pouzenc
Footsteps of Elvis, Naantali, Finland: Dennis Livson, Markku Veijalainen
Govinda Gallery, Washington: Chris Murray
Hatch Show Print at the Country Music hall of Fame, Nashville, Tennessee: Jim Sherraden
International Center of Photography, New York: Brian Wallis
Library of Congress, Washington, Maryland
Life magazine, New York: Sandy Green
MEC Productions, Paris: Dominique Laisney
MPO, Boulogne-Billancourt: Loïc de Poix, Chairman of The Board
Musée de la Photographie, Charleroi: Marc Vausort
National Archives Maryland, Washington
National Civil Rights Museum, Memphis, Tennessee: Beverly C. Robertson
Rock'n'Soul Museum, Memphis, Tennessee: John Doyle
Smithsonian Institution, Washington, Maryland: Susan Ostroff
Soulsville, Stax Museum of American Soul Music, Memphis, Tennessee: Marc E. Willis, Carol Drake, Tim Sampson
University of Memphis Libraries—Mississippi Valley Collections, Memphis, Tennessee: Chris Ratliff, Ed Frank, Jim Cole

Photography Agencies
Corbis, Paris: Frédéric Sommer
Getty Images, New York: Eileen Flanagan, Gregory Spencer
Getty images, Paris: Françoise Dubreuil
Magnum Photos, London: Anna Stevens
Magnum Photos, New York: Tom Wall
Magnum Photos, Paris: Catherine Rouvière
Showtime, Toronto, Canada: Dave Booth
Sipa Press, Paris: Macha Gorina-Bellanger

Partners
Philips: Jean-Marie Bourel

This book was published on the occasion of the exhibition *Rock 'n' Roll 39-59*, presented at the Fondation Cartier pour l'art contemporain in Paris from June 22 to October 28, 2007.

Exhibition
Chief Curators: Alain Dominique Perrin and Gilles Pétard
Curators: Isabelle Gaudefroy and Katell Jaffrès assisted by Noémi Joly and Ilana Shamoon
Creative Consultant: Gregg Geller
Intern: Camille Leboulanger
Exhibition Design: Nathalie Crinière and Eve-Marine Basuyaux
assisted by Charlotte Billon, Agence NC
Graphic Design: Clément Vauchez and Thomas Dimetto, Atelier La Bonne Merveille
Registrar: Corinne Bocquet
assisted by Alanna Minta Jordan
Intern: Emily Nechanian
Installation Coordinator: Christophe Morizot
Installation: Gilles Gioan
Film Production: Tatiana Maksimenko
Film Direction: Mathieu Zeitindjioglou
Film Researcher: Le Chaînon manquant
Sound Design: Gérard Chiron
Sound Clip Preparation: Maxime Munoz
Sound Clip Texts and French Voice: Frédéric Lecomte
English Voice: Jean-Jacques Burnel
Sound Studio Installation: Klaus Blasquiz
Light Design: Nicolas Tauveron
Descriptions: Sébastien Donadieu

Exhibition Book
Design: Atalante/Paris
Publications: Sophie Perceval
assisted by Adeline Pelletier and David Lestringant;
interns: Agathe Dejoie, Solène de Bure, and Marin Sarvé-Tarr
Photoengraving: Steidl, Göttingen
French/English Translation: Charles Penwarden

The Exhibition *Rock 'n' Roll 39-59* is organized with the support of the Fondation Cartier pour l'art contemporain, under the aegis of the Fondation de France, and with the sponsorship of Cartier.

Fondation Cartier pour l'art contemporain
Director: Hervé Chandès
assisted by Virginie Bergeron
Chief Financial Officer: Sylvie Dumas
assisted by Magali Bourcy
Development Manager: Sonia Perrin-Amara
assisted by Cécile Chauvot
Curators: Hélène Kelmachter, Grazia Quaroni, Leanne Sacramone, Katell Jaffrès, Ilana Shamoon
Publications: Sophie Perceval
assisted by Adeline Pelletier
Special Project Managers: Audrey Ganzin, Noémi Joly, and David Lestringant
Registrar: Corinne Bocquet
assisted by Alanna Minta Jordan
Press: Linda Chenit
assisted by Hélène Cahuzac
Bookshop, Visitor Services: Vania Merhar
Nomadic Nights: Isabelle Gaudefroy (programming), Frédérique Mehdi (production), Camille Chenet (assistance), Laure Belaz (coordination)
Administration: Michèle Geoffroy, Ursula Thai
Human Resources and Accounting: Fabienne Pommier assisted by Cornélia Cernéa
General Services: François Romani
Installations: Gilles Gioan
Landscape Gardener: Metin Sivri

Éditions Xavier Barral
Director: Xavier Barral
Publications: Annette Lucas and Pierre Vorméringer
Fabrication: Stéphane Crémer
International fabrication rights: Sylvie Leuthenmayr
exb.fr

Texts Credits

Rock Begins by Robert Palmer
Rock Begins, *The Rolling Stone Illustrated History of Rock and Roll*, 3/e. Eds. Anthony DeCurtis, James Henke, Holly George-Warren, Jim Miller. New York: Random House, Inc., 1992. © 1992 Straight Arrow Publishers, Inc. © 1976, 1980 Rolling Stone Press. All Rights Reserved. Used by Permission.

Elvis And The Fifties by David Halbertsam
Copyright © 1993 by The Amateurs Limited. Used by permission of Villard Books, a division of Random House, Inc.

Elvis Presley by Alfred Wertheimer
From *Elvis at 21: New York to Memphis* copyright © 2006 Alfred Wertheimer. All rights reserved. Published by Insight Editions (www.insighteditions.com).

Five Styles of Rock'n'Roll by Charlie Gillett
Copyright © 1970 by Outerbridge & Dienstfrey. Used by permission of Souvenir Press Ltd.

Quotes

P. 33: Quoted by David Halberstram in *The Fifties*. New York: Villard Books, 1993; p. 54: Quoted by Lewis A. Erenberg in *Swingin' the Dream: Big Band Jazz and the Rebirth of American Culture*. Chicago: The University of Chicago Press, 1998; p. 64: Ace Collins, ess, 1998; p. 64: Ace Collins, *Turn Your Radio On: The Stories Behind Gospel Music's All Time Greatest Songs*. Grand Rapids, Michigan: Zondervan Publishing House, 1999; p. 72: Quoted by Deanna R. Adams in *Rock'n'Roll and the Cleveland Connection*. Kent: Kent State University Press, 2002; p. 91: Barry Hansen, "Rhythm & Gospel", *The Rolling Stone Illustrated Story of Rock and Roll*. New York: Random House, 1992; p. 109: Quoted by Guthrie p. Ramsey Jr in. *Race Music: Black Cultures from Bebop to Hip-Hop*. Berkeley: University of California Press, 2003; p. 157: Quoted by Gertrude Samuels in "Why They Rock'n'Roll—And Should They?", *New York Times Magazine*, January 12, 1958; p. 166: Quoted by *Photoplay Magazine*, December, 1956; p. 285: Nick Cohn, *Awopbopaloobop Alopbambooom: The Golden Age of Rock*. New York: Da Capo Press, 1996; p. 295: Quoted by Robert Palmer in *Rock & Roll: An Unruly History*. New York: Harmony Books, 1995; p. 311: Quoted by Rick Coleman in *Blue Monday: Fats Domino and the Lost Dawn of Rock'n'Roll*. New York: Da Capo Press, 2006; p. 345 : Quoted by Myles Palmer in *Small Talk, Big Names: 40 Years of Rock Quotes*. Edinburgh: Mainstream, 1993; p. 375: Robert Palmer, *Rock & Roll: An Unruly History*. New York: Harmony Books, 1995.

Images Credits
Introduction

p. 2-3: © Ed Feingersh, Library of Congress, Washington D.C., Prints & Photographs Division, Look Magazine Photograph Collection, 56-6625-D. Originally published in "The Great rock'n'roll controversy," *Look*, June 26, 1956; p. 4-5: © Phillip Harrington, Library of Congress, Washington D.C., Prints & Photographs Division, Look Magazine Photograph Collection, 56-6706-C. Originally published in "Elvis Presley–he can't be–but he is," *Look*, August 7, 1956; p. 6-7: © Phillip Harrington, Library of Congress, Washington D.C., Prints & Photographs Division, Look Magazine Photograph Collection, 56-6706-I. Originally published in "Elvis Presley–he can't be–but he is," *Look*, August 7, 1956; p. 16: © Marion Post Wolcott, Library of Congress, Washington D.C., Prints & Photographs Division, FSA/OWI Collection, 1a34344r; p. 17: © Jack Delano/Library of Congress, Washington D.C., Prints & Photographs Division, FSA/OWI Collection, 1a33879r; p. 18: © Russell Lee, Library of Congress, Washington D.C., Prints & Photographs Division, FSA/OWI Collection, 3c29128; p. 19: © Russell Lee, Library of Congress, Washington D.C., Prints & Photographs Division, FSA/OWI Collection, 8c51155; p. 20: © Marion Post Wolcott, Library of Congress, Washington D.C. D.C., Prints & Photographs Division, FSA/OWI Collection, 8a41393; p. 21: © Marion Post Wolcott, Library of Congress, Washington D.C., Prints & Photographs Division, FSA/OWI Collection, 8a41455; p. 22: © Russell Lee, Library of Congress, Washington D.C., Prints & Photographs Division, FSA/OWI Collection, 8c23357; p. 23: © Russell Lee, Library of Congress, Washington D.C., Prints & Photographs Division, FSA/OWI Collection, 8c23366; p. 24-25: Life Magazine/Time & Life Pictures; p. 26-27: © Corbis; p. 28: © Philippe Halsman/Magnum Photos; p. 29: © J.R. Eyerman, © Time & Life Pictures/Getty Images; p. 30: © O. Winston Link, Alain Dominique Perrin Collection, London; p. 31: © Nina Leen, © Time & Life Pictures/Getty Images; p. 32: © Loomis Dean, © Time & Life Pictures/Getty Images; p. 34 (above): © Esther Bubley, Library of Congress, Washington D.C., Prints & Photographs Division, FSA/OWI Collection, LC-USZ62-75338; (below): © Hulton Archive/Getty Images; p. 35 (above): © Elliott Erwitt/Magnum Photos; (below): © Marion Post Wolcott, Library of Congress, Washington D.C., Prints & Photographs Division, FSA/OWI Collection, 3c15416; p. 36: Library of Congress, Washington D.C., Prints & Photographs Division, Visual Materials from NAACP Records, LC-USZ62-110591.

The Roots of Rock 'n' Roll

p. 44-45: © Atelier La Bonne Merveille, Paris; p. 46: © Marion Post Wolcott, Library of Congress, Washington D.C., Prints & Photographs Division, FSA/OWI Collection, 8c30475; p. 48-49: Gilles Pétard Collection, Paris; p. 51-53: Léon Dierckx Collection, Brussels; p. 55: © Cornell Capa/Magnum Photos; p. 56-61: Gilles Pétard Collection, Paris; p. 62: Mitch Diamond Collection, Boston (www.kardboardkid.com). Photo Charles Mayer, Boston; p. 63: Pete Howard Collection, Los Angeles (www.postercentral.com); p. 65: © Wayne Miller/Magnum Photos; p. 66 (above): © Marion Post Wolcott, Library of Congress, Washington D.C., Prints & Photographs Division, FSA/OWI Collection, 8c09856; (below): © Marion Post Wolcott, Library of Congress, Washington D.C., Prints & Photographs Division, FSA/OWI Collection, 8c14222; p. 67 (above): © Marion Post Wolcott, Library of Congress, Washington D.C., Prints & Photographs Division, FSA/OWI Collection, 8c09930; (below): © Marion Post Wolcott, Library of Congress, Washington D.C., Prints & Photographs Division, FSA/OWI Collection, 8c14223; p. 68-71: Gilles Pétard Collection, Paris; p. 73: © Clemens Kalischer; p. 74: © Wayne Miller/Magnum Photos; p. 75-76: © Ernest C. Withers, courtesy Panopticon Gallery, Boston; p. 78-79: David Swartz Collection, New York City. Photo Sheldan Collins, Spontaneaous Accomplishments, LLC; p. 81: © Clemens Kalischer; p. 82: Photo Yale Joel, © Time & Life Pictures/Getty Images; p. 83: © Frank Driggs/Michael Ochs Archives/Getty Images; p. 84-85: Mitch Diamond Collection, Boston (www.kardboardkid.com). Photo Charles Mayer, Boston; p. 86: Pete Howard Collection, Los Angeles (www.postercentral.com); p. 87: Gilles Pétard Collection, Paris; p. 90: © Ernest C. Withers, courtesy Panopticon Gallery, Boston; p. 92-93: Gilles Pétard Collection, Paris; p. 94-95: David Swartz Collection, New York City. Photo Sheldan Collins, Spontaneaous Accomplishments, LLC; p. 96-99: Gilles Pétard Collection, Paris; p. 100: Mitch Diamond Collection, Boston (www.kardboardkid.com). Photo Charles Mayer, Boston; p. 101: Rock and Roll Hall of Fame and Museum Inc. Collection, Cleveland; p. 102-103: David Swartz Collection, New York City. Photo Sheldan Collins, Spontaneaous Accomplishments, LLC; p. 104-107: Gilles Pétard Collection, Paris; p. 108: © Wayne Miller/Magnum Photos; p. 110-111: Gilles Pétard Collection, Paris; p. 112-113: Léon Dierckx Collection, Brussels; p. 114-115: Mitch Diamond Collection, Boston (www.kardboardkid.com). Photo Charles Mayer, Boston; p. 117: © Bettmann/Corbis; p. 118: © The Associated Press. Originally published April 24, 1956, courtesy Library of Congress; p. 119-120: Photo © Don Cravens, © Time & Life Pictures/Getty Images; p. 121: © John Bryson/Time & Life Pictures; p. 122-124: Life magazine/Time & Life Pictures.

The Rock 'n' Roll Explosion

p. 134: © Eve Arnold/Magnum Photos; p. 135-136: © Bruce Davidson/Magnum Photos; p. 137 (above): © Wayne Miller/Magnum Photos; (below): © Robert W. Kelley, © Time & Life Pictures/Getty Images; p. 138-139: © Eve Arnold/Magnum Photos; p. 140-147: © Bruce Davidson/Magnum Photos; p. 148: © Michael Ochs Archives/Getty Images; p. 150-151: © Bettmann/Corbis; p. 152-153: © Ed Feingersh, © Look Magazine; p. 154-155: Life Magazine/Time & Life Pictures; p. 156: © Robert W. Kelley, © Time & Life Pictures/Getty Images; p. 158-159: Michel Aphesbero Collection, Bordeaux; p. 160: © Bettmann/Corbis; p. 161: © Jean Bubley and the Estate of Esther Bubley, courtesy Howard Greenberg Gallery, New York City; p. 162-163: © Michael Ochs Archives/Getty Images; p. 164-165: © Jean Bubley and the Estate of Esther Bubley, courtesy Howard Greenberg Gallery, New York City; p. 167-171: Alfa Juke-Box Collection, Paris. Photo © Patrick Gries, Paris; p. 175-237: © Alfred Wertheimer, All Rights Reserved. Courtesy Staley Wise Gallery, New York City; p. 240: © Michael Ochs Archives/Getty Images; p. 242: © Ernest C. Withers, courtesy Panopticon Gallery, Boston; p. 243: Gregg Geller Collection, New York City; p. 244-245: Victor Pearlin Collection, Boston; p. 247: © Michael Ochs Archives/Getty Images; p. 248-250: © Ernest C. Withers, courtesy Panopticon Gallery, Boston; p. 252-253: Pete Howard Collection, Los Angeles (www.postercentral.com); p. 254: David Swartz Collection, New York City. Photo Sheldan Collins, Spontaneaous Accomplishments, LLC; p. 256-257: Michel Lenoir Collection, Paris; p. 258-259: Barry Weinstein Collection, Boston; p. 260: Mitch Diamond Collection, Boston (www.kardboardkid.com); p. 261: Gregg Geller Collection, New York City; p. 262: Michel Aphesbero Collection, Bordeaux; p. 263-264: Gregg Geller Collection, New York City; p. 265: © 2007 Reed Business Information, a division of Reed Elsevier Inc., courtesy Library of Congress, Washington D.C.; p. 266-267: Gilles Pétard Collection, Paris; p. 268: Pete Howard Collection, Los Angeles (www.postercentral.com); p. 269-270: Michael J. Malone Collection, Seattle. Photo © Tim Henegan; p. 272-275: Michel Aphesbero Collection; p. 276: Courtesy Line Renaud, Paris. Photo D.R.

The Golden Age of Rock 'n' Roll

p. 284: Gilles Pétard Collection, Paris; p. 286-287: © Ed Feingersh, Library of Congress, Washington D.C., Prints & Photographs Division, Look Magazine Photograph Collection, 56-6625-A; p. 288-289: © Ed Feingersh, Library of Congress, Washington D.C., Prints & Photographs Division, Look Magazine Photograph Collection, 56-6625-J; p. 290-291: Michel Lenoir Collection, Paris; p. 292: Terry Stewart Collection, courtesy Rock and Roll Hall of Fame and Museum, Cleveland; p. 293-294: Gilles Pétard Collection, Paris; p. 296: Michel Lenoir Collection, Paris; p. 297: Gilles Pétard Collection, Paris; p. 298: Mitch Diamond Collection Boston (www.kardboardkid.com). Photo Charles Mayer, Boston; p. 299: David Swartz Collection, New York City. Photo Sheldan Collins, Spontaneaous Accomplishments, LLC; p. 300: © Don Bronstein, Gilles Pétard Collection, Paris; p. 302-303: Michel Lenoir Collection, Paris; p. 304-305: Gilles Pétard Collection, Paris; p. 306-307: Barry Weinstein Collection, Boston; p. 308: David Swartz Collection, New York City. Photo Sheldon Collins, Spontaneaous Accomplishments, LLC; p. 309: Mitch Diamond Collection, Boston (www.kardboardkid.com). Photo Charles Mayer, Boston; p. 310: © Charlotte Brooks, Library of Congress, Washington D.C., Prints & Photographs Division, Look Magazine Photograph Collection, 57-7561-A; p. 312-313: © Charlotte Brooks, Library of Congress, Washington D.C., Prints & Photographs Division, Look Magazine Photograph Collection, 57-7561-B; p. 316: © Charlotte Brooks, Library of Congress, Washington D.C., Prints & Photographs Division, Look Magazine Photograph Collection, 57-7561-G-13; p. 317: © Charlotte Brooks, Library of Congress, Washington D.C., Prints & Photographs Division, Look Magazine Photograph Collection, 57-7561-I-28-3-15; p. 318: Courtesy Rick Coleman et Antoine "Fats" Domino. Published in Rick Coleman, *Blue Monday*. Cambridge: Da Capo Press, 2006; p. 319: Gilles Pétard Collection, Paris; p. 320-321: David Swartz Collection, New York City. Photo Sheldon Collins, Spontaneaous Accomplishments, LLC; p. 322: Gilles Pétard Collection, Paris; p. 323: Barry Weinstein Collection, Boston; p. 324: © Michael Ochs Archives/Getty Images; p. 326-327: Gilles Pétard Collection, Paris; p. 328-329: David Swartz Collection, New York City. Photo Sheldon Collins, Spontaneaous Accomplishments, LLC; p. 330-334: Gilles Pétard Collection, Paris; p. 336-337: © Bettmann/Corbis; p. 338: Barry Weinstein Collection, Boston; p. 339: Michel Lenoir Collection, Paris; p. 340: Pete Howard Collection, Los Angeles (www.postercentral.com); p. 341: Mitch Diamond Collection, Paris (www.kardboardkid.com); p. 342-343: Michel Aphesbero Collection; p. 344: © Michael Ochs Archives/Getty Images; p. 346-347: Michel Lenoir, Paris Collection; p. 348: Copyright Lew Allen with permission of Maria Elena Holly by CMG Worldwide Inc.; p. 349: David Swartz Collection, New York City. Photo Sheldon Collins, Spontaneaous Accomplishments, LLC.; p. 351-359: Copyright Eggleston Artistic Trust, Cheim & Read, New York City. Used with permission, all rights reserved; p. 360: © Michael Ochs Archives/Getty Images; p. 362-363: David Swartz Collection, New York City. Photo Sheldon Collins, Spontaneaous Accomplishments, LLC; p. 364-365: Michel Lenoir Collection, Paris; p. 366: © Ernest C. Withers, courtesy Panopticon Gallery, Boston; p. 368: © Showtime Music Archives, Toronto; p. 369: Michel Lenoir Collection, Paris; p. 370: © Michael Ochs Archives/Getty Images; p. 371: Michel Lenoir Collection, Paris; p. 372: © Michael Ochs Archives/Getty Images; p. 373: Rock and Roll Hall of Fame and Museum Inc. Collection, Cleveland; p. 374: Courtesy Hank Thompson, Raleigh; p. 376: © Don Cravens, Library of Congress, Washington D.C., Prints & Photographs Division, Look Magazine Photograph Collection, 58-7685L24; p. 377: David Swartz Collection, New York City. Photo Sheldan Collins, Spontaneaous Accomplishments, LLC.; p. 378: Pete Howard Collection, Los Angeles (www.postercentral.com); p. 379: Michel Lenoir Collection, Paris; p. 380: Courtesy Rock and Roll Hall of Fame and Museum Inc., Cleveland; p. 381: © Ralph Crane/Life Magazine/Time & Life Pictures; p. 382-385: Gilles Pétard Collection, Paris; p. 386 (above, l): Rock and Roll Hall of Fame and Museum Inc. Collection, Cleveland; (above, r): Mitch Diamond Collection. Boston (www.kardboardkid.com). Photo Charles Mayer, Boston; (below, l): Courtesy of Hank Thompson, Raleigh; (below, r): David Swartz Collection, New York City. Photo Sheldan Collins, Spontaneaous Accomplishments, LLC.; p. 387 (above): David Swartz Collection, New York City. Photo Sheldan Collins, Spontaneaous Accomplishments, LLC.; (below): Courtesy of Hank Thompson, Raleigh; p. 388 (above, l): Michel Lenoir Collection, Paris; (above, r): Gilles Pétard Collection, Paris; (below): Michel Lenoir Collection, Paris; p. 389 (above, l): Gilles Pétard Collection, Paris; (above, r; below, l): Michel Lenoir Collection, Paris; (below, r): Gilles Pétard Collection, Paris; p. 391: © 1990 Sharyn Felder. Used by permission only. All rights of every kind are reserved throughout the world; p. 394-398: Victor Pearlin Collection, Boston; p. 400-402: ARChive of Contemporary Music, New York City; p. 404: Victor Pearlin Collection, Boston; p. 406: ARChive of Contemporary Music, New York City.